Indo-China:
Signposts in the Storm

J. Davidson

Longman

LONGMAN MALAYSIA SDN. BERHAD
25, First Lok Yang Road, Singapore 2262.
Wisma Damansara, Jalan Semantan, Kuala Lumpur

Associated companies, branches and
representatives throughout the world

†*First published* 1979
†*Second impression* 1981

ISBN 0 582 72603 4

Printed by Singapore Offset Printing (Pte) Ltd.

959
D28~
11 9375
oct. 1981

For permission to reproduce the photographs mentioned below, the
Publishers are indebted to the following:

Editions du Seuil, Paris, France for the photo of General Leclerc & Ho
Chi Minh from *Histoire du Vietnam 1940—1952* by P. Devillers; UPI for the
photo of President Ngo Dinh Diem with US Ambassador General Maxwell
Taylor.

The illustration on the cover is a photograph taken by the author of a rubbing of
Angkor.

Introduction by the Right Honourable Mr. Malcolm MacDonald O.M.

For my family, who also were there

LAOS

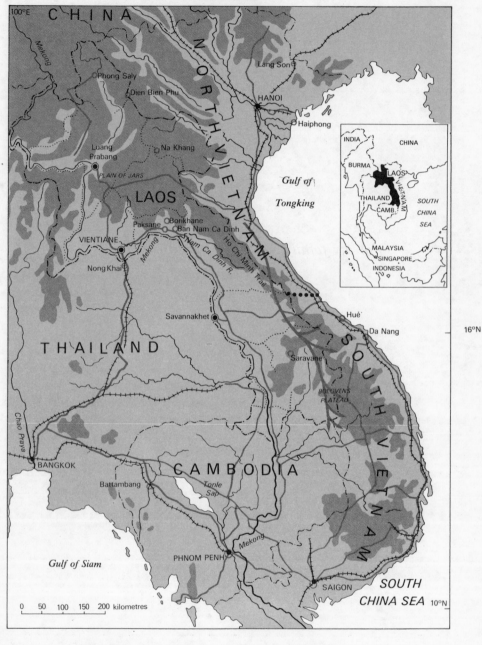

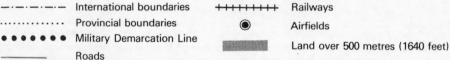

- —·—·—·— International boundaries
- ·············· Provincial boundaries
- ●●●●●●●● Military Demarcation Line
- ——— Roads
- ++++++++ Railways
- ◉ Airfields
- ▨ Land over 500 metres (1640 feet)

VIETNAM

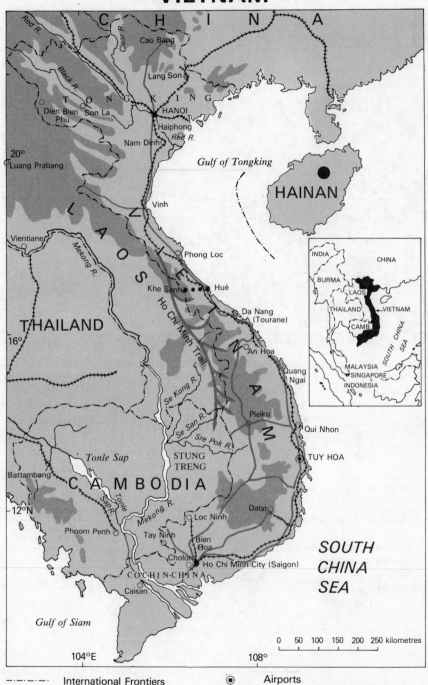

C H I N A

Red R.
Clear R.
Cao Bang
Lang Son
Black R.
T O N G K I N G
Dien Bien Phu
Son La
HANOI
Haiphong
Nam Dinh
Red R.
20°
Luang Prabang
Gulf of Tongking
HAINAN
Vinh
Vientiane
Mekong R.
L A O S
Phong Loc
Khe Sanh
Hué
V
I
E
T
Da Nang
(Tourane)
16°
THAILAND
Ho Chi Minh Trail
An Hoa
N
Quang
Ngai
Se Kong R.
Se San R.
Pleiku
A
Sre Pok R.
STUNG
TRENG
Qui Nhon
M
TUY HOA
Tonle Sap
Battambang
C A M B O D I A
Mekong R.
Dalat
12°N
Sap R.
Tonle
Sap R.
Loc Ninh
Phnom Penh
Tay Ninh
Bien Hoa
Cholon
Ho Chi Minh City (Saigon)
COCHIN-CHINA
Caisan
SOUTH
CHINA
SEA
Gulf of Siam

INDIA
CHINA
BURMA
LAOS
THAILAND
VIETNAM
CAMB.
SOUTH CHINA SEA
MALAYSIA
SINGAPORE
INDONESIA

0 50 100 150 200 250 kilometres

104°E   108°

- · - · -   International Frontiers
• • • • •   Military Demarcation Line
————   Roads
⊙   Airports
+++++++   Railways (mainly closed in South)
▓▓▓   Land over 500 metres (1640 feet)

KHMER REPUBLIC

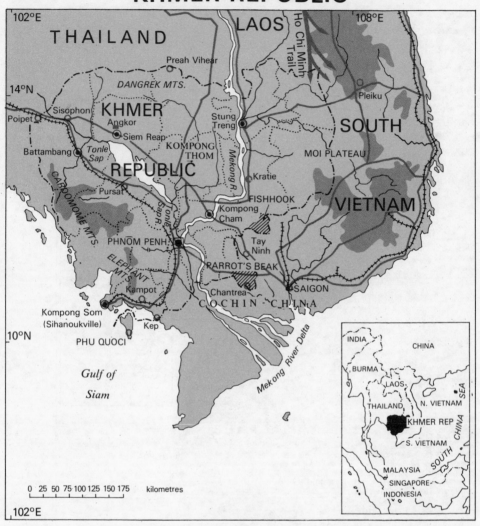

102°E   108°E

THAILAND

LAOS

Ho Chi Minh Trail

Preah Vihear

DANGREK MTS.

14°N

Poipet

Sisophon

KHMER

Angkor

Siem Reap

Battambang

Tonle Sap

REPUBLIC

Pursat

Pleiku

Stung Treng

KOMPONG THOM

SOUTH

MOI PLATEAU

Kratie

Mekong R.

FISHHOOK

Kompong Cham

VIETNAM

CARDAMOME MTS.

Tonle Sap R.

PHNOM PENH

Tay Ninh

ELEPHANT MTS.

PARROT'S BEAK

Kampot

Chantrea

COCHIN CHINA

SAIGON

Kompong Som (Sihanoukville)

Kep

PHU QUOCI

10°N

Gulf of

Siam

Mekong River Delta

INDIA

CHINA

BURMA

LAOS

THAILAND

N. VIETNAM

KHMER REP

S. VIETNAM

MALAYSIA

SINGAPORE

INDONESIA

SOUTH CHINA SEA

0 25 50 75 100 125 150 175   kilometres

102°E

—·—·—·— International boundaries
············· Provincial boundaries
———— Main roads
++++++++ Railways

◙ International Airports
⊙ Airfields
▨ Land over 200 metres (656 feet)

Contents

Preface

The French War in Indo-China against Ho Chi Minh lasted almost a decade: the subsequent American involvement against Hanoi nearly twice as long. It is now commonplace that these conflicts in Indo-China during the last thirty years had massive impact far beyond South East Asia and, despite the prolonged suffering of the Indo-Chinese peoples, this global impact is likely to provide the principal interest for history. It did not arise by chance. From the beginning, the Communist Vietnamese leadership sensed the significance to them of the world beyond Vietnam. Over the years, they consistently sought international feed-back for their cause. Their military actions were often linked to political objectives thousands of miles from the battle-field; to aims in Europe and the United States; sometimes even, to objectives in Moscow and Peking. The demonstrations on Vietnam which took place in Europe and the United States often reflected the spontaneous idealism of youth. In a number of cases they were also part of an effective orchestration for the Hanoi cause.

In the 1970s, this drive for the widest possible feed-back has an accepted place in the armoury of most revolutionary causes. But in the 1940s and 1950s, and even into the 1960s, this war beyond the lines was not always fully appreciated by French and American leaders. This could never have been said of Ho Chi Minh. An awareness of a wider world was a key feature of his leadership. His first seizure of power in Indo-China came in the dying days of Japanese authority in 1945, at a time when he believed American views on post-war decolonisation would help his cause. A year later, in 1946, he recognised that a limited French return was the only way to ensure the withdrawal of the Chinese Nationalist army of occupation. Sadly, the relationship with the French foundered, but eventually the French war drifted into peace talks. By this time the Communist Vietnamese were besieging the strong French garrison at Dien Bien Phu. Their capture of the fortress came on 7 May 1954, just one day before the Indo-China conference opened in Geneva. In similar fashion, the Communist Vietnamese all-out offensive against Saigon and the other cities in South Vietnam, in the early part of 1968, coincided with the first rounds of the United States Presidential Primaries, and was pointed directly at United States public opinion.

The timetable for the Communist Vietnamese in their peace talks with the Americans during the latter months of 1972 was again closely related to their assessment of what might happen in Washington. This time, the Communist leadership weighed the temptation on an Administration; the wish to be able to declare in advance of an election that it had settled the long and bitter conflict in South East Asia. But these were years when President Nixon and Doctor Kissinger were riding high. Washington did not settle. After a few anxious weeks, which spanned the Presidential election, there was return to the negotiating table. The Communist Vietnamese recognised the mood in Washington. The upshot was the 1973 Paris Agreement on ending the war in Vietnam.

Watergate would, however, shortly cast its shadow of distrust and discredit. It would have been out of character if Hanoi had not measured the stress on President Nixon at this time. North Vietnamese pressure increased and, for the Indo-Chinese peoples themselves, the Paris Agreement very soon revealed itself as hollow and temporary. In the year of the 'ceasefire', another one hundred thousand Vietnamese soldiers were killed or maimed. But increasingly the views of the United States Congress gained sway. And with it purpose for peace. The Congress cut military aid to Saigon, and maintained their view despite the outspoken opposition of Doctor Kissinger. In August 1974, the pressure on Richard Nixon forced his resignation. Without Vietnam, would there have been Watergate? Some observers believe that the continuing tragedy of Vietnam sharpened the knife which cut down the President. Eight months later, the Vietnam war was over. Hanoi had achieved its objective of wearying America of involvement in Indo-China. Whatever the criticism which can be made of the Hanoi leadership, it cannot be accused of a narrow strategic concept.

Later analysis may question the extent to which the direct interests of the United States really were involved in Vietnam. Or, even if they were at one time engaged, how long this stage endured. It can hardly be denied that, for a number of years, successive American Administrations themselves contributed to the global impact which served the purposes of the Communist Vietnamese. For a long time, Washington itself chose to see Indo-China as a key area of challenge in its global confrontation against "international communism". Is it a reasonable judgment that the United States became too deeply engaged, and remained locked in longer than they needed?

However the question is answered, it does seem that the most significant results of the war related to the world scene, and that this was because of the impact on the United States itself. Yet fair observers should also consider what the Asian map might look like today if there had not been the prolonged American intervention.

For France, the Indo-China war was quickly followed by the Algerian tragedy. The two events paved the way for the years of Gaullism and anti-American sentiment. For the United States, the involvement in Indo-China, which resulted in the longest war in the country's history, played a very large part in the nation's upheavals of the 1960s. The decision of President Lyndon Johnson not to seek a further term as President stemmed directly from his reappraisal of the American position in Indo-China — of the reappraisal required to 'heal the wound' in the United States. Indeed, the dishonesty of Watergate itself, stemmed not too remotely from White House interest in the leak of the American secret documents and classified material on Indo-China comprising the Pentagon Papers. At about the same time as Watergate there was also exposure of the "secret" American bombing in Cambodia which had begun in 1969. This bombing was aimed at the Viet Cong concentrations and strongholds in the Eastern part of the country, but often killed innocent Cambodians in no way involved in the conflict. There was an intention to save American lives. Even so, the action was an excess of authority and a deception of Congress. In the field of United States policy, and the executive authority of the President, the consequences of the United States involvement in Indo-China has still fully to be measured.

President Carter has promised "to get the country moving again", — but not in the mood of President Kennedy's inaugural address. At that time it was "We will go anywhere, pay any price, to defend the cause of freedom around the world". These were words which, in all fairness, could have been justified as reflecting the mood of the nation at the time they were spoken. President Carter's rhetoric is pitched lower, and mirrors the more reflective mood of the United States in the aftermath of Vietnam. Indeed, one of the more powerful of the forces responsible for the achievement of the new Presidency could have been a sense that the nation's compass had somehow gone wrong: that the machinery of government was no longer responding as it should to the developing moods of the nation. President Ford's worthy service to restore the nation's faith in its government was properly recognised by his successor in his first words as President.

There can still be argument as to the extent Vietnam was in itself causative, and the fundamental American problem of two decades. Or, if it was merely the largest symptom of a deeper problem for the United States in coming to terms with a world in transition, where, for all its strength, America itself was not immune from change and trial. The comfort for the Western world is that in the end the United States solved its own problem. But the world has still to evaluate the new American mood. How will the more reflective stance of the American people affect the future American policies toward Asia, Europe and

Africa? If, at the end of the day, Vietnam was, after all, less than vital to American security, what of commitments elsewhere?

The immediate story of Indo-China is of more than thirty years of war. This, in turn, is part of a larger framework of colonialism and decolonisation. In 1945, General Smuts observed that the caravan of mankind was on the move again. Nowhere was this more true than in Asia. And the thirty years of Vietnam conflict — like the Russo-Japanese war at the turn of the century — have already acquired symbolism in relation to Western and Asian values. Any foolish certainty that what was West was best is already long past.

Events in Indo-China have already been studied in depth by many writers. Moreover, with the publication of the Pentagon Papers and of President Johnson's memoirs, some of the inner United States thinking is now generally available. The memoirs of President Nixon and of Doctor Kissinger are not yet published, but it would be surprising if they did not soon appear. In addition, although it belongs almost to the beginning of the story, the section of the despatch from Lord Mountbatten to the Combined Chiefs of Staff, covering his 1945 post-surrender tasks as the Supreme Allied Commander in South East Asia, has only fairly recently been published. The delay of 25 years before its publication related to the political sensitivities of the former colonial powers. In the 1970's, these sensitivities seem far distant from today's world. This is yet another measure of the immense change in international attitudes and relationships since 1945.

Given that so much has already been written, either by those directly engaged, or by professional historians pursuing their trade at arm's length, what is left is in a sense self service for those who have found interest in the subject. It is with the obvious diffidence of an amateur, — and with all the benefit of hindsight — that I have endeavoured to put together this further brief study of events in Indo-China. It ends with the final Communist success on 30 April 1975 when their troops entered Saigon, and the subsequent formal unification of Vietnam on 2 July 1976. In particular, I have tried to identify turning points. I have also sought to make some assessment of the sway of nationalism.

The Communist involvement in Indo-China was of course self-proclaimed. Even so, the ideological strand was only one of a number which comprised the conflict. The Communist Vietnamese victory was also due to their success in gaining for themselves the banner against imperialism in their country, and capturing the tide of local sentiment against outsiders and their ways. But how will the tide flow in the future? Now that the direct Western involvement is over, is there a possibility that the Vietnamese leaders could run the risk of appearing to their neighbours as new imperialists, with ambitions beyond their borders? And, if this were so, what would be the Chinese reaction? Or is there regional acceptance of a Vietnamese will for peace; and will this blossom? And what is the outlook for Cambodia? Has the blood-letting now run its course, or may it merely be about to change direction?

The questions about the real motivation of Hanoi, which are touched on above, were often asked during the costly years of Western military involvement in Indo-China. Was the inspiration of Ho Chi Minh and his followers militant Communism or Nationalism? Or what blend of the two? And, to the extent that Nationalism was an element, how wide or narrow the base? At one extreme, was it Tonkinois (North Vietnamese) Nationalism and Irridentism hardened by the living conditions of North Vietnam, and disciplined by Communism, spilling over, like the Nazi German expansion of the 1930s, to neighbours of their kin who might have preferred no part of it? Or, at the other extreme were there some veins of unity within Indo-China as a whole, even if these stemmed only from a common legacy of French colo-nialism? To what extent were the borders and divisions on the map representative of real differences between peoples?

There are other questions. To what extent may the policies of France and the United States have contributed at various moments in their respective conflicts to the hardening of the forces against them? Would North Vietnam have shaped as it did if the country had not been tempered by the years of conflict? Might there instead have been a mellowing, rather than a sharpening of Communist Vietnamese purpose, and the development of an Asian Yugoslavia? As their own war came to an end, many Frenchmen were drawn to the view that they had been fighting for an American interest. Yet what was the American interest? And how was it identified and re-identified as time passed? The point sounds basic, but was it always fully appreciated that, with the commitment of its regular armed forces, a great power crosses a Rubicon. Thereafter, whatever the original interest, the stake tends to lift to the larger interest of prestige in battle. If there does have to be some degree of involvement, do the American methods in the Eisen-hower years, and the special technique in Laos, offer useful guides?

America was drawn massively into Indo-China. The American interest became direct. The Soviet Union and China avoided this degree of involvement. In the early days of the Indo-China conflict, in the 1940s, the Soviet Union saw South East Asia as far less important than France and Western Europe. Support for Ho Chi Minh was viewed merely as electoral liability for the French left. Similarly, in the 1970s, the Soviet Union gave priority to its policy of détente with the United

States. In the years between, were there missed opportunities for gestures of goodwill and reconciliation which could have halted the suffering in Vietnam, Cambodia and Laos? Were there any valid parallels from events elsewhere in the final stages of the Western presence in Asia? And do the years when Malaysia and Singapore faced confrontation from Indonesia suggest any pointers?

There are also practical issues which especially face a great democratic power as it develops its external policy. This policy can to some extent, be endorsed by the electorate and the results of the Presidential elections in the United States in the 1960s, and in 1972, suggest electoral endorsement for American policies in Indo-China. But major external commitment demands more than a simple electoral majority; or even a substantial electoral majority. The requirement is for the widest possible consensus, and for this consensus to be sought on the main issue. In British affairs, the special referendum on membership of the European Community proved a useful formula.

It is proper to ask how a democracy best escapes the inertia and drag of policies which are not working out. It is a question more easily posed than answered. Flexibility does not come easily for there is a tendency for patterns of events to become set. In the aftermath of Munich, it was often suggested that things might have turned out for the better if more positive action had been taken against Hitler. For Britain, this way of thinking led, in the end, to Suez. On the other hand, the Korean War started in the aftermath of what appeared to be an American intention to withdraw. All of these were events which, in their time, appeared to offer a guide to the management of the next crisis. But successive crises are never quite the same. The military textbooks stress maintenance of the aim. Yet, where there is responsibility to democratic process, the only practical course is often one of almost continuous adjustment.

The aim in this study was to try to perceive the main historical signposts in the Indo-China drama and to offer some comment on them. Its content follows largely in the wake of material previously published in book form or in the press: a continuing problem has been what to omit. The philosophies of those who support Communism and of those who oppose it are not argued. Effort has been made to try to see all sides. The practical issue, and it is one more easily stated than resolved, has been that of determining the middle ground on a long drawn-out international tragedy. Even so, there is, I think, a balance to be found from the mass of material available. With the Hanoi success and the end of United States' military action in the area, some conspectus of the whole Western involvement in Indo-China can begin to be drawn.

The bibliography at the end outlines the books to which I have referred in the preparation of the study. In addition, I have had the privilege of discussing the events of 1945 with Earl Mountbatten of Burma, the wartime Supreme Allied Commander in South East Asia. I have also had the pleasure of a number of talks with the Right Honourable Mr. Malcolm MacDonald, Governor-General of the British Dependent Territories in South East Asia from 1946 to 1948; British Commissioner-General in South East Asia from 1948 to 1955; and acting co-Chairman of the 1961 Geneva Conference on Laos. Some events I saw first hand.

Finally, the acknowledgement. The study could not have been attempted without the blessing of the Diplomatic Service whose grant of sabbatical absence opened the door to the enterprise. May I also mention the kindness which I received at the University of Kent at Canterbury. It is the fashion to thank those who have made a study possible, while, at the same time, disassociating them from responsibility for the results. I can but repeat my sincere appreciation to my Department, and to my kindly academic hosts, for the opportunity given me to gain insight into the hundred years of Western involvement in Indo-China: an involvement which culminated in one of the most complex and tragic international problems of the middle of the twentieth century. In addition, may I thank Professor George Thomson and Dr. Michael Leifer for all their encouragement and assistance as I sought to complete the narrative.

James Davidson
Brunei 1977

Unhappily, events in Indo-China have emerged too much as apprehended. Suffering has continued, especially for the Cambodians and for the Vietnam boat people. Outside pressures have persisted. Russia and China stand strongly opposed. Moscow is served by Hanoi's present dependence, and is prepared to underwrite Vietnamese hegemony in Indo-China. Peking is determined to stay this expansionism and to deny Soviet influence. A major Chinese punitive action against Vietnam took place in February 1979. Unless Vietnam releases its grip on Indo-China, it would be surprising if that were the last such confrontation.

"Be harsh: give death", was the motto offered by Himmler, the Nazi S.S. leader. Coldness and contempt for humanity were the S.S. hallmarks. The philosophy was brutality. The upshot was massive genocide. Alas, the Nazis have not been unique. Within Cambodia, the Pol Pot regime had achieved a level of horror which similarly shocked the world before it was overthrown by Hanoi. The Vietnamese admittedly acted out of realpolitik. They too threaten Khmer identity — albeit far less bloodily. Most of the Khmer people seek an independent Cambodia: — but not under Pol Pot. After that nightmare, Cambodians dream of a return to the harmony of their country before 1970. The dream deserves the widest international support.

James Davidson, 1980

Introduction

This book contains a narrative of an important piece of modern history — the succession of events which have occurred through the last forty years in the lands which at their beginning were known as French Indo-China, and are now the independent states of Vietnam, Cambodia and Laos.

James Davidson has an extensive first hand knowledge of South East Asia, first as a naval officer and later as a diplomat, which goes back many years. Most recently he has served with distinction as High Commissioner in Brunei, the historic and colourful Sultanate across the South China Sea from Vietnam and Cambodia.

He writes the story of Indo-China well. His account begins with some glimpses into the far more distant past, when for a thousand years much of present day Vietnam was governed directly as part of China's vast realm and then for about another thousand years its rulers accepted an at least nominal Chinese suzerainty. In the mid-Nineteenth Century, when the Empires of the British, the French, the Dutch and others were spreading ever more widely round the world, the French acquired partly as colonies and partly as protectorates, the five territories called Tonkin, Annam, Cochin China (the trinity which now compose Vietnam), Laos and Cambodia. Davidson describes the variety of ethnic groups in those differing lands, and the historic quarrels and political complexities which, through the centuries — and right up to today — have hampered friendly relations between them; complexities which have also sometimes involved the nearby Thais.

Most of the book is concerned with the troubles which started to erupt in Indo-China after the "hot" World War ended in the mid 1940s, setting off internal upheavals in those small countries, upheavals which in turn led to intrusions into their affairs by external Great Powers now waging their "cold war". The chapters recount the only partially successful efforts of the French to re-establish their Imperial rule in 1946; the nature of the mostly Nationalist, but partly Communist, Independence movement in Vietnam, some of whose leaders felt reluctantly compelled to launch a guerilla war against the French; the spill-over of fighting into Laos and Cambodia, where the quest for independence from French rule might otherwise have been

conducted more peacefully; the gradual political and military defeat of
the French through the next eight years; the 1954 Geneva Conference
which sought to establish early Independence for the three Indo-
Chinese states in ways accepted by the French, but not by the
Americans in the case of Vietnam: the collapse in 1956 of the
implementation of the Geneva Agreement on Vietnam; the consequent
resumption of fighting between a now predominantly Communist
North Vietnam and an anti-Communist South Vietnam, with the
former receiving material aid from Russia and China, and the latter
receiving increasingly strong military support from America; the
renewed extension of the war into Laos; the 1961—62 Geneva
Conference which succeeded for a while in limiting that extension; and
thereafter the succession of events which in all the three lands
culminated in the defeat of the Americans and their non-Communist
allies, and the establishment in them all of Communist governments.
The Communist North Vietnamese strength of purpose is illumined;
and the American predicament is evenly and fairly presented.

In the course of his narrative Davidson sketches pen-portraits of
several of the fascinating Oriental and Occidental characters who
played important parts in the drama: Ho Chi Minh, Emperor Bao Dai
and Ngo Dinh Diem in Vietnam, Prince Sihanouk in Cambodia, and
also some of the principal French and American personalities who were
involved. And, in addition to a well-researched account of the dramatic
events which one after another composed the sad tragedy of Indo-
China, wider international affairs come under scrutiny. There is much
shrewd commentary, and Davidson speculates whether the worst of the
misery of Indo-China need have occurred, or whether instead the piece
might, with deeper understanding, have had a happier ending.

I myself happened to watch the succession of acts from close
quarters because of near-by and partly overlapping activities in which I
was engaged during much of those times in South East Asia; and I have
little doubt that the outcome could have been better. I believe that if at
any time in the late 1940s the French had recognised the inevitability,
and indeed desirability, of the Vietnamese, Cambodian and Laotian
peoples being freed from Imperial rule — as the British then did
regarding the Indians, Pakistanis, Burmese and Singhalese — they
could by peaceful negotiations have ensured that they would, at an
agreed pace, all become independent nations maintaining especially
close friendly association with France. Again, I believe that if the
Americans had accepted the proposals of the 1954 Geneva Conference,
a similar satisfactory settlement could have been achieved. It is true
that Vietnam would almost certainly have become a Communist state,
but I think that it would have been (with the sincere accord of China

and the less sincere acquiescence of Russia) a non-aligned nation in the same way as Tito's Communist Yugoslavia became in Europe. Cambodia and Laos would probably have become non-Communist independent nations retaining friendly relations with the West. And France and America would not have suffered the heavy blows they did. No doubt some fresh problems would have arisen — but I must not ruminate further on the "might have beens".

This wise book marks signposts in the past, and draws warning against ill-thought out distant great power interference. Happily, the ASEAN nations themselves are now, together, marking out their own signposts toward regional peace and prosperity in South-East Asia.

I highly commend Davidson's book to the reading public.

MALCOLM MACDONALD

ASEAN — *The Association of South-East Asian Nations which was formed on the 7th August 1967, is a regional grouping comprising Indonesia, Malaysia, the Philippines, Singapore and Thailand.*

1   The Geographic Setting

THE geography of Indo-China bears very closely on its past and present; the name itself is descriptive. It is a region of contact where China touches "The Indies". It has been shrewdly observed that to land in Vietnam from the West is to feel that one has already arrived in the Chinese world; the arrival from the East, however, has some feeling of having already left China. It is also a region of geographical contrast. There are extensive areas of low-lying watery land with rich soil: there are spiky mountain ranges and wooded plateau areas. What is however common to all the three countries of Indo-China, — to Vietnam, Cambodia and to Laos, is a terrain which favours guerilla war.

The climate of the region is governed by the monsoons which stem from the pressure changes over the Asian land mass between summer and winter. Traditionally, the cycle of rice cultivation, and hence the peasant's round, is one of almost endless activity at certain seasons with little to do at other times. From November to March there are north-easterly winds bringing a relatively cooler air flow. From May to September there is a south-west monsoon drawing in moist air from the Indian Ocean and bringing a good deal of rain. This rainfall is heavier on the high ground and on the East Coast than in the Mekong Delta. The bad weather also tends to come earlier in the North than the South. This climatic variation bore very directly on the military situation. There was a tendency toward less military activity in the wet season, when large areas of the terrain were flooded, than in the dry months of the year. Low cloud during the wet season and in the period immediately before the wet season also inhibited air activity.

Because of the war, the demographic figures have to be offered with some qualification. According to a 1970 United Nations estimate, North Vietnam then had a population of the order of 22 million; South Vietnam about 18 million. For Cambodia the figure was 7 million. For Laos, 3 million. As for the concentrations, Saigon was the largest town and, as the war closed in, its population exceeded 3 million. Estimates of the population of Hanoi usually ranged around the 1 million mark. Before 1970, Phnom Penh had a population of about half a million. A refugee influx swelled this to about 2 million by 1974. When the

1

revolutionary forces of the Khmer Rouge captured the city in April 1975 it is generally accepted that they enforced the evacuation of most of these people into the countryside.

Vietnam is both geographically and in population terms by far the largest of the Indo-China countries. Its area is about 120,000 square miles; bigger than Britain but smaller than France. In the days of division between North and South Vietnam the area of each was about 60,000 square miles. It is a standard observation that Vietnam is shaped like "two rice baskets joined by their carrying pole", but what is not always appreciated is that the two rice baskets and centres of population, the one in the North around Hanoi, the other in the South around Saigon, are more than 600 miles apart: indeed the overall length of the country from North to South is almost 1,000 miles. The dumbell shape which comprises the now unified Vietnam stretches between the seventh and twenty-third parallels North. To the West, except in the region of the Mekong Delta, the dumbell is marked by an inhospitable mountain line. Beyond the mountains lies the valley of the Mekong, Laos, Cambodia and Thailand. The Mekong, flowing from China, and on its way marking the boundary between Laos and Thailand, passes through Laos and Cambodia before reaching the sea in the delta area of South Vietnam.

What is now the Northern part of Vietnam used to be known as Tonkin, and the mountainous and sparsely populated area of North and North West Tonkin was in the early days a favoured stronghold for Ho Chi Minh and his followers. The central part of Vietnam used to be known as Annam, and this was indeed the Chinese name for the mediaeval Vietnamese State. It derived from An-Nan — pacified South! In more recent times, the name Annam has also sometimes been used to mean the whole of what is now Vietnam. The term Cochin China was applied by the French to the area of the Mekong Delta.

The population of Northern Vietnam is concentrated in the Red River Delta: that of the South in the Mekong Delta. Over the centuries, there have been repeated partitions of Vietnam between the 16th and 18th parallels — roughly half way between the two. After 1954 the division lay along the 17th parallel. Historically, there is also said to have been something of a social divide — the North more eminent than the South, due perhaps to being more adjacent to China, the former suzerain. Traditionally, the North may have had the prestige of intellect and leadership; certainly its climate is less intensely tropical than that of the South. It was the combination of all these factors which prompted the French to site their capital of Indo-China in Hanoi rather than Saigon. As for the people of Vietnam, the French of Indo-China distinguished sharply between the Tonkinois of the North and the people of the South. According to General Salan, an Indo-China veteran and a Commander in Chief during the war, "They may be the same race, but they are terribly different: ce sont des frères enemis".[1]

Again referring to the South, Salan says, "Cochin China (the Mekong Delta area) owes its beginning to people from the sea: Khmers (Cambodians) and Chams (a nation of the South overcome by the Vietnamese some centuries ago) are at the base of its civilisation. The hallmark is a liberal state of mind. Its people are closer to us and to Western civilisation than are those of the North who bear the mark of centuries of Chinese influence: the North is a harder country and the people there claim the rich South as living space. We (the French) have achieved some precarious osmosis of this mixture". Salan quotes a traditional proverb of the South about the North: "We speak the same language but we each have our own cooking pot". But this was never accepted by those seeking the unity of Vietnam. Indeed to Ho Chi Minh and his followers, Salan's view was of the very essence of 'Divide and Rule'.

The lower Mekong Valley is immensely fertile. Cambodia and South Vietnam, which gain most benefit, are traditional rice surplus areas and have rich fisheries. The North, on the other hand, has a history of rice shortage, and the rice production in the Red River Delta is very dependent indeed upon an intricate irrigation network. A system of dams, dykes and canals, some of it hundreds of years old, controls the tributaries and regulates the water flow. But the rice production of the North was usually less than its need. It would have been natural therefore for Ho Chi Minh and his lieutenants to have seen the two Vietnamese economies as complementary, and to have related the anthracite and other mineral resources of the North with the rice and rubber of the South. Certainly the French themselves saw all the economies of Indo-China as complementary.

This wider view has been held by others. During the 1950s and 1960s, the United Nations Economic Committee for Asia and the Far East (ECAFE) considered the Mekong basin as a whole and developed a number of ambitious ideas for its future. Under this United Nations auspices, Cambodia, Laos, Thailand and South Vietnam along with a number of foreign donors, including the United States and Britain, worked in collaboration for some years toward major development of the lower Mekong basin. Inevitably, the Indo-China conflict impeded progress. For example, a major irrigation scheme at Prek Thnot in Cambodia was attacked by the Communists during the course of 1971. But much is still on the drawing board and capable of being applied to help the countries of the area.[2]

Once a reasonable stability returned to the region, an enlarged 'Mekong Committee' might perhaps be harnessed to new international aid arrangements and have some role in providing help for the reconstruction and development of the area as a whole. Political factors wholly govern the possibility of progress. The nature of any development to be undertaken would be relevant both politically and socially. One school of thought envisages billion dollar development on the Mekong itself, to provide irrigation and the supply of massive quantities of electricity. Another sees the wiser course, to begin with, as step by step local development of tributary rivers and a balance more toward irrigation than electricity generation. When the experts are divided, it is not easy to form judgement. In any case, some political cooperation must come first. There could be hazards in trying to move too fast toward large projects spanning frontiers and toward the creation of electrical generating capacity too much in excess of any existing industrial requirement. In this geographical/development area, modesty and a realistic prospect of accomplishment are probably the best signposts to success. It would also be surprising if the new Communist Governments in Vietnam, Cambodia and Laos did not incline toward development favouring the peasant.

What can be said with certainty is that the Mekong and its use is central to the life of the region. Over considerable stretches it is also a boundary and not infrequently a source of incident. The regulation of shipping along its navigable lengths has, in the past, been another cause of dispute, and this could recur in the future. Near to the point where the Mekong enters Cambodia from Laos, there are rapids and obstacles to navigation. But for hundreds of miles below this point the river is wide and navigable and rich in fish, and deserving the name of 'Great River' by which it is known to the peoples of Cambodia and Vietnam.

It is also a great river in a very practical sense. Close to Phnom Penh, it joins with another big river, the Tonle Sap, which runs northwest from the Cambodian capital to the Great Lake of Cambodia and thence by streams to Angkor. When the Mekong is in full flood, its mass of water effectively causes the Tonle Sap to back up towards its source. During the wet monsoon the Tonle Sap does not run down to the sea. It runs back towards the Great Lake of Cambodia until mid-October or thereabouts. After that, it turns and runs like a normal river to the sea. This turning of the water, bringing a very rich fish catch, used to be a major event in the Cambodian calendar. During the 1960s, Prince Sihanouk would personally participate in the Fête des Eaux which marked the occasion.

The vegetation of the region has obvious military relevance. More than half of Indo-China is forest, comprising both dense rain forest and more temperate woodland; everywhere there is much cover. There are also the rice areas. In addition, there are considerable areas in the

South given over to the growing of rubber. These had very special military significance.

In Vietnam and Cambodia, as in Malaya, the Communists frequently used rubber plantations as strongholds. The combination of relatively cleared ground, and shelter from observation and attack from the air, held obvious benefit. Another military factor was that the labour in the rubber plantations in South Vietnam and Cambodia was often of North Vietnamese origin. Despite the war, the rubber plantations of Indo-China, which were largely French-owned and managed, succeeded in maintaining normal commercial operations for a surprisingly long time. Rumour sometimes suggested a degree of Communist and capitalist understanding. Before 1970, when the shooting spread into Cambodia, the Chup plantation in the Eastern part of the country was widely believed to contain the headquarters of the Communist forces in the South.

The Indo-China communications system largely reflected French priorities, and an impulse to make the most of the region's geographical/economic resources. The railway line from Haiphong to Kunming in China was finished in 1910. A line between Hanoi and Saigon was finished in 1936. The cities of Hanoi, Saigon and Phnom Penh were graciously recast in French colonial style and a number of trunk roads — often tree lined as in France — were built to link these and other places. There was thus a main road between Saigon and Hanoi (a Northern stretch of which became known during the French war as the Street Without Joy); and between Saigon and Phnom Penh. Over much of the region, these and other main roads are often dykes, exposed elevations over sea level landscapes of rice fields and patches of woodlands. Elsewhere, routes are often cuts through hilly forest. Roads of either sort are vulnerable to guerilla attack. Throughout the area, there are airfields, legacy of the years of war. These aided communications. At the same time they could turn into traps. Almost everywhere, the nature of the communications and of the countryside lent itself as backdrop to Mao Tse Tung's four line formula for revolutionary war:

> "When the enemy advances, retreat;
> when the enemy halts, harass;
> when the enemy avoids battle, attack;
> when the enemy retreats, press him".

In contrast to Vietnam, with its differences between North and South, Cambodia seemed during the 1950s and 1960s, to be a homogenous country — not merely in terms of race and religion but also in the style of life. The plainlands, which make up about three quarters of the country, are its rice bowl. They are bounded to the East by the Moi plateau and on the West by mountain ranges: and the strongholds of the Khmer revolutionary movement were initially established in these areas away from the plain.

The capital, Phnom Penh, derives its name from a devout widow named Penh who, some centuries ago, dedicated a temple on a small hill (Phnom). The city lies about 150 miles from the sea, at the heart of the Cambodian plain, where the Mekong and Tonle Sap rivers come together. It looks out to a wide expanse of water, and can be reached by ships of about four thousand tons and up to about 15 foot draught. After 1970, when the war came to Cambodia, the Mekong river passage became a lifeline. But it was an exposed lifeline, especially in the dry season when the safe channels for navigation were restricted, and ships making the passage were vulnerable to hostile gunfire from the banks of the river. For this reason ships travelled in convoy, and each convoy was a military operation involving patrol craft and aircraft and army activity ashore. A guide to the hazard was that even in 1971 the insurance rate for the "Smokey Joes", the battered old cargo ships and tankers, which kept Phnom Penh supplied, was between 15 and 20% per voyage.

The deep water port of Cambodia is at Kompong Som, sometimes known as Sihanoukville, in South-West Cambodia. The direct distance from Phnom Penh was only 100 miles, but the connecting road could easily be cut. The significance of Kompong Som diminished after 1970. Previously, it had been an important entrepôt for the supply of the Communist forces in South Vietnam.

Laos, the third of the Indo-China countries, is by far the least developed. It is completely landlocked, stretching nearly 600 miles from North to South. It is bounded on the North by China, the East by Vietnam, the South by Cambodia and on the West by Thailand and Burma. The largely mountainous terrain limits economic development. Vientiane, the capital, is on the Mekong and has a population of about 100,000. Luang Prabang, the former royal capital, has a population of about 20,000. The exploitation of the mineral possibilities, such as tin, which are known to exist, is hampered by communications difficulties. But a side effect of the war was an improvement of communications between Laos and Thailand. A direct rail connection was made from Bangkok to Nong Khai on the Thai side of the Mekong opposite Vientiane.

Another relatively recent communications development in the country has been the building by the Chinese of all weather roads in Northern Laos. The purpose of these roads was said to be the connection of the Chinese road system in Yunnan with the road system of North Vietnam. But some observers believed that the development was intended to give China an independent intervention capability in the

Bullock-cart, Cambodia 1970, similar to the cart of a 1000 years earlier shown on the cover illustration.

A typical wet season scene — Cambodia, 1970.

area should the need arise. During the years of conflict, there was almost continuous North Vietnamese involvement in Laos, and both in the North and in the South certain communications were virtually taken over. In Northern Laos, this took the form of denying to the royal government in Vientiane the provinces bordering North Vietnam. Sometimes there was also pressure against the modest local authority close to Vientiane itself. In Southern Laos, the North Vietnamese effort was mainly concentrated on setting up and maintaining the network of trails in the Eastern border area, which became known as the Ho Chi Minh trail. This network linked the Communist support area in the North with its military spearhead in the South and was vital to the Communist cause. On the other side of the coin, there were covert United States and Thai operations involving the Meo tribes people of Northern Laos. The base for this activity was Long Chen, not far from the border of North Vietnam. A few years ago, reports by a United States Senate Committee ascribed the responsibility for the activity to the CIA and defined the whole enterprise as 'the Clandestine War'. Press reports at the time stated that this CIA activity came to an end soon after the 1973 Peace Agreement on Vietnam and Laos.[3]

Although they are now historical, some of the internal sub-divisions of the war should also be mentioned. Laos was divided and numbers of the population were for many years under Pathet Lao Communist control. In Cambodia, pro-Communist forces were, from the fairly early days of the war, entrenched close to the capital, and the writ of the government at Phnom Penh did not run in a number of provincial centres. For almost all of the Cambodian war, considerable areas of the countryside and at least half the Khmer people were under Communist control.

In South Vietnam on the other hand, although a number of countries recognised the Provisional Revolutionary Government of South Vietnam well before the final Communist victory, and indeed large areas of the countryside were under Communist control throughout, most of the provincial centres remained held by Saigon until late in the war. In the aftermath of the 1973 Agreement, a number of newspaper reports suggested the development in the South of a "Third Vietnam" under the direct authority of the Provisional Revolutionary Government.[4] This took in the Communist held regions along the hilly spine of the South as well as other areas of traditional Viet Cong strength. There were reports of road works designed to link them together and consolidate their populations. The capital of this "Third Vietnam" was at Loc Ninh, a long time Viet Cong stronghold about 60 miles North of Saigon and almost on the Cambodian border. As for the status within the Communist camp of the Provisional Revolutionary Government of South Vietnam, this was a matter on which there were different views. Some observers saw it as an entity in its own right; others as a mere appendage of the government at Hanoi. What can certainly be said is that Hanoi consistently proclaimed the unification of Vietnam as its major objective.

1 Salan: *Mémoirs*, p. 440.

2 See also *Far Eastern Economic Review*, 19 September 1976.

3 *Financial Times*, 29 January 1974.

4 *Sunday Times*, 7 January 1974.

2   The Historical Background

THE term Indo-China is more than a geographic description. It also defines much of the history. Vietnamese origins are usually held to lie in Chinese expansion southwards well over two thousand years ago. Communities formed by the ancestors of the Vietnamese existed in the Red River Delta in about 200 B.C. At this time, a Chinese war lord conquered the area and combined it with the South Chinese provinces of Kwangsi and Kwangtung to form an independent kingdom. This kingdom was later annexed by China, and for a thousand years it remained under Chinese rule. During this time, there were a number of insurrections against Chinese authority and, in the end, the region to become Vietnam achieved its independence. Even so, there was continued leaning toward Chinese ways and culture. "China overshadows Vietnam geographically, demographically, linguistically, politically and culturally. Other influences may intrude for a while but China is always present".[1] The ethnic element is manifest. The Vietnamese look Chinese. But a factor of human perversity intervenes. It is true that Vietnam, sometimes described as the "lesser dragon", has its origins close to China, yet, over the centuries, the ruling dynasties of Vietnam have continuously sought to assert their own practical independence from China. At the same time, they have also sought to impose their own domain upon others.

The Han dynasty, of about the same period as the Roman Empire, brought under Chinese rule the area known as Tonkin, the forerunner of the Northern Vietnam of today. During this period, there were resistance movements, one of which, according to contemporary Vietnamese legend was led by two sisters called Trung, who now have a prominent place in the Communist Vietnamese Pantheon. But for nearly ten centuries the Chinese were the rulers. Thereafter, although claiming suzerain status, direct Chinese authority seems to have lapsed. During the thirteenth century the Mongol rulers of China launched an invasion of Vietnam, but it was defeated, and this episode was proclaimed by Ho Chi Minh in a resistance call during the 1940s. About a hundred years after repelling the Mongol invasion, Vietnam was again attacked from the North, this time by the Ming rulers of China. But once more the Chinese were defeated; on this occasion after a decade of guerrilla war. As part of the settlement, however, and to discourage further direct Chinese intervention in Vietnamese affairs, appropriate homage was paid to Peking. Meanwhile, the Vietnamese of Tonkin had their own ambitions. After bitter fighting, they themselves eliminated their Southern neighbour, the kingdom of Champa, a kingdom about half way down the Vietnam coast, which derived its culture from India. Subsequently, they established themselves over the Khmers in the Mekong Delta, and Khmer reserve about the Vietnamese is one of the most fundamental of the facts of life in Indo-China. The hostility between these two peoples is a feud of long standing.

Although the lack of Chinese success discouraged further direct attempts to impose their rule on their troublesome Southern neighbour, it remained the practice for parties contending for power in Vietnam to seek Chinese blessing. "The dragon throne was a kind of Papacy both in its own right and in that of its clients".[2] On the whole, the Chinese seem to have asserted their suzerainty more in relation to a certain residual claim to territory than in seeking specific rule over the people of that territory. The closer to the Chinese border, the closer the relationship. Thus there was a relatively definite claim over the frontier of Tonkin, formally ceded to France in 1883. The claim was less in Annam, and virtually non-existent in Cochin China where, indeed, the Vietnamese presence itself entered only relatively late in the day.

Historically and geographically, the Chinese influence in Indo-China stems from the North and from the land. The 'Indian' influence, on the other hand, lies in the South, and stems, at least in part, from the sea. In human and historical terms, its focus is in the land which is now Cambodia and some of the adjoining areas of Southern Laos and Southern Vietnam. The Khmers, the people of Cambodia, are racially homogenous and very distinct indeed from their Vietnamese neighbours and, as already mentioned, the feud between these two peoples runs deep.

The Cambodians are a brown-skinned people with almost two thousand years of Hindu and Buddhist recall. This alone makes them very different from the Vietnamese. Their language also differentiates them from the Vietnamese. The earliest Chinese records, of nearly two thousand years ago, described them in these terms: "The men are ugly and black and their hair is curly."[3] Possibly there might be Melanesian, Indonesian or Polynesian strains. Perhaps interestingly, New Zealand visitors to Cambodia have sensed some Khmer likeness to the Maori.

Whatever the distant origins, during the first centuries A.D., Indianisation proceeded apace within the area of present-day Southern Cambodia. It was fostered by the contact of visiting travellers and traders, and, by about the fifth century, the principal country of the region, which went by the name of Funan, was thoroughly Indianised. Indianisation operated strongly at the top, through the importation of Brahmin priests and Brahmin ceremonial to confer legitimacy on those who had achieved power, and to add status to occasions. (Indeed, to jump well over a thousand years, even after the deposition of Prince Sihanouk, his half-brother's wedding in Phnom Penh was an occasion for Brahmin as well as Buddhist ceremonial.) The Sanskrit language was used by the ruling class, and the legal code comprised various Hindu elements. The then art of the country, examples of which could until fairly recently be seen in the museum at Phnom Penh, plainly reveals its debt to India.

At some time during the sixth century, the Kingdom of Funan was overrun by its Northern neighbour, Chenla, which also had an Indianised society. Then followed a period of some confusion in which the two states seem to have come together to become Kambuja, the direct forerunner of the present-day Cambodia. By now, a recognizable Khmer type had emerged. Khmer features today are much the same as the features of the Khmers on their sculpture of a thousand years ago. Indeed, more than the physical likeness remains unchanged. To give just one example, the bullock cart in use today in Cambodia has graceful curved shafts: the appearance is exactly the same as that of the bullock carts captured for history in the sculpture of Angkor and other temples in Cambodia.

Then, during the eighth century, Kambuja came under pressure from Java and the sea, and the Khmers moved inland from their first homeland, not far from the present day Phnom Penh. They travelled about two hundred miles to the North, along the Tonle Sap river and settled close to the region which has become famous as Angkor, with its great complex of temples and massive architecture and related irrigation works. Now came the Khmer explosion. From Angkor, the Khmer realm spread out over much of South East Asia. The rulers developed the cult of the God King, associated with the Hindu God Siva, and the kingdom reached its greatest extent in the twelfth century under a King Jayavarman VII — a figure with whom Prince Sihanouk liked to be compared.

After this came decline, associated by some students of Khmer history with the widespread adoption within the country of the Theravada branch of Buddhism with its modest philosophy. The kingdom came under pressure from the Thais and, in the fifteenth century, Angkor itself was abandoned. The Khmers went back down the waterways of Cambodia to the heartland near Phnom Penh, from which they had headed North about seven hundred years before. For much of the outside world, their temple civilisation remained for centuries as a legend, rather like King Solomon's mines; and, for the Khmer state, the centuries from the middle 1400s to about 1850 were a struggle for survival against their powerful neighbours, the Thais to the West, and the Vietnamese to the East.

During this period Khmer survival was aided by the mountain spine of Vietnam which limited Vietnamese expansion westward; but, at around the beginning of the eighteenth century, the Mekong Delta was lost to the Vietnamese. Subsequently, Thailand established a suzerain status over the rest of Cambodia and this persisted until the reunification of Vietnam and the restoration of the Vietnamese empire which took place at the beginning of the nineteenth century. Thereafter came increased conflict between the Vietnamese and the Thais for the control of the remnant of Cambodia. By the middle of the last century, it appeared to the Khmer King, Ang Duong, that his Thai and Vietnamese neighbours were about to make a final partition of his country along the line of the Mekong. He accepted French protection and, a few years later, this was finalised by his son, Norodom, in a Protectorate Treaty of 1863. The Indian influence during the very long period of history, from the first beginnings of Cambodia to the final link with France, was never direct. But it had a living pulse. It was the influence of religion, and of travellers and traders, and, above all, of culture.

For several centuries up to the late 1700s, the history of Vietnam, at that time called Annam, had frequently been one of civil war between North and South. The elongated shape of Vietnam, and the differences between the interests of North and South, were always a complication to central control. In the sixteenth century, there had been two states, often in conflict; and again in the eighteenth century. But in contrast with Cambodia, where the centuries were a long period of decline, there was always outgoing Vietnamese vitality. As for Laos, the Principalities were on the margin.

In 1777, the Nguyen Dynasty in Southern Vietnam was overthrown in a revolt led by the Tay Son brothers who, in 1786, conquered Northern Vietnam also, thereby once again unifying the country. Prince Nguyen Anh, who continued to resist in the South, came into contact with a French missionary called Pigneau de Behaine. Pigneau succeeded in persuading France to intervene on behalf of the Nguyen Dynasty, and achieved a treaty under which France would help Nguyen in return for a number of privileges. Although the French Government later changed its mind about intervention, Pigneau himself went ahead. He recruited a force of a few hundred Frenchmen and, with this military force, played a key role in bringing about the final Nguyen victory in 1802.

In that year, Nguyen Anh was proclaimed Emperor of Vietnam under the name of Gia Long, "Praiseworthy Excellence". He established an Imperial Court at Hue, a city just South of the 17th parallel. Gia Long also undertook the traditional insurance of obtaining from the Emperor of China his investiture as a tributary ruler. His profession of loyalty was respectful: "Prostrate upon the ground, I hope that your Majesty will deign to show me pity. I am not more than a tiny tributary of your Empire and my strongest desire is to be sprinkled by the rain of your generosity. While my thoughts fly toward you and the fumes of incense rise, I address this petition to you".[4]

In this fulsome message, Gia Long described himself as King of Nan Yueh (*Nan* being South, *Yuéh* being a term sometimes applied to a region of South East China). The Chinese Emperor, Chia Ching, preferred that his vassal's country should be called Yueh Nan (South *of* Yueh) to avoid any suggestion that it embraced purely Chinese territory. The name Yueh Nan was applied and local pronunciation turned this into the 'Viet Nam' by which the region is known today.[5]

By the nineteenth century, however, the weakness of Chinese power invited foreign interference in the traditional Chinese areas of suzerainty. In China itself, Britain became the principal Western influence. In Indo-China, the French moved in. In both cases, the flag followed national footsteps. The British those of her traders, the French those of her priests.

From the seventeenth century, French Catholic priests had been active in Indo-China, and, in Vietnam, had achieved the considerable secular and scholastic success of the Romanisation of the local script previously based on the Chinese ideogram. In terms of Vietnamese separation from the Chinese connection, this achievement suggests a landmark.

The Catholic priests, with their *mission civilisatrice* coupled with their religious vocation, may however have moved too strongly against local sentiment. In 1835, a French priest called Marchand was accused of involvement in a plot against Minh Mang, then the ruler at Hué. Minh Mang does not seem to have shared the tolerant attitude toward the Church of his father, Gia Long. Marchand was executed, and for many Frenchmen the manner of his execution by "the death of a thousand cuts" made Marchand, like Gordon in the Sudan, a martyr whose death had to be avenged. By the mid 1850s, the French Fathers were under increasing pressure from the then Emperor of Vietnam, Tu Duc, a great grandson of Gia Long. One of his first proclamations was to the effect that the Christian religion was contrary to nature, since it did not sufficiently honour dead ancestors. Meanwhile, in France itself, the Catholic and Nationalist revival under Napoleon III provided a spur for direct French intervention in the area. The French Navy in the Far East was instructed to take action. Briefly, there was also some Spanish participation to avenge the Catholic martyrdom and, in 1858, a joint Franco-Spanish force took Tourane (now Danang). Shortly afterwards, Saigon was occupied by a French force under Admiral Rigault de Genouilly and, in 1862, the greater part of Cochin China, at the Southern end of Vietnam, was formally ceded to France. The Western presence in Indo-China was now established and, given the background, it was inevitable that it would expand.

Apart from prestige, economic reasons also provided some motive power. Perhaps the Mekong, with a nearby delta port of Saigon, might provide a backdoor to the riches of China? A young French Naval officer called Francois Garnier who was to play a large part in pressing the French interest forward, conceived an exploration of the upper Mekong. This, and the romance which captured France of Henri Mouhot's travel to Angkor, led into Laos, and into Cambodia, where the Khmer monarchy, foreshadowing Khmer ethnic apprehension of a century later, had already recognised that the suzerainty of a power stronger than her neighbours was a vital protection against a carve up of the country by them. In 1863 Cambodia became a French protectorate. By now Southern Indo-China was largely French.

The confidence of the local Governors and Commanders-in-Chief, Admirals of the French Navy, as so often at certain key moments later, was absolute. Thus Admiral Dupré in 1873 telegraphed Paris: "Tonkin est ouvert; necessité absolue l'occuper: demande aucun secours: succés assuré."[6] (Tonkin is wide open: clearly necessary to occupy it: need no help: success assured.) Then, as a century later, but perhaps with more reason, the sometimes siren call of glory beckoned. Once again, a French Catholic priest was much involved: this time Monseigneur Paul Puginier, the Vicar Apostolic of Western Tonkin. Like Bishop Pigneau, eighty years previously, Puginier believed that France had a special rôle to play. However, within twelve months, Tonkinois resistance led to the death in action, close to Hanoi, of Francois Garnier who was spearheading the French occupation effort: the decision of the government in Paris compelled Dupré to withdraw, and another ten years were to elapse before France would be established in Tonkin.

Even then, the hostility of China had to be overcome before the French position was secure. The steady increase of French influence in the 1860s and 1870s caused mounting concern in Peking, not merely in relation to affairs in Tonkin on the southern border of China proper, but in relation to the whole realm of China. Then, as now, the centre of gravity of China lay North of the Yangtse, and the borderlands of greatest interest to China were those of the North. The central issue for the Manchus was probably the extent to which events in Tonkin might be seen by other nations threatening their Empire as a pointer to Chinese will elsewhere; for example, in Korea (soon to fall to the Japanese); in Sinkiang (where the Russians loomed close); in Tibet (where there was British pressure); above all in North China itself.

The formula chosen by China was to operate by proxy through an irregular force (or brigand group, dependent on the view taken). This force, which had its base in the general area of South China and the Tonkin border, was known romantically as the Black Flags.[7] It was in some ways a precursor of the 'volunteers' of the Chinese Peoples Army who intervened in Korea in 1950 and whose possible intervention in Indo-China had also to be taken into account. The Black Flags of the 1880s achieved a certain success as the French pressed North to the Chinese border. In 1883, in a battle close to Hanoi, the Black Flags cut to pieces a French column led by a Captain of the French Navy called Rivière.[8] The reaction of the French Government under Jules Ferry was immediate. An expeditionary force numbering some thousands of men was despatched to Tonkin and a distinguished French Admiral called Courbet was given command. To begin with, all went reasonably well for the French and, in a battle at Sontay, a little way north of Hanoi, the Black Flags suffered a major defeat.

At this stage there was some negotiation. France undertook to recognise the Southern frontiers of China proper. China, without explicit withdrawal of suzerainty, agreed to recognise all existing and future treaties between France and Vietnam. Despite differences on the nature of the financial indemnity sought by France, a draft agreement between the two countries was signed at Tientsin in May 1884.

Following this, the French sought to formalise their position at Hué, the imperial capital of Vietnam, by requiring the ceremonial destruction of the silver seal presented eighty years previously by the Chinese Emperor Chia Ching to his Vietnamese vassal, Gia Long. All now seemed settled. Then, as so often in the history of Vietnam, a local military initiative defeated the efforts of diplomacy. On 23rd June, there was a sharp engagement in the frontier area. The French suffered a number of casualties. War was resumed; this time on a larger scale. The French ultimatum now required full and immediate Chinese compliance with the Tientsin Treaty and payment of a considerable indemnity. In addition, the French envisaged the seizure of certain Chinese territory pending Chinese acquiescence. On the island of Formosa, the port of Keelung was attacked. On 23rd August, Admiral Courbet's squadron, which had established itself at the famous teaclipper Pagoda Anchorage near Foochow, destroyed a large part of the Chinese Navy. On 27th August, an imperial decree from Peking proclaimed that China was at war with France.

Once more, Formosa became a French objective. In addition, Courbet occupied the strategic island group known as the Pescadores, midway between Formosa and the mainland. At this stage, the diplomacy of the Chinese Maritime Customs Service, British controlled then as it was until its demise in the late 1930s, made an effective intervention. Sir Robert Hart, the Inspector General of the Customs Service, sounded Paris on the possibility of settlement based upon Chinese agreement to abandon its suzerain position in Tonkin. During March 1885, an agreement was finalised.[9]

But as had happened before in the political and military affairs of Indo-China, and would happen again, a matter which seemed settled turned out otherwise. Effective orders failed to reach those in command of the troops, or were not heeded by them. A battle with heavy French casualties took place on the frontier near Langson, where, almost sixty years later in 1940, nearly a thousand French soldiers would fall in yet another 'accidental' battle, this time against the Japanese Army of South China. The battle of Langson, at the end of March 1885, did not however destroy the settlement already negotiated, even though in Paris the Government of Jules Ferry was fiercely attacked by Clemenceau and was forced to resign. On 11th June 1885, the Treaty between France and China was finally accomplished. With it, the suzerain Chinese authority over Tonkin was extinguished — at any rate for the time being.

Meanwhile, the years between 1858 and 1885 had seen the consolidation of French power internally over Indo-China as a whole into what was to become the Union Indo-Chinoise. By the end of the century, the effort of the colonial community had turned the region into a rich asset for France. The leadership of Paul Doumer, one of the greatest of the French Governor Generals, played a notable part.

But there was another side. These years were the high noon of Western colonisation, and the economy of the French Empire in Indo-China was completely linked to that of the metropolitan country: for example, the French home tariffs were applied to all non-French goods entering Indo-China. And there was more than the linking of an already established pattern of trade. The pattern of development was also very largely governed by French needs.

The French were by no means alone in this policy of linking colonial development to metropolitan needs. And, by the metropolitan ethic of the day, it was not an unreasonable policy. Moreover, in the French colonies, as in the colonies of the other Western powers, there were many who sought to ameliorate and improve conditions for the local community. But, in general, it was the case that all over South East Asia, the local economies were adjusted to the metropolitan capitalist values.

At the same time, all this seemed natural. Indeed, from one point of view the Western contact conferred a blessing by hastening progress. On occasion, it also brought security. Even so, a number of observers believe that the disruption of the existing rural economies to meet the needs of the West caused deep unhappiness in the local community. The old community structure suffered. With hindsight, it can be seen that the creation of a proletariat serving an alien economic interest, however benevolent, would probably bring trouble. But, at the time, this was by no means clear. Neither was the extent to which resentment could grow against the outsider, however well meaning.

The structure of the Union Indo-Chinoise emphasised the power of France. The component territories of the Union were Cochin China, Annam, Tonkin, Cambodia and Laos. An Emperor of Annam reigned over Annam and part of Tonkin. Likewise, Kings reigned in Cambodia and Laos. But everywhere, the French Administration was supreme. The final right to make kings, as, for example, Prince Sihanouk in 1941, rested with the French Governor General as Agent of France.

Indeed, in the case of Sihanouk, he was a choice slightly out of the direct line, and the background has interest. King Norodom of Cambodia, who had accepted the French Protectorate in 1863, lived until 1904. At French instigation, his sons had been passed over and his brother Sisowath was appointed to the Throne. The latter reigned until 1927 and was succeeded by his son Sisowath Monivong, who reigned until 1941. Monivong's son Monireth now appeared a natural claimant. However, the French considered Monireth too independent-minded. They therefore brought about the selection, as King, of Prince Norodom Sihanouk, a great-grandson through the paternal line of the old King Norodom. At the time, Sihanouk was considered a more malleable choice. It was also thought that this choice might reconcile dynastic disagreement between the Sisowath and Norodom branches of the Royal family, but the breach remained. One of the most able members of the Sisowath line, Prince Sisowath Sirik Matak, was in fact closely associated with General Lon Nol in the events which led to the deposition of Sihanouk in March 1970.

The consolidation of French rule in Indo-China took place at more or less the same time as the consolidation of the French posses- sions in Africa. It was natural, therefore, that French colonial concepts should be centralised and, to begin with, the governing concept was that of *assimilation*: the people of the colonies would become French. Later, as the practical problems of assimilation became more obvious, there was retreat toward *association*. But, if only as an example of the basic French concept of a *mission civilisatrice*, it was fact that in Cambodia, at war in 1971, and with a French Ambassador long absent for political reasons, more than four hundred teachers from metropolitan France were still engaged in providing education and in cementing the cultural link.

The concept of providing education without, however, opportunity to match, posed problems in relation to local nationalist aspirations, which were to dog the French administration of Vietnam until its end in 1954. One authoritative publication states, for example, that until 1936 Cambodians were only employed at the lowest administrative levels within their own country.[10] In terms of population, for every British administrator in British India there were, proportionately, thirty French administrators in Indo-China.[11]

For the Indo-Chinese Union as a whole, which was established in 1903, there was a Governor General. In Annam, as in Cambodia and Laos, local monarchies with their court existed beside the French administration, embodied in a Résident Supérieur, who exercised effective control and authority. In Tonkin, although formally part of Annam, there was a direct colonial administration. There was also a direct colonial administration in Cochin China. Up to the beginning of the Second World War, French policy in Indo-China did not envisage effective self government for the Union as a whole or in part. In 1939, Bao Dai, the Emperor of Annam visited Paris to try to persuade the Popular Front Government that France should relax her administrative stranglehold on his country. The attempt was fruitless.[12]

So much for the internal picture.

Externally, the situation was governed by Chinese weakness and by the Anglo-French entente of 1904. During the 1890s, France had acted determinedly to limit Thai advance toward the Mekong Delta. This had led to differences between France and Britain. The Anglo-French entente established, in effect, an Anglo-French hegemony in South East Asia, with Thailand a buffer state between, and this situation stood until the end of the 1930s.[13]

[1] Duncanson: *Government and Revolution in Vietnam*, p. 23.
[2] Duncanson, p. 43.
[3] Briggs: *The Ancient Khmer Empire*, p. 16.
[4] McAleavy: *Black Flags in Vietnam*, p. 17.

⁵ *Ibid.* p. 18.
⁶ Lê Thánh Khôi: *le Vietnam*, p. 373.
⁷ McAleavy, p. 100.
⁸ *Ibid.* p. 204.
⁹ *Ibid.* p. 269.
¹⁰ The American University: *Cambodian Handbook 1973*, p. 32.
¹¹ Duncanson, p. 103.
¹² Lancaster: *The Emancipation of Indo-China*, p. 76.
¹³ Lyon: *War and Peace in South West Asia*, p. 17.

3   The Origins of the Indo-China Independence Movements

T
HE history of Vietnam illustrates many examples of the independent nature of its people. Their reaction to the French presence was no exception. It is true that the French were accepted by the hill peoples, the Montagnards, who to some extent saw the French as protectors against the Vietnamese themselves. But, elsewhere in Vietnam, the French did not achieve the degree of rapport which they did in Cambodia and Laos. There were many reasons for this. Perhaps not least of them, the fact that the dynamic character of the Vietnamese was offended by the social structure of the colonial system. In very approximate terms, this comprised a French *élite*; then a middle class in which the Chinese community were strongly represented; and, below this, the mass of the Vietnamese themselves. There were exceptions, but this was sufficiently close to the reality to be a factor for trouble. Yet, even if there had been more opportunity for the Vietnamese, it is not really possible to say that their final reaction would have been any different. Sooner or later, they would have reacted against outside intervention, however well meaning. The achievements of the colonial period in its hey-day, in bringing security and in development, cannot be ignored. But there is the other side. The run of events does suggest that colonists cannot usually afford to remain a minority for very long.

In Indo-China, the years of French occupation were years of continuing resistance by various local groups. This resistance, always much stronger in Vietnam than in Laos or Cambodia, was carried out by different elements. At first, the mandarins and aristocrats sought the badge of leadership and, in the late 1880s, the Royal Family of Annam were the main spring of a guerrilla movement which in military terms was a precursor of the Viet Minh and Viet Cong of 60 or 70 years on. Indeed, over the years, three Emperors of Annam were deposed by the French. These depositions took place in 1885, 1907 and 1917. In this last case, the then Emperor, Duy Than, was personally involved in a plot against French rule. Subsequently, the nationalist movement increasingly gained ground among intellectuals and schoolteachers. Finally, came the Communists under Ho Chi Minh.

A major landmark in Indo-China, as in India (where Congress for the first time proclaimed independence as its objective), was the Japanese victory over the Russians in 1905. Vietnamese activists themselves by far the most active of the indigenous political aspirants, turned their eyes to Japan. The Vietnamese Prince, Cuong De, who was a direct descendant of the Vietnamese Emperor, Gia Long, who had united the country at the beginning of the 19th century, was involved. Cuong De had placed himself at the head of the Nationalist movement, and fled to Japan when the local situation grew too difficult for him. There, he was to be heard of again in the events of fifty years later. But in the years just before the 1914 war, perhaps because of some requirement for Western finance for development, Japanese pan Asian ambitions were muted. In 1910, Japan expelled a number of prominent Vietnamese nationalists and dissolved the previously active Vietnamese student association in Japan.

South China now took over from Japan as the overseas base of Vietnamese nationalism. For this nationalism, the China of Doctor Sun Yat-sen was a happy forcing ground. In the aftermath of the first World War, which further stimulated Vietnamese nationalism, Canton was the main meeting place for Ho Chi Minh, now becoming known in South Vietnam, and Borodin, the Soviet organiser of revolution in Asia. This was not Ho's first contact with Soviet Communism. In 1922, and again in 1924, he had been a visitor to Moscow. But then, as later, Ho Chi Minh saw clearly that Marxism as a doctrine would by itself awaken no echo in the Vietnamese masses who were peasant and traditionalist. It was necessary therefore to proceed in two stages: first, along with other elements, to establish Vietnamese independence on a basis of nationalism: then a second revolution to establish a completely Socialist regime.[1]

Along with nationalist leaders from other countries, who saw opportunity at Versailles in 1919, Ho Chi Minh did in fact submit an appeal at that time to the Allied leadership.[2] Ho Chi Minh's memorandum, a copy of which is said to be on display at the Revolutionary Museum in Hanoi, seems to have asked for equality in Vietnam for the colonial people, and for greater local autonomy. It stopped short though of a bid for complete independence from France. The memorandum had no effect. Thereafter came the contact with Moscow and with Borodin in Canton.

The Chiang Kai-shek break with the Communists in 1927 completely changed the position for Ho Chi Minh. He no longer had a secure base close to his own country and, despite his founding of the Indo-China Communist Party in 1929 or 1930, he does not himself appear to have been in the front line in the disturbances in Annam at about this time, in which, first the rival Vietnamese Nationalist party, and then his own Communist party, were both separately involved.

The Vietnamese Nationalist party, the Viet Nam Quoc Dan Dang, usually referred to as the VNQDD, had been founded in the mid 1920s by a middle class group of journalists and school teachers. It was modelled on the Kuomintang of Chiang Kai-shek, and its activities took in extortion and assassination as adjuncts to its proclaimed objectives, which were predominantly nationalist. In 1929, it sought to induce disaffection among Vietnamese troops in the French forces, and four companies of troops at Yen Bay were persuaded to mutiny to coincide with some planned terrorist activity elsewhere. The French security services got on top, and there was drastic action against the Nationalist Party membership. Those who survived fled across the Chinese border into Yunnan. In the following year, the Communists organised disturbances at Vinh. Several thousand country people were persuaded to march and demonstrate. Once again the French reaction was drastic. The trail led clearly to the Indo-China Communist party and its leader.

Despite his apparent absence from the scene, Ho Chi Minh was regarded by the French as one of the principal instigators of the trouble and was tried *in absentia* for complicity in the events, and was sentenced to death. By this time, Hong Kong was Ho Chi Minh's chosen sanctuary, and this led to an interesting British involvement in his life. The name Ho Chi Minh had not yet appeared and, except in the relevant documents of the British courts concerning him, the name generally used in description of the North Vietnamese leader was Nguyen ai Quoc. In the legal documents, the name used was Sung Man-cho, "a person of Chinese origin". For the purpose of telling the story here, the name Nguyen ai Quoc is used.

The story[3] begins at the end of 1930, when Nguyen ai Quoc entered Hong Kong without permit. After some months of illegal residence, he was arrested by the Hong Kong police on 6th June 1931 in a police raid on premises entered using a magistrate's warrant issued under the Seditious Publications Ordinance (1914). Although no seditious material was apparently found, Nguyen ai Quoc was detained. He was not, however, brought before a magistrate's court within the time laid down in the search warrant, and the Hong Kong court reports also refer to "other irregularities".

These various irregularities saved Nguyen ai Quoc when his lawyers appealed against a Hong Kong government deportation and ship order directing that he be placed on board a named French ship due to sail from Hong Kong for Indo-China. Given the absence of appropriate extradition machinery, it was argued that this order went beyond the right of the Hong Kong Government merely to expel from its territory any person who had entered the colony illegally. And, although his true identity was manifestly known, Nguyen ai Quoc himself chose not to admit to it, and held formally to the identity of Sung Man-cho. The governing factor was of course the political aspect. Nguyen ai Quoc had been tried in absentia in Indo-China and had been condemned to death by the colonial tribunal at Vinh and, although this sentence had since been commuted to hard labour, other charges were outstanding against him. Some of these, such as incitement to murder, carried the death penalty. With the French Government taking a detailed interest in the case, it had the making of a cause célèbre.

The first test of the matter was in the Hong Kong Courts by way of habeas corpus proceedings in which Nguyen ai Quoc's counsel, briefed by a well-known Hong Kong solicitor, Mr. F. H. Loseby, established the invalidity of the deportation order. This was on 20th August 1931.

Following this, and despite some apparent reserve on the part of the Governor, a second and more carefully prepared deportation order was served on Nguyen ai Quoc. Once again, the issue was questioned in the Hong Kong Supreme Court. This time, on 11th September 1931, the Court validated the deportation order, which yet again included the direction that Nguyen ai Quoc should be put on a French ship for Indo-China. Almost at once, however, the Hong Kong Court gave Nguyen ai Quoc permission to appeal to the Privy Council in London.

At this stage, the French authorities indicated that if Nguyen ai Quoc were returned to Indo-China, the Résident Superieur 'would use his authority to avoid capital punishment'. There also appeared, at this time, to have been some differences of opinion within Whitehall concerning the case. The Colonial Office now favoured Nguyen ai Quoc being required to leave Hong Kong as soon as possible — but with no direction as to his destination. The Foreign Office advised that the matter should await the decision of the Judicial Committee of the Privy Council. Events followed this second course.

The case was due for hearing before the Privy Council on 27th June 1932, with Sir Stafford Cripps, who had only recently ceased to be Solicitor General, appearing for the Hong Kong Government, and D.N. Pritt, the well-known left wing lawyer, appearing for Nguyen ai Quoc. Pritt outlined the position in his biography:[4] "it did not take Cripps long to see what a bad showing the case would make for the Hong Kong Government and for the Colonial Office, and he approached me with the suggestion that the matter should be disposed of by letting Ho leave the colony under his own steam, going wherever he wished. Ho had, of course, always been willing to do this, and there was consequently no difficulty in dealing with the matter in that way so the appeal was never argued in open Court".

The agreed terms were approved by the Judicial Committee of the Privy Council on 21st July 1932: the Council comprising the Lord Chancellor, Lords Irwin, Tyrrell, Betterton and Avory. The main points were:

(a) The Hong Kong Government had the right to deport Nguyen ai Quoc.

(b) But the deportation order ought not specify the particular ship on which he should leave.

(c) The appellant should not be placed on a French ship or be sent to French territory.

(d) The Hong Kong Government would help the appellant reach his chosen destination.

(e) The appellant would receive £250 costs.

The story was not quite ended. Nguyen ai Quoc now decided that he would like to travel to Britain. Once again, Stafford Cripps became involved. He advised that, while Nguyen ai Quoc had to leave Hong Kong and was not to be put at risk, he could only go where he would be accepted, and the Home Office had made it clear that he would not be accepted in Britain. Meanwhile, the French continued to watch their target who, at the end of 1932, apparently managed to travel to Singapore and back. On 19th January 1933, Nguyen ai Quoc was once more arrested by the Hong Kong police. Three days later, he was quietly shipped for Shanghai on board the S.S. Anwhei. He did not actually leave harbour on board her but, to disguise the trail, was taken out to the ship in a Government launch after dark and embarked outside Hong Kong harbour. The British involvement was at last ended.

Between 1933 and 1936 Ho Chi Minh was in Moscow at the Lenin School:[5] then, from 1936 to 1941, in China. He returned to Vietnam in 1941, and had a brief spell as a prisoner of the Nationalist Chinese before final emergence in full light in Vietnam in 1943 as a partisan leader, well regarded by the American liaison officers in South China. Throughout his years away from his own country, Ho Chi Minh appears however to have maintained a firm grip on the Indo-Chinese Communist party. In particular, during the immediate pre-war years, he appears to have influenced the party to follow the international Comintern line, which developed in the face of the growing fascism in Europe and Asia, toward co-operation with other nationalist groupings and the formation of a "popular front". At the same time, the Indo-Chinese Communist party maintained its own clandestine net, "awaiting a hatchet blow to the existing order from outside, which would give it the opportunity to seize power".[6] No great imagination was needed to expect that the hatchet blow might come from Japan.

To return to Ho Chi Minh. By 1933, and by now known generally as Nguyen ai Quoc (Nguyen the Patriot), he was already over forty years old. Born in 1890, near Vinh, close to the 17th parallel, which for more than twenty years after the 1954 Geneva Conference marked the line of division between North and South Vietnam, he was of middle class Vietnamese stock. His father is said to have been a man of nationalistic leanings, which were absorbed by the young Ho Chi Minh and, after an education at the Hué Lycée, Ho Chi Minh's political views began to get him into trouble with the authorities. In 1912, he left Vietnam, and is reputed to have spent some time in London as an apprentice pastry cook at the Carlton Hotel before involving himself in political life in France, first as a member of the Socialist Party, later as a member of the Communist Party. Thereafter, the contact with the Comintern. The record of the man is of political prudence, personal charm, great capacity to plan (or plot, according to the point of view taken), Communist belief and nationalist determination.

An almost contemporary Vietnamese patriot was Ngo Dinh Diem who, during the late 1950s and early 1960s, was to stand so strongly against Ho Chi Minh. Ngo Dinh Diem also came from middle Vietnam near Vinh. His family, however, was Catholic and mandarin, and by the early 1930s, Diem was holding high office under Bao Dai the Emperor of Annam. But not for long. He found the over-riding French sovereignty an affront, and withdrew from public life. He lived for nearly ten years in relative obscurity near Hué. In 1945, he refused an offer to join Ho Chi Minh, and another to join Bao Dai. Then more refusal of power, although lobbied from time to time by various parties, until emergence in 1954 as the central political figure in South Vietnam.

The years between 1951 and 1954 appear to have been crucial in establishing United States interest in Diem. Following some contact in Tokyo between Diem and Professor Fishel of Michigan State University, the University apparently sponsored a visit by Diem to North America. Subsequently, there were some very positive assertions that in their contact with Diem and his regime, Michigan State University had acted as the agent of the CIA. Indeed, Fishel himself, is quoted[7] as having said, "after two years I surfaced — to use a CIA term — to become head of the MSU program". This MSU program was a U.S. Government financed "public administration" program with some emphasis on police work. During his visit to the United States, Diem spent much time at Maryknoll seminaries under the jurisdiction of Cardinal Spellman, and gradually became known in American political circles as an effective lobbyist for the anti-

Communist cause in Vietnam. Supreme Court Justice William Douglas was impressed with him and arranged a breakfast meeting with the then Senator John Kennedy and with Senator Mike Mansfield, later to become Senate Majority Leader. The two senators had been critics of the French rôle in Vietnam and strongly propounded an independent nationalist alternative. Diem appeared to them to be suitable leadership material.[8] A characteristic of Diem, like Ho Chi Minh, was nationalist determination.

There were also royal patriots. Bao Dai, the Emperor of Annam, may have appeared the playboy, but at least, in the view of General Catroux,[9] the French Governor in 1939 and 1940, and of General Salan later, Bao Dai was a key national figure. And the judgment of Dean Acheson, Secretary of State in the Truman Administration was that "Bao Dai had ability and claims to stature and leadership as the legitimate claimant to the throne, which could have been an important asset in Vietnam. His handicap was long residence on the French Riviera, and the suspicion of being a captive King".[10] Certainly, Bao Dai's 1945 appeal to de Gaulle to grant independence to Vietnam was one of great dignity and patriotic force.[11] Unfortunately, the nature of the French administration limited for too long the rôle of the Emperor. In Cambodia, where Sihanouk sensed that the continued existence of the Khmer nation jammed between the Thais and the Vietnamese was the all important objective, the priorities were different.

Similarly, in Laos, the Princes represented a basic patriotic element and, within Vietnam, in addition to the political parties seeking constitutional change, various newly formed religious sects, notably the Cao Dai and the Hoa Hao, also had a nationalistic role. Each of these sects had hundreds of thousands of adherents in their local areas. Their beliefs, however, are by no means easy to define.

The Cao Dai flourished in Southern Vietnam. The sect, which combined elements of Catholicism, Hinduism and Spiritualism worshipped the Cao Dai (Supreme Being) who was said to communicate with members through the spirits of the dead. It was founded in Saigon in the mid-1920s. It offered 'protection', and developed an elaborate organisation which in some ways followed Roman Catholicism. In 1927, its 'Holy See' was established at Tay Ninh, close to the Cambodian border. Their clergy were headed by a 'Pope', and their 'Saints' included Victor Hugo. By 1940, there may have been as many as one million Cao Dai adherents.

The Hoa Hao sect, whose strength was also in Southern Vietnam came to the fore a little later than the Cao Dai. Its leader Huynh Phu So, who prophesied the defeat of the French by the Japanese, advocated a simplified form of Buddhism and, like the Cao Dai, the sect offered 'protection'. To touch briefly on the future, both sects were to clash with the Communists in the years ahead. In 1947, they, along with others, openly broke with the Communists and declared their support for Bao Dai.

The 1930s also saw a bonus to the various nationalist causes through concessions of free speech and association to French colonial peoples. This was a spin off from the election in France of a Popular Front Government. It applied particularly in Cochin China, which by virtue of its colonial status, enjoyed a more liberal regime than the protected territories of Annam and Tonkin. The act of liberalisation provided an opening for various left wing factions and, as the Japanese war with China developed in the late 1930s, and the Second World War broke out in Europe in 1939, the local force best equipped to challenge French power in Indo-China was the Communist party of Ho Chi Minh. And this was so, even though Ho Chi Minh himself was outside of Vietnam at this time.

[1] Devillers: *Histoire du Viet Nam*, p. 58.

[2] Fall: *Ho Chi Minh*, p. x.

[3] Public Records Office 1931/82837; 1932/92610; 1933/13790. Hong Kong Law Reports for 1931 and 1932 (Vol. XXV p. 62).

[4] D.N. Pritt: *Autobiography: Right to Left*, pp. 137–138.

[5] Bernard Fall: *The Viet Minh*, pp. 30, 32 and Wood's 'Selected' speeches of Ho Chi Minh.

[6] Duncanson, pp. 147, 148.

[7] Gettleman: *Vietnam: History and Documents*, p. 260.

[8] *Ibid.* p. 248.

[9] General Catroux: *Deux actes du drame Indo Chinois*. General Salan: *Memoirs*.

[10] Dean Acheson: *Present at the Creation*, p. 671.

[11] See p. 38.

4 *Japanese Hegemony: 1940 – 1945*

IN July 1937, Japan set off the so-called China incident: in fact, war with those areas of China which could be reached by the Japanese Armed Forces. For Chiang Kai-shek and the Nationalist Government, the safe supply route from Tonkin to South West China was now of vital importance. This importance was also well appreciated by the Japanese who, from August 1937 onward, sent numerous notes of protest to Paris against its use. For the French in Indo-China, the traffic was highly profitable. All their pressure was for its continuance and for increased French military strength in the area. To the Japanese, the traffic came close to provocation. At the beginning of 1939, they occupied Hainan island off the Gulf of Tonkin. A month later, they seized the Spratley islands which at that time were nominally French.

For Chiang Kai-shek, there was in fact some solace in the Japanese occupation of Hainan. Chiang was convinced that the Sino-Japanese War would at some stage become part of a wider Pacific War in which the United States would be an ally. Such a war was bound to end in defeat for Japan, and within his circle, Chiang spoke optimistically of the Japanese action against Hainan as an event which guaranteed this war.[1] But for the French, the pressure was now on and, shortly before the outbreak of the Second World War, General Catroux was named as Governor General of Indo-China. This was the first time for more than fifty years that a General (or an Admiral) had been chosen for the appointment. Catroux arrived the day war broke out. His mandate from Paris was to ensure the maximum contribution to the metropolitan war effort. His own immediate assessment was that not a soldier could be spared.[2] The armies of Japan loomed nearby, large and menacing, their blockade of China hampered by a recently announced French decision in favour of allowing war material for Chiang Kai-shek to continue to enter China by the route of Haiphong and the Red River railway to Yunnan.

By mid 1940, the French defeat in the West had changed the balance even more adversely against the French position in Indo-China. Catroux's first response to the famous call of 18th June by de Gaulle was a message to the metropolitan government, by now in Bordeaux, recommending that in Asia the Anglo-French alliance should continue.

There was no reply. On 19th June, Catroux received a Japanese ultimatum to close the supply route to China and to accept a Japanese Control Commission to confirm the closure. Given the military balance, Catroux had little option but to accept, and to hope that the Japanese would not raise their bid. Elsewhere in South East Asia, the British attitude at this critical moment was not so very different. On 27th June 1940 (in the aftermath of Dunkirk) Singapore was closed to military traffic to China, as was the Burma Road between 17th July and 17th October.[3]

Meantime, before a first meeting with General Nishihara, Chief of the Japanese Control Commission, which was due to take place on 29th June, Catroux sought help from the United States and Britain. In particular, he asked America for 120 aircraft and for certain anti-aircraft equipment, to redress the balance between the French aircraft strength of about 20 machines and the nearby Japanese strength of about 300 machines. The French Ambassador in Washington replied that Summer Welles, the United States Under Secretary of State, had said there could be no assistance. Then, on 27th June, Catroux met in Saigon with Admiral Sir Percy Noble, the British Naval Commander-in-Chief in the Far East. Apart from the overriding political factors imposing constraint at this time, the British Admiral also made it clear that much as he personally would wish to help, he lacked the means to do so. Of his all important force of 15 submarines, 12 had already been detached outside the area because of the critical situation in Europe. Of the three which remained in the Far East, two were undergoing refit. In private conversation with the French Naval Commander, Noble also made an unsuccessful attempt to persuade him to sail the French Fleet in the Far East to British ports. At about the same time, Catroux heard from Vichy that "foreign activities in French territory were unacceptable",[4] and received the somewhat impractical instruction to "halt negotiations" with the Japanese.

While Catroux was facing these major governmental issues, he was also under considerable personal pressure. For his acceptance of the Japanese terms he had earned a black mark from the disorganised French government, which itself had just signed the armistice with Germany. Perhaps Vichy also recognised his leaning away from them in the appalling conflict of loyalty which faced all Frenchmen at this time; and Catroux learnt, during June, of the Vichy intention to replace him by his immediate colleague, Admiral Decoux, the French Naval Commander in the Far East. At that stage, the two men, still saw broadly eye to eye. By early July, however, Decoux's views had changed, and it is reasonable to think that the British attack on the French fleet at Oran on 3rd July may have been a factor in this. Thereafter, he was much more a man of Vichy and anxious to assume authority. This he did on 20th July. Shortly after, Catroux, by now in Singapore, rallied to de Gaulle.

The problems facing Decoux were daunting. On his Northern border, the Japanese army had the bit between their teeth: inside Indo-China, there was some upsurge of independent local nationalism. All this was coupled with the pressing task of maintaining French identity nearly ten thousand miles from France in the wake of the recent major disaster to France herself.

Within days, the Japanese had increased their demands. No longer were they satisfied with the cut-off of supplies to China. Their requirement now was for military facilities within Indo-China. Decoux appears to have counselled against concessions, but Vichy decided otherwise and, on 30th August 1940, agreement was reached as follows[5]:

(a) Japan would recognise French sovereignty in Indo-China.

(b) France would recognise Japanese pre-eminence in the Far East and would grant Japan appropriate military facilities in Indo-China.

(c) The application of the agreement would be settled by the local French and Japanese military commanders.

"The business seemed settled: it was not".[6] The discussion on the application of the agreement took place against a background of increased Japanese pressure. At sea, the Japanese navy made a demonstration in force in the Gulf of Tonkin. On land, the Japanese army in South China massed to attack. By 21st September, however, detailed agreement had been reached giving Japan the use of a number of airfields in Northern Indo-China. A subsequent extension of this agreement covered airfields in the South, one of which was used a year later by the aircraft which sank the *Prince of Wales* and *Repulse*. The Japanese were also given the right to station some thousands of troops in the country. Sadly however, the agreement of 21st September came too late to avoid bloodshed.

The leadership of the Japanese forces in South China had the itch for battle. On 22nd September, in professed ignorance of the agreement reached the previous day, a major Japanese attack developed across the frontier at Lang Son, about 70 miles north of Haiphong. The attack took place in the same area where the French army had suffered so heavily nearly sixty years before. In the fierce fighting which followed in September 1940, well over eight hundred French soldiers lost their lives.[7] There is some feeling among a number of French people that this onslaught, which took place a whole year before Pearl Harbour, is insufficiently known in the English speaking world. In the immediate aftermath, the Japanese army entered Haiphong, but in relatively limited numbers, and nearly five years were to pass before Japan would seek finally to oust French authority.

For the French administration, the year 1940 still, however, had its headaches in store. In Cochin China, there were some relatively amateur Communist uprisings (the hand of Ho Chi Minh and his military commander Giap being absent). These were fairly soon contained. An altogether larger development, and one which thirty years later was to hold a place in the very forefront of the political judgment of Prince Sihanouk, were the Thai attacks at the end of the year against Laos and Cambodia. Certainly, at sea, the French reaction was effective, and on 17th January 1941 a small French squadron under Captain Bérenger sank a substantial part of the Thai Navy capable of putting to sea in a battle off the South Coast of Thailand adjoining Cambodia. Admiral Decoux described this victory as the first success of 'France vaincue', and one which would accord Bérenger a place in history as the victor of Koh-Cheng. Understandably, as the Governor General and Commander-in-Chief, he also claimed a share of the honour.[8] But a land battle in Western Cambodia went much less well. And once again, Decoux received a Japanese ultimatum which, after Lang Son, could not be taken lightly. The upshot was a settlement involving the loss to Thailand of some Laotian territory, along with the Cambodian provinces of Battambang and Siem Reap.

Decoux's memoirs of his years in Indo-China indicts the Japanese for conspiracy with the Thais. He also mentions, as matters contributing to his problems, the then recently signed Treaty of Friendship between Britain and Thailand, and the detention by the Royal Navy in the Gulf of Aden, in October 1940, of the French transport *Esperance* carrying much needed reinforcements from Djibuti to Indo-China.[9] In local terms, the episode was a gain to Thailand at Vichy's expense. On the larger canvas, it marked a further extension of Japanese influence as events moved toward war in the Pacific.

Throughout this period, the French position in Indo-China was manifestly vulnerable. Decoux's memoirs frequently refer to his tightrope, and to his pride that the tricolour continued to fly over the country. Decoux's own summary of his "foreign policy" as the area was enveloped by the Pacific War reads as follows[10]:

(a) To defend French sovereignty in Indo-China against the Japanese.

(b) To observe as strict a neutrality as possible.

(c) Not to exceed the obligations toward Japan agreed by the French Government.

(d) To limit where possible the effect of these obligations.

(e) To maintain the status quo where the frontier with China was open.

(f) To ensure that such joint defence agreements as existed were not put into practice.

Decoux also records his counsel to the French of Indo-China. Once again a few brief headings spell out his policy.[11]

(a) Union, Cohesion, Silence. To be silent is to serve.

(b) Resistance to propaganda or initiatives which would divide the French of Indo-China, and put them one against the other.

(c) Resistance to the Japanese to be discreet so as not to produce a dangerous reaction.

(d) Union and discipline of all the French of Indo-China so that the country might return intact to France at the end of the war.

(e) Action in the social domain to the benefit of all.

Internally, within Indo-China, the war years were marked by two main trends. One of these was the way the Decoux administration sought increasingly to come to terms with the indigenous interest while still preserving the special French position. Schools and hospitals were built in increasing numbers, and new opportunities were provided for local people. Late in the day, an attempt was being made to improve contact between the French and the Indo-Chinese peoples and to "win the hearts and minds" of the population. The other trend was the military and political expansion, especially in North West Tonkin, in the lee of the Chinese army of Yunnan, of the Viet Minh under Ho Chi Minh and Giap: this 'Viet Minh' being the old Indo-China Communist party expanded to take in other Vietnamese independence groups.

The Viet Minh was set up in 1941, with some Chinese Nationalist support, following a congress at Ching Hsi in South China. At this congress, the Vietnamese Communists joined with other Vietnamese Nationalists to form the League for the Independence of Vietnam: the Vietnam Doc Lap Dong Ming Hoi, better known as the Viet Minh. But within the Viet Minh, the Communists held the posts of influence. Ho Chi Minh was the Secretary-General. It was not long before the Chinese Nationalists had second thoughts about the Viet Minh, and extended their sponsorship elsewhere.

At this time, as on a number of occasions, Ho Chi Minh followed the course of prudence, and played down Communist objectives. To have done otherwise would have sharpened further the latent hostility toward the Viet Minh of Chiang Kai-shek and the Chinese Nationalist leadership. Indeed, for a while, Ho Chi Minh was their prisoner.[12]

However, in the middle years of the Japanese occupation, he was released. The circumstances are by no means clear, but it is sometimes suggested that the reason related to the organisation and supply of intelligence. Whatever the reason, it would be surprising if Ho Chi Minh had not been expected to keep reasonably in line with the Nationalist Party of Vietnam whose ideas parallelled those of the Chinese Nationalists. It was at about this time, and connected by some with the intelligence task, that he became known as Ho Chi Minh, a name which roughly translates as "he who enlightens".[13]

Once safely back in Tonkin, Ho Chi Minh extended his political authority. He also re-insured with elements of the U.S. Office of Strategic Services carrying out intelligence and aircrew rescue duties in Southern China and Northern Vietnam. According to some observers, he gained marks by guerilla operations against the Japanese.[14] Equally, there is a view that the Viet Minh studiously avoided action against the Japanese.[15] What is generally accepted, however, is that, in June 1945, as the overall Japanese position was crumbling, Ho Chi Minh was strong enough and politically astute enough to establish a "liberated area" in the hills of Thai Nguyen, north of Hanoi, a stronghold to which the Viet Minh returned when driven out of Hanoi in December 1946.

But outside of Tonkin, the Viet Minh writ was a lesser force. In the South, during the last months of Japanese authority, the Kempetai, the Japanese security police, apparently spread their favours among other Vietnamese beneficiaries. Ngo Dinh Diem is said to have been among those who were helped by the Kempetai.[16] The Cao Dai and Hoa Hao sects with their blend of the religious, the political and the para-military were also beneficiaries. In certain areas of Cochin China, the sects became the masters. What distinguished the Viet Minh, however, was that although their main political and military power was in the North, there were at least some elements of their strength in most parts of Vietnam. Under Ho Chi Minh, they could make a reasonable claim to be a nationwide force.

Externally, there was also movement. A key event was the re-establishment, under de Gaulle in 1944, of a French Government in Paris. By the beginning of 1945, there were clear signs that for Japan in the East, as for Germany and Italy in the West, a day of reckoning was close. Towards the end of 1944, Decoux's previous full powers became subject to the judgment of a Gaullist orientated *Council of Indo-China*. "Some judgments to lead to tragedy then followed: the military resistance leaders understood neither the mood of the people of Indo-China nor the sentiment of the leadership of China and the United States."[17] Notably, this concerned the timing of action to be taken — or not taken — by the French forces in Indo-China against the Japanese occupation army.

Unhappily, French security was ineffective, and their planning was soon penetrated by the Japanese Security Police, the Kempetai. The Japanese quickly became aware that Gaullist policy envisaged a clash of arms at an appropriate moment: certainly in the case of any American landing. Decoux appears to have continued to counsel prudence, but alongside his formal authority, real command of the French forces in Indo-China now lay with the elements of the Council of Indo-China led by the Gaullist nominee, General Mordant. A query by Decoux to Paris brought a top secret telegram from M. Pleven, Minister for the Colonies, to Decoux, which noted the latter's unpublished "act of subordination" to the Paris Government, and emphasised Mordant's military responsibilities. The same telegram also envisaged a Jour J (D Day) for French armed action at an appropriate moment.[18] For the Japanese, apprehensive of the possibility of allied landings in Indo-China, there was a military requirement to strike first.

On 9th March 1945, Decoux was faced with a final Japanese ultimatum requiring French forces to be placed at once under Japanese command. Decoux demurred and, after a period under arrest in Hanoi, was transferred to a rubber plantation near Loc Ninh — a region later to become well known during the war of the 1960s and 70s as a Viet Cong stronghold. The Japanese acted fiercely to achieve their objective. For many of the French administration, the upshot was brutal .... All over Indo-China, massacre and execution at the hands of the Japanese was commonplace.[19] At Langson, where the French garrison carried out a spirited defence against a strong Japanese attack before eventually being overwhelmed, the two senior French Army officers, General Lemmonier and Colonel Robert, and the civilian Administrator, M. Auphelle, were executed by the Japanese. They were forced to dig their graves, and were then beheaded. Many others in the French garrison were shot out of hand. The ripples reached as far as London. The reserve of the United States Government toward the French position in Indo-China was well known. Because of this Mr. Churchill telegraphed Field Marshal Wilson in Washington, to make a private approach to General Marshall, the Chief of Staff of the United States Army. "It would look bad in history if we let the French force in Indo-China be cut to pieces by the Japanese through ammunition shortage if we could save them. The Prime Minister hopes we can agree on not standing on punctilio in this emergency."[20]

But there were elements of French heroism to redeem the misjudgments which had brought on the Japanese action, and had disregarded intelligence reports of the impending Japanese attack, and had indeed cancelled a State of Alert ordered by General Sabattier, the French Commander in Tonkin. Some of the French forces in the North were able to break out, and a column under General Alessandri made the long march over the mountains to safety in Yunnan, and, in all 6000 French troops got away, approximately half of them soldiers from France itself, the remainder Indo-Chinese troops. With re-equipment, this force could have been the spearhead of a French return. But it was no part of Chinese Nationalist policy to aid the return of French authority to Indo-China, "and there was marked reluctance to re-arm and re-equip the French survivors."[21] Some of the events of the future were already casting their shadow.

The Japanese action of 9th March was intended to batter the French authority, and it achieved this purpose. The French hold was broken, and, in the view of Admiral Decoux, all the misfortune to follow stemmed from French failure, after 1944, to continue to follow his counsels of prudence.[22] The action was also intended to spur local nationalism, and, on 11th March, in response to Japanese pressure, Bao Dai dutifully announced the independence of Vietnam. On the next day, Sihanouk followed suit with an announcement of Cambodian independence. In Vietnam and elsewhere in Indo-China the result was administrative breakdown. The situation was made to measure for the Viet Minh.[23]

[1] Henry McAleavy: *The Modern History of China,* p. 306.

[2] Catroux, pp. 8–25.

[3] Churchill: *The Second World War,* Vol. II, p. 225 and p. 440.

[4] Catroux, pp. 40–87.

[5] Devillers, p. 77.

[6] Pedrazzani: *La France en Indo Chine: de Catroux à Sainteny.*

[7] Fall, p. 19.

[8] Decoux: *A la Barre de l'Indo Chine,* p. 141.

[9] Decoux, pp. 128–144.

[10] Decoux, p. 212 and p. 263.

[11] Decoux, p. 366.

[12] Duncanson, p. 153.

[13] Lancaster, p. 114.

[14] Gettleman: *Vietnam History and Documents,* p. 47.

15 Lancaster, p. 116.

16 Duncanson, p. 151.

17 Devillers, p. 119.

18 Decoux, p. 309.

19 Pedrazzini, pp. 133–140.

20 Churchill: *The Second World War,* Vol. VI, p. 632.

21 Lancaster, p. 111.

22 Decoux, p. 484.

23 Duncanson, pp. 156–157.

5 1945 – 1946 Transition and Opportunity: The French Return

BY the beginning of 1945, it was clear that Japan had lost the war. But the desperate Japanese resistance in the Pacific Islands did not point to its early end, and it would be no criticism "that the Allied Command was not fully prepared politically, militarily and logistically for the immediate imposition of its authority in Japanese occupied South East Asia."[1] In addition, however, major delay and difficulty arose from the instruction issued by General MacArthur, the American Supreme Commander, who had been given special authority,[2] that the documents of surrender in theatres other than his own might only be signed after his own had been signed: moreover, that no landing or reoccupation by military forces might be made until after formal surrender in Tokyo. The very real vigour of the allied reaction in South East Asia was restrained, above all, by external factors.[3]

On 6th August, had come the first atom bomb on Hiroshima and, three days later, the second bomb on Nagasaki. On 10th August, the Emperor Hirohito, in an historic broadcast, his first ever to his people, told the Japanese that they had been defeated. On 15th August, Japan capitulated. In South East Asia, strong naval forces were already well out at sea in the heavy weather of the South West monsoon, poised for reoccupation of Japanese held territory. For about two weeks, they had to mark time pending the Japanese surrender in Tokyo on 2nd September 1945.[4]

The international background at this moment bore very directly on the future of Indo-China. President Roosevelt, long affronted by de Gaulle, had made no effort to conceal his reserve toward any continued French presence in Indo-China, apparently having in mind some possible Sino-American tutelage of an independent Vietnam — perhaps even some Russian involvement.[5] The post war scene in the Far East had come up on the margin at the November 1943 Combined Conference of Allied Leaders; and General Stilwell who doubled as Lord Mountbatten's Deputy in South East Asia and as Commander of U.S. forces in China, recorded President Roosevelt's view on Indo-

China as expressed to him at this time. The view was blunt: "NOT TO GO BACK TO FRANCE".[6] Inevitably, this bias against the reimposition of French colonial rule still coloured some American official thinking, although Roosevelt himself had died a few months previously. In China, the government was that of Chiang Kai-shek; anti-Communist but also anti-colonial; at any rate as far as the colonies of others were concerned: yet perhaps having its own territorial ambitions, an aspect unlikely to have been lost on Ho Chi Minh. In Britain, a Labour Government had come into power which was committed to the liquidation of its own imperial position in India. But the message from de Gaulle which reached Indo-China on 15th August was on a somewhat different frequency: "France was now ready to resume its responsibilities for the benefit of all".[7]

This announcement related both to de Gaulle's special statement of 24th March on Indo-China, and to the principles to govern post-war French colonial policy which had been laid down at a Free French conference at Brazzaville in January 1944 at which de Gaulle himself had been present. The preamble of the political recommendations laid down that "The aims of the work of civilisation which France is accomplishing in her possessions exclude any idea of autonomy and any possibility of development outside the French Empire bloc. The attainment of self government in the colonies even in the most distant future must be excluded."[8]

Within Indo-China itself, the situation hardly pointed this way. It had been agreed at the Potsdam Conference that Indo-China should be divided into two separate occupied zones: the forces of Chiang Kai-shek would have responsibility North of the 16th parallel: those of Admiral Mountbatten, the Allied Commander in South East Asia, would have responsibility South of this line. (In the view of Lord Mountbatten "this decision caused great difficulty at the time, and sowed the seed for ever greater conflicts in the years to come".)[9] Formally, the Japanese surrender was to the Allies. But, on the spot, the Japanese leaned towards passing power to Ho Chi Minh and the Viet Minh who, pending the arrival of any allied forces, also represented the focus of power.

The mood of the moment was well conveyed in a message sent by Emperor Bao Dai to de Gaulle on 20th August pleading for a recognition of the nationalist tide now flowing so strongly:

> "I address myself to the people of France, to the country of my youth. I also address myself to its Head of State and Liberator, and I would like to speak more as a friend than a Head of State.
>
> You have too much suffered during these fateful years not to understand that the Vietnamese people, with twenty centuries of history and glorious past, can no longer accept foreign rule.

You would understand still better if you were able to see for your-self the situation here, and to sense the heartfelt wish for independence. Even if you were able to re-establish French rule here it would not be obeyed; each village would be a nest of resistance; each collaborator an enemy; and your French colonists would themselves seek to leave this atmosphere.

I beg you to understand that the only way to safeguard French interests and the French cultural heritage in Indo-China is by frank and open recognition of the independence of Vietnam, and by renouncing any idea of re-establishing French authority here under whatever form.

We would so easily be able to reach understanding and friendship if you were to cease to claim to be our masters.

I appeal to the idealism of the French people and the wisdom of its Head of State, and I pray that the peace and happiness now for all the peoples of the world will equally be assured to all the people of Indo-China." [10]

There does not appear to have been any reply to this message. Meanwhile, the Viet Minh continued to consolidate their position, and a few days later, at the Imperial Capital of Hué, Bao Dai signed a formal act of abdication. Once again the dignity of his words merits quotation in full.

"The happiness of the Vietnamese people. The independence of Vietnam. To achieve these ends we have declared ourselves ready for any sacrifice, wishing that our sacrifice may help the country. Recognising that at this moment the union of all our fellow countrymen is a necessity for our country, we reminded our people on 22nd August that in this decisive time for the nation, unity meant life and division death.

Given the powerful democratic impulse developing in the North of our country, we fear that conflict between North and South may be inevitable if we await the opening of a National Congress. We know that if such a conflict were ever to arise it would plunge all our people into suffering and help our invaders.

We cannot escape a sentiment of sadness at the thought of our glorious ancestors who, during four centuries, have struggled for the greatness of our country. We cannot fail to experience regret in looking back at the twenty years of our reign, during which we have hardly been able to give significant service to the nation.

In spite of this, and strong in our belief, we have decided to abdicate and to transfer power to the Democratic Republic Government.

At the moment of relinquishing our throne, we would only wish to express three wishes:

(a) We ask the new government to take care of the dynastic temples and of the royal tombs.

(b) We ask the new government to treat as brothers all the parties and groups who have waited for the independence of Vietnam, even though they may not belong to the popular movement: thus to give them the chance to join in the re-building of the country and to show that the new regimè is itself built on unity.

(c) We ask everyone, including the royal family, to stand together to support the new government so as to consolidate our
national independence.

As for ourselves, during twenty years of reign we have certainly
known many sorrows. From now on, we are happy to be a free citizen of
an independent nation. We will not permit anyone to misuse our name
or that of the royal family, to sow discord among our fellow citizens.

Long live the independence of Vietnam.
Long live our Democratic Republic."[11]

Events were now moving fast. During the night of 23rd August
two separate parachute operations took place over Indo-China.[12] One
was in the South. Colonel Cédile, the French Commissioner designate
for the South and two companions dropped near Tay Ninh, about fifty
miles from Saigon, with instructions to assert French authority and to
offer to the Viet Minh de Gaulle's terms of 24th March, which held out
for Indo-China a special position within the French Community, "an
autonomy proportionate to its evolution and attainments."[13] But at
this stage, the local leadership of the Viet Minh, already holding power
and awaiting the arrival of British troops to take over the Japanese
positions, showed no wish to transfer authority to Cédile. In due course,
it was through these British troops that authority was subsequently
transferred to Cédile. But this comes later. Before then, on 31st August,
Cédile contacted Decoux at Loc Ninh. Decoux, who appears to have
believed that he still had an effective rôle to play was formally told that
his mandate in Indo-China was terminated. Indeed, within six weeks he
was in France under arrest. Decoux's memoirs reveal his personal
bitterness alongside a certain lack of awareness of the new tides now
flowing in the world.[14]

Meanwhile, the other parachute operation in the North had fared
less happily. Here, the French team was led by Colonel Pierre Messmer,
the French Commissioner designate for the North who, many years
later was to become the Prime Minister of France. Shortly after
landing, Messmer and his two companions were detained and held by
the Viet Minh. After some weeks in captivity, during which Captain
Brancourt the medical member of the team died, Messmer and
Lieutenant Marmont, the only other survivor, made an epic escape to
the Chinese lines. During this time, another man, Jean Sainteny, a
notable leader of the Resistance in France, was appointed
Commissioner in Messmer's place.

But events had already moved. During August, Ho Chi Minh had
acted decisively to assert his authority in Hanoi and on 22nd
September, he had proclaimed the independence of Viet Nam under
the Viet Minh. "Le Viet Minh sert actuellement de base a l'union et à la
lutte de notre peuple. Affiliez vous au Viet Minh, apportez lui votre

soutien et faites qu'il se renforce davantage."[15] (The Viet Minh is now the basis of the unity and struggle of our people. Join the Viet Minh. Give it your support. Help it grow stronger.) With the occupation army of the Chinese Nationalists expected shortly, Ho Chi Minh also appealed for discipline. His Declaration of Independence borrowed deliberately both from the United States Declaration of Independence and from the 1791 Declaration of the French Revolution.[16] Its opening words enunciated that all men were born equal, and possessed inalienable rights, among them life, liberty and the pursuit of happiness.

The declaration went on to assert that, after 1940, the French in Indo-China had failed to respond to Viet Minh proposals for action against the Japanese. "The truth is that we have wrested our independence from the Japanese and not from the French: the French have fled: ... The Japanese have capitulated: the Emperor Bao Dai has abdicated." Finally, came an appeal to the allies: "we are convinced that the allied nations, which at Teheran and San Francisco have acknowledged the principles of self determination and equality of nations, will not refuse to acknowledge the independence of Vietnam: ... a people who have fought side by side with the allies against the fascists during these last years: such a people must be free and independent."

Then, on 6th September, a small British team arrived in the South to look after prisoners of war. On 12th September, the first major unit of the British forces came ashore in Saigon. It was part of Major General Gracey's 20th Indian Division, a division comprising both British and Indian troops. The instructions given to its Commander were to occupy no more of Indo-China than was required to secure control of the Japanese:[17] explicitly, that Field Marshal Count Terauchi, the Supreme Commander of the Japanese Expeditionary Force (South), whose headquarters were in Saigon, should clearly understand his personal responsibility for ensuring that his forces fulfilled their surrender obligations effectively and in detail.

By now, however, the situation was close to flash point. Some French elements were in combative mood, among them units of the colonial army recently released from captivity. Likewise, certain Vietnamese, and there were a number of hideous atrocities.[18] In this extremely difficult situation General Gracey, whose brief was to beware of involvement, believed he had no alternative but to establish martial law. His proclamation, which prohibited all political demonstrations and processions, covered however all of Southern Indo-China, and not merely the required allied key points, and Lord Mountbatten who saw political pitfalls counselled negotiation.[19]

Mountbatten was also anxious about being sucked into a military commitment for which adequate forces might not be available. The 3rd and 9th French Colonial Infantry Divisions (D.I.C.'s), which had been designated for service in Indo-China, were both still in Europe and, although Mountbatten urged that their arrival should be speeded up, their advance elements could hardly be expected to reach Saigon before the beginning of November.

Within 48 hours, there was a crucial development. To quote from Mountbatten's despatch: "On 23rd September General Gracey had agreed with the French (Cédile) that they should carry out a coup d'état; and with his permission, they seized control of the administration of Saigon and the French government was installed. Considerable fighting took place during the night, but British/Indian troops had taken over the security of all important positions". The situation was one of enormous complexity, not least because of the use of Indian troops and the state of public and political opinion in India. At a meeting in Singapore on 28th September, to which Gracey and Cédile were summoned, Lord Mountbatten stressed the importance he attached to the early commencement of negotiations between the French and Viet Minh. It was a turning point: judgment after the event cannot lightly be made.

Gradually, the French position consolidated. General Leclerc, a man of great quality, whose armoured division had won fame in the war in Europe, and who had, since August, been Commander-in-Chief under Mountbatten of French forces in the South East Asia command, arrived in Saigon on 5th October.

On taking over Military Command in Indo-China, Leclerc was counselled by Mountbatten that the rising tide of Asian nationalism was not a factor to be ignored, and that the open hand of friendship offered the best hope for future partnership between the former colonies of the West and the old metropolitan powers.

Mountbatten's farewell words were:[20] "You are now going to share responsibility for Indo-China with d'Argenlieu (now appointed as High Commissioner), I beg you to understand that you cannot put back the past: there is a new situation". To which Leclerc replied: "What you say makes sense but is not French policy. I have been told we must strengthen our military position to be able to negotiate friendly terms". Even so, within the limits of his directive, Leclerc did his very best toward the nascent nationalism represented by Ho Chi Minh's government in Hanoi.

On 9th October, an agreement signed in London between the British Foreign Secretary and the French Ambassador, M. Massigli, recognised French responsibility for the civil administration. Step by step, the French re-established their grip on the provinces in the South, where Viet Minh strength was relatively weak,[21] while the British forces briefly maintained their position in Saigon until the departure of General Gracey in January 1946. The success achieved by Leclerc was considerable. Within three or four months, the French presence had been effectively reasserted in the Southern part of Vietnam and Cambodia. Indeed, in Cambodia, Leclerc flew to Phnom Penh and personally arrested Son Ngoc Thanh, who had been put in power by the Japanese when they superseded the Vichy French administration earlier in the year. Leclerc realised however, that despite the presence of Viet Minh forces under a capable leader called Nguyen Binh, the South was the soft skin. The hard nut in the North had still to be cracked.

As had been agreed at Potsdam, Chinese forces arrived to carry out the occupation of Indo-China, North of the 16th parallel. The task fell to four Chinese armies totalling nearly 200,000 men under General Lu Han, the Chinese military Commander of Yunnan, who some time later defected to the Communists.

"The Chinese troops entered Tonkin as if it were a conquered province".[22] They also brought with them various tame Vietnamese emigré elements to help their position, and they were warmly welcomed by the Chinese community numbering some hundreds of thousands, most of them merchants and traders. During October 1945, General Ho Ying-chin the Chinese Chief-of-Staff, visited Hanoi, and, while saying that China had no wish to annex North Vietnam, went on to add that China would be happy to help the country toward independence, and to announce that for the present French shipping would not be permitted to enter Indo-Chinese waters north of the 16th parallel.[23] Ho Ying-chin was too close to Chiang Kai-shek for the Chinese position not to be clear. Not only were the Chinese preventing the return to Indo-China of the troops who had made their escape into Yunnan after the Japanese action of 9th March; they also continued to hold in semi-internment the French troops who had been confined by the Japanese. At this stage, there was certainly no indication that the Chinese Nationalist leadership had in mind any early return of French power.

The significance of these various Chinese actions and declarations was not lost on the Viet Minh leadership, who had no wish to exchange one colonial master for another. Ho Chi Minh also appreciated the risk to his régime inherent in the occupation of Tonkin by the forces of a Government already engaged within China against Mao Tse-tung and his Communist followers. Ho Chi Minh's qualities of prudence stood him in good stead. Quite deliberately, he put the brakes on his own party.[24] Increasingly, he stressed the image of Uncle Ho, whose legend spanned the party lines. Indeed, on 11th November, he publicly dissolved the Communist Party. Clearly, he maintained the all important private network. Even so, the public gesture was meaningful.

Ho Chi Minh sought to prove to the Chinese Nationalists that he wished to bridge the divisions in North Vietnam and, on 19th November, he concluded an agreement with the Vietnamese Nationalist Party. This was sensible window dressing, and the "election" to be held early in 1946 was allowed to go forward. Unsurprisingly, it was won by the Viet Minh, who continued to lean on the prestige of the former Emperor Bao Dai and maintained his status as "Principal Counsellor to the Government". Indeed, Sainteny recounts that Ho Chi Minh rebuked one of his Ministers who referred to Bao Dai as "Counsellor": "The title is Monseigneur:"[25] Later on, this was also the title by which Sihanouk liked to be addressed, when Head of State of Cambodia, after ceasing to be King.

In the immediate aftermath of the election, Ho Chi Minh made the following statement to the correspondent of the French daily paper *Résistance.*[26] "We bear no ill will against France and her people. We admire them greatly and have no wish to break our links with the French people. But we ask that France takes the first step. We wish it all the more as we see other nations involve themselves in our own affairs." The statement went on to underline Vietnamese readiness to fight for independence.

In Saigon, General Leclerc recognised that the Viet Minh apprehension about the Chinese presence North of the 16th parallel, would be played as a high card in re-establishing French influence in Tonkin. But, at any rate to begin with, this was not a card to be played suggesting the use of force. Return could only be through negotiations, and negotiating channels were already in existence: — in Chungking through normal diplomatic channels; in Hanoi, through Sainteny the French representative with the Viet Minh.

A negotiating pattern emerged surprisingly quickly which, to some, may have suggested elements of concealed and personal inducement for the Chinese involved. For a price pitched high, but not impossibly so, China appeared to be prepared to leave North Vietnam. The price was the surrender by France of her concessions at Shanghai, Tientsin, Hankow, and Canton: plus gift of the Yunnan railway and the establishment of free port and transit facilities through Haiphong into China. The French leased territory at Kuang Chow Wang, in the nearby Liau Chau peninsula, had already been given up shortly before. Subject to agreement, and to final signature on 1st March, the relief by the French army of the Chinese troop in the North might take place between 1st and 15th March.

The French negotiation with the Viet Minh also proceeded at a surprisingly fast pace, helped along by Viet Minh suspicion that China wished to retain her present considerable influence in Tonkin. For the Viet Minh it was a choice between the devil and the deep blue sea. It would be surprising, however, if Ho Chi Minh's views had not been very considerably weighed by the news of 30th January 1946 that General de Gaulle had withdrawn from power in France. The assumption of authority by Felix Gouin, and the replacement of Jacques Soustelle, the Minister of the Colonies, by Marius Moutet suggested a possible turning point in favour of the Viet Minh.

Meanwhile in Indo-China, General Leclerc, for his part, was prepared to go some way along the road toward recognition of Vietnamese independence to bring the country back into the French sphere. But inside Indo-China there were other views which counted. In particular, Leclerc clashed with Admiral d'Argenlieu, Carmelite monk, regular Naval Officer, and faithful Gaullist, recently arrived as French High Commissioner in Indo-China. D'Argenlieu was profoundly opposed to the concept of the independence demanded by the Viet Minh. At this stage, Paris supported Leclerc, and on 25th February a joint Viet Minh/French communiqué was published announcing that President Ho Chi Minh had discussed with M. Sainteny, the French representative in Hanoi, the possibility of official negotiations between France and Vietnam.[27] The President recalled that the Vietnamese position was *independence and co-operation*. M. Sainteny made known that France agreed to recognise the right of Vietnam to its own Government, Parliament, Army and foreign exchange. The question of Vietnamese diplomatic representation was discussed. There was agreement on the need for detente.

The negotiation continued under way, and the Viet Minh sought Chinese help to improve the terms. They also started to move their own public opinion toward settlement. Finally, on 6th March, a Franco-Vietnamese convention was signed. An English translation of the full French text is at Appendix A. Its main terms were:[28]

(a) The French Government recognised the Republic of Vietnam as a free State, having its own Government, Parliament, Army and finance, as part of the Indo-Chinese Federation and the French Union. Concerning union (of Tonkin, Annam and Cochin China), the French Government undertook to ratify the decisions of a referendum.

(b) The Vietnam Government declared itself ready to welcome the French Army when, in conformity with international agreements it would relieve Chinese forces.

(c) On signature of the agreement, both parties would take all measures to avoid incident, and to create the atmosphere for friendly negotiations bearing on:
   (i)   Vietnamese Diplomatic Relations.
   (ii) The future status of Indo-China.
   (iii) French cultural and economic interests in Vietnam.

(d) The French military presence would diminish by one-fifth
each year, to phase out completely after five years.

Ho Chi Minh's own view of the convention is illustrated by the
widespread support he sought to obtain for it among his political peers,
among them Bao Dai. When Sainteny made his formal call on Ho Chi
Minh on 6th March, the former Emperor was by his side. In Sainteny's
view this was to "licence by this presence the authority of Ho Chi Minh
as Head of the Government and also his action in concluding an
entente with France."[29] Ho Chi Minh said to Sainteny, "You have won.
You know I wanted more than this. But one cannot have everything at
once."[30]

The Viet Minh leadership was indeed sufficiently anxious about
the reaction of their own public opinion that they arranged a large
public meeting in Hanoi the day after the signature. Giap, as military
leader explained the problem with candour. His main points were:[31]

(a) The agreement had good and bad elements. It was something
that France recognised the Democratic Republic of
Vietnam as a free country.

(b) The Viet Minh aim was a united Vietnam. Although France
had wanted to keep Cochin China separate, she had now
agreed on a referendum. 'The result of this was certain'.

(c) The leadership was far from happy about the return of
French troops but had accepted the position. Why? Because
there was no real option.

(d) France now had America, China and Britain on her side. The
Democratic Republic was on its own.

Ho Chi Minh, who was received with great warmth, also spoke.[32]
He stressed that the agreement opened the way to international
recognition. French troops would be under allied orders, and the agreement stipulated that after five years they would be gone. Surely it was
better to avoid the sacrifice of tens of thousands of lives and reach
independence through negotiation. "Keep calm and maintain
discipline," he told his people, "I will not let you down".

On the same day that the convention was signed, a powerful and
well prepared French assault force which had left Saigon a week earlier
arrived off Haiphong. The arrival was not without incident. The local
Chinese Commander professed that he could not permit any landing to
take place, and his artillery opened fire. The French reacted with
determination and after an hour of heavy engagement, with some dead
on both sides, the battle was won. The determination of General
Leclerc had secured the return of the French presence to Tonkin. What
remained to be seen was the way in which the convention establishing
this presence would be observed by the two sides.

[1] Duncanson, p. 157.

[2] General Order No. 1 approved by the President of the United States and the Prime Minister of the United Kingdom.

[3] Lord Mountbatten's report, p. 184.

[4] *Ibid.* p. 184 also personal experience.

[5] The public papers and addresses of Franklin D. Roosevelt, 1944–5. *Vichy and Threshold of Peace,* pp. 562–3.

[6] Tuchman: *Sand against the wind.* Stilwell, p. 405.

[7] Pedrazzani, p. 150.

[8] Lancaster, p. 123.

[9] Mountbatten, Section E preface.

[10] Devillers, p. 138.

[11] Devillers, p. 139.

[12] *Ibid.* pp. 150–160. Hammer: *The struggle for Indo-China,* pp. 8–11.

[13] Hammer, p. 43.

[14] Decoux, pp. 341–347 and 476–480.

[15] Pedrazzani, p. 157.

[16] Fall: *Ho Chi Minh,* p. 141.

[17] Mountbatten, pp. 285–287.

[18] Devillers, pp. 156–162.

[19] Mountbatten, p. 287.

[20] Personally recounted by Lord Mountbatten.

[21] Devillers, pp. 156–162.

[22] *Ibid.* p. 191.

[23] *Ibid.* p. 193.

[24] Devillers, p. 200.

[25] Sainteny: *Ho Chi Minh and Vietnam,* p. 58.

[26] Devillers, p. 204.

[27] Devillers, p. 218.

[28] *Ibid.* p. 225.

[29] Sainteny, p. 59.

[30] *Ibid.* p. 64.

[31] Giap: *Peoples War,* p. 27.

[32] Devillers, p. 240.

6 1946 — The Slide to War

GENERAL Leclerc, who on his way to Indo-China had spent several weeks in Ceylon at Admiral Mountbatten's headquarters, appears to have shared the latter's touch for the new Asian nationalism. The general, whose considerable war record included leading French forces back into Paris and Strasbourg, made sure that when his column reached Hanoi, every tank and truck bore the colours of Vietnam as well as the French tricolor. Similarly, Leclerc arranged that the guard for his residence should comprise both French and Vietnamese soldiers. From the beginning, Leclerc sensed the aspirations of the new nation; and a staff officer's note annotated *Read and Approved* by the general himself listed his views as follows:[1]

   (a) Take on nothing we cannot carry through.

   (b) Limit French involvement to what is essential, and avoid interference in internal Vietnamese matters.

   (c) Accept that common structures can only be built in common, and concentrate on co-operation.

   (d) Ho Chi Minh and his team have the confidence of the country. Entente with them is essential.

Leclerc's impressive personality clearly came across well to Ho Chi Minh. Their meeting went smoothly, and Sainteny recalls that with Ho Chi Minh there was never reason to fear the sort of "breach of good manners" as when Giap had introduced himself to Leclerc with the words "the top resistant of Vietnam is pleased to meet a top resistant of France." Sainteny says that Leclerc's attitude was one of some reserve. Perhaps a trick may have been missed. The future would amply justify Giap's right to have made the claim. But in any case Leclerc's own stay in Indo-China was coming to an end, and local authority lay increasingly with Admiral d'Argenlieu in Saigon, and the Admiral's views were very different to those of the General.[2] Thus, during the month of the landing in the North, "I marvel that with such a splendid expeditionary force its leaders prefer negotiation to battle"; and, on 20th March, at a reception for the King of Cambodia, d'Argenlieu publicly invoked Munich in speaking of the policies of Leclerc. The central issue was the nature of post-war Indo-China. The French traditionalists had in mind a dominion, with something considerably less than full sovereignty embracing all its units. They were also anxious, not without some reason, about North Vietnamese influence in South Vietnam.

During 1946, the Viet Minh, whose armed forces were steadily growing in strength, were almost continually in dialogue with the French authorities on these issues. At the end of March, Admiral d'Argenlieu, flying his flag in the cruiser Emil Bertin, visited Along Bay in North Vietnam, and received Ho Chi Minh on board his flagship. The Vietnamese sought early and conclusive negotiations. The Admiral (unlike Mountbatten in India) was in no hurry. The Vietnamese asked for talks in Paris, since they believed that a solution in their favour would be more likely to emerge at talks in the metropolitan country than in the colony. The Admiral offered Dalat, a hill resort in Southern Vietnam. Eventually, agreement was reached on a preliminary meeting at Dalat. Ho Chi Minh himself did not attend, but Giap was a leading member of the Vietnamese delegation and spoke in fiery terms against French offers which fell well short of independence.[3] The upshot was agreement to meet again in France.

On the Vietnamese side, the argument consistently returned to 'Independence (for all Vietnam) and Alliance'. In a statement reported in Le Monde on 14th July, Ho Chi Minh spelt this out.[4] "On the political plane the contacts between France and Vietnam must lead to a treaty. The basis of this treaty must be the right of self determination and, provided there is action in the common interest, we accept association with France on economic and cultural matters within the French Union. An Indo-Chinese Federation can justify itself by the necessity for some economic co-ordination, and Vietnam, which is wealthier than her two neighbours, is ready to help them. But Vietnam stands firm against the Federation becoming a Governorate General in disguise."

Ho Chi Minh then had this to say about Cochin China where military elements of the Viet Minh were already active, "It is Vietnamese land. Before Corsica was French it was Vietnamese." Finally, he spoke of French interests, stressing Vietnamese readiness to give a special place to France in the new Vietnam.

These statements were intended for the French people as well as the French Government, and followed the opening, on 6th July, of the Fontainebleau conference on Vietnam. The Vietnamese side were hopeful that this conference in France, with General de Gaulle withdrawn from authority, and with strong Socialist influence present, might be more productive than their dialogue with d'Argenlieu. Indeed, they believed that d'Argenlieu had sought to sabotage the possibility of agreement by a recent proclamation, apparently on his own authority, of a Provisional Republic of Cochin China with all significant powers reserved to France.[5]

This was an unhappy adventure. On 1st July, the French authorities in Saigon named as President of this Republic of Cochin China a widely respected Doctor of Medicine called Nguyen Van Thinh. Thinh was a moderate who had been active in the politics of Vietnam since before the war. It seems that Admiral d'Argenlieu felt that with the Fontainebleau conference so close he could not wait any longer for authorisation from Paris for action which he believed necessary.[6]

On 10th November Doctor Thinh hanged himself. According to General Salan, he committed suicide out of frustration and unhappiness. Thinh had become increasingly disturbed at the false position in which he found himself, "Despite the inauguration of a seemingly independent Republic within the French Union the French authorities in Saigon continued to treat the local authority as a lesser French department".[7]

Meanwhile, the Viet Minh leadership was outraged. On 1st August, Pham Van Dong, who was already one of Ho Chi Minh's closest colleagues, slammed the point home. How could d'Argenlieu's action square with the convention of 6th March? On 11th August, *Le Monde* reported that the leading political figures of the South saw the leftward leaning of Hanoi as the obstacle to Vietnamese unification.[8] But this leftward leaning was not yet striking the echo which might have been expected with the men of the left in Paris. Indeed, although the Communist line would change later, Maurice Thorez, the Communist Vice-President of the Council of Ministers, had said to Sainteny in advance of the talks: "The agreements are satisfactory: we have nothing to add or subtract if the Vietnamese do not respect the terms: let the guns speak for us".[9]

The Fontainebleau conference dragged on. French public opinion was not yet running sufficiently strongly to sway the traditional position on Indo-China; a position which, on 27th August, was endorsed by de Gaulle, whose views from retirement would not be lost on the Bidault government. "United with the overseas territories which she opened to civilisation, France is a great power: without these territories she would be in danger of no longer being one".[10] It can only be a matter for speculation as to the upshot, had de Gaulle acceded to Ho Chi Minh's various requests for a meeting with him. Sainteny says he believed that Ho Chi Minh was deeply hurt that neither de Gaulle nor Leclerc received him.[11] Yet, for Leclerc, some element of caution was understandable. He had already come under criticism for "liberal meddling".

On 12th September, the conference broke up, leaving unsigned a draft *modus vivendi* representing what had appeared to be the bare minimum of agreed views. Two days later, after a personal meeting with Bidault, Ho Chi Minh put his signature to the document which made economic and cultural concessions to France: "I have signed my death warrant" were Ho Chi Minh's words to his detective escort; and, to Sainteny and Moutet, the Socialist Minister for the Colonies: "Don't let me leave this way: give me some weapon against the extremists: you will not regret it".[12]

An English translation of the text of this important document is at Appendix B.

The effect of the modus vivendi has been well summarised, as permitting the resumption of French economic activity in the North, while maintaining the status quo on political and military matters. More dubiously, it was also taken by some French opinion as permitting the immediate collection by France of the customs duties on which the all-Indo-China budget was largely based. These duties, mainly paid by French citizens, had been counted on by the Viet Minh to more than make good the local revenues lost as a result of their decision to free the peasants from all taxation. A number of disputes were to arise over the collection of customs duties, and one of these would be the fuse which finally set off the explosion which, a few months, later triggered the French War in Indo-China.

The customs problem, and increased Viet Minh military activity in the South, which were to bring the situation to flash point, developed during the first half of October. The modus vivendi said that joint commissions would work out how, and by whom, the country's currency should in future be issued, and how, and for whose benefit, the customs duties should be collected.[13] On 10th September, four days before the signature of the modus vivendi, the French authorities in Hanoi announced that France would take full and sole control of the customs at Haiphong as from the middle of October: after the modus vivendi this order was not amended ....[14] At Haiphong considerable sums of money were involved: especially the money of rich Chinese traders, and, whatever the French legal and financial rights may or may not have been, they may also have felt that any customs duties collected by the Viet Minh would go straight to the purchase of yet more arms for them. There was a heightening of tension and, unhappily for the cause of peaceful settlement, these were weeks when Ho Chi Minh was out of touch, returning by sea from France on board the French Navy sloop *Dumont d'Urville*, and Giap, his military deputy, had commenced to make the running.[15] Giap was now the leader of a force of 30,000 men with a reasonable stock of arms, and his relative youth and his temperament probably worked in the direction of the use of this force.

On 20th October Ho Chi Minh reached Haiphong. Despite the tension, the magic of 'Uncle Ho' had suffered no diminution with his own faithful, and Ho Chi Minh still proclaimed Franco-Vietnamese co-operation. Meanwhile, the military wing of the Viet Minh under Giap had taken advantage of this 'co-operation' to crack down on its only local political rival, the Vietnamese Nationalist Party,[16] whose Chinese Nationalist backers had departed just a few months before. The thread of co-operation was thin but not yet broken.

From now on, however the path lay downhill, and both sides were helped along the slope by some of their leading military. The level of Vietnamese terrorism mounted, especially in the South, and certain French units responded with equal ferocity. Perhaps less forgivable than the reaction of the fighting man on the ground were certain incidents for which the headquarters of Admiral d'Argenlieu was believed responsible. On two occasions, vital messages from Ho Chi Minh to Paris, which might have led toward peaceful settlement, were apparently delayed at d'Argenlieu's headquarters in circumstances which have been considered to arouse suspicion.[17]

On 11th November, Ho Chi Minh sought urgently to communicate to Bidault his anxiety about the "unilateral French action creating French customs facilities at Haiphong". "At this moment, when the mixed commissions envisaged in the modus vivendi of 14th September are commencing negotiations, it cannot escape you that this action may have grave consequences ... I am sure you will wish to consider instructions to withdraw measures counter to the Franco-Vietnamese entente". This message, which could have been in Paris the next morning, did not reach Paris until 26th November. In the meantime the incident took place which led to war.[18]

On 20th November, a French patrol craft at Haiphong, arrested a Chinese junk on suspicion of smuggling. The Viet Minh militia, the Tu Ve, then obstructed the French boat and detained its crew. Colonel Debès, the French Commander at Haiphong, alerted strong forces, and there was some shooting. At this stage the local liaison committee met and managed to achieve a cease-fire and the release of the French prisoners.[19] But by the afternoon the Viet Minh had not obeyed French instructions to remove barricades put up in the Vietnamese quarter of the town. At this stage, there was more prolonged fighting but, once again, the local liaison committee succeeded in patching up a cease-fire.

From Saigon, General Valluy, the military Commander, and also at this time acting as High Commissioner while d'Argenlieu was in Paris, told General Morlière, the senior French officer in the North, to make it a condition of negotiation with Ho Chi Minh that all Viet Minh forces evacute the Haiphong area.[20] From an immediate military standpoint, it was perhaps understandable that Valluy should wish for complete military control of Haiphong. But Morlière appreciated that it was a wish which could not be achieved without major use of force and, on

22nd November, he reassured Saigon that the incident of 20th November was now settled. The ceasefire still held.

On 22nd November, General Valluy, in Saigon, received a message from d'Argenlieu, passing on M. Bidault's approval that the Haiphong incident be used to teach the Vietnamese a lesson. At this stage, Valluy apparently bypassed Morlière, and directly instructed Debès at Haiphong "to use all the means at your disposal to become master of Haiphong and bring the Vietnamese army to a better understanding of the situation".[21] On 23rd November, Debès issued an ultimatum in Haiphong requiring Vietnamese evacuation within two hours. The Vietnamese said they had to await instructions from Hanoi. After a brief delay, the French guns opened up, and Admiral Battet, whose flagship the cruiser Suffren was involved, estimated that civilian dead could have numbered as many as six thousand.[22] By 28th November, the French were masters of the town, the airport and the harbour of Haiphong.[23]

The senior French liaison officers in Hanoi still did their best to reduce the tension.[24] Admiral d'Argenlieu and his Deputy, General Valluy, tilted the other way. A message which Ho Chi Minh sent on 15th December to Léon Blum, the new French Prime Minister, and which, like the message of 11th November, could have reached France next day, did not reach Paris until 26th December.[25] The key part of the message was a proposal that both sides should revert to their pre-20 November positions. Meanwhile, the soldiers prepared. Giap withdrew battalions from Hanoi and other towns, and reinforced the Viet Minh stronghold about fifty miles north of Hanoi. Elsewhere tunnels and bunkers and road blocks were prepared. General Valluy also pushed forward preparation for battle. On 17th December, during the course of a lightning visit to Sainteny in the North, Valluy is reported to have said, "The Viets want a scrap. We will show them".[26]

Strain and tension mounted. In Hanoi, each side feared attack by the other and, at this critical moment, Ho Chi Minh was a sick man — and those hostile to him would say conveniently so. In mid-December, he wrote to Sainteny:[27] *"M. le Commissaire and Dear Friend, The atmosphere is now tense. It is very sad. While waiting for the decision from Paris, I am counting on you and M. Giam (Ho Chi Minh's Foreign Minister) to find a way to improve the position. Please accept my best wishes for yourself and Madame Sainteny"*. Sainteny, who says in his book "if only I could have had the precise instructions from Paris" (where the government was in flux), was constrained to write to Ho Chi Minh during the course of 19th December, giving his government twenty-four hours to find and punish those responsible for recent attacks on French military and civilians.[28]

Also, in mid-December, General Valluy had written to General
Salan, who at that time was in Paris. "You can tell Juin (General Juin)
and de Lattre (General de Lattre) that I am grateful for the kind words
they send: they seem to approve of me: they did not approve of Leclerc:
even so, I need better liason from Paris to be up-to-date on the
ambience: ... the 'Civil Servants' pursue their illusions, but the conflict
is close: ... each day brings us toward a face to face with the Viet Minh
who have not digested our return to Tonkin and want to throw us in the
sea".[29]

By nightfall on 19th December, both sides were poised for action.
Elements in the Viet Minh leadership, counting on a favourable
response from the Government of Léon Blum, may still perhaps have
wished to restrain their followers, but time had run out. After dark,
organised Viet Minh military action broke out and, although the
French had received some intelligence warning, and were partially
ready, numbers of French civilians, men, women and children, were
among those killed. Sainteny himself was injured when the armoured
car in which he was travelling was blown up on a mine. In turn, the
French garrison reacted with vigour and, by the evening of the
following day, had re-established security in the city. The 9th Colonial
Infantry Division, which had learnt its street fighting in 1945 in
Europe, in the battles for the towns of Alsace, defeated the Viet Minh
in the streets of Hanoi, but was unable to prevent its withdrawal. And,
when Ho Chi Minh's residence was occupied in the afternoon of 20th
December, it was found that he and his close collaborators had already
made their escape.

Outside the city, the Viet Minh army under Giap was virtually
intact, and indeed strong enough to besiege Nam Dinh, the third city of
the North, until the spring of 1947. The battle was engaged and, on 21st
December, came the proclamation of Ho Chi Minh of a fight to the
finish. "The French colonists are once again seeking to subjugate us.
Unite without thought of ideology or race or religion. Struggle with
what you have: picks, spades, sticks. Save the country. We will win.
Long live the independent, indivisible Vietnam".[30]

The war, which was to last another eight years, had now begun.
Before its end, it would cost the French army "... two sons of Marshals
of France, twenty sons of Generals, 1300 Lieutenants, 600 other officers
and more than 75,000 N.C.O.s and men dead in Indo-China".[31]

Meanwhile, in Paris, General Leclerc had this to say to General
Salan, already mentioned as one of the most experienced officers of the
French Army in the affairs of Indo-China; "Why have we not respected
the agreement of 6th March? Why have we not got on with the
referendum instead of dragging on with these miserable customs talks,

which have now put light to the barrel of powder? I am utterly disheartened: how are we now to get out of it? we had managed all right: now we are racing toward the war I had sought to avoid: where will we find the men and material? We have not got enough". General Salan observes in his mémoirs that Leclerc, who was preoccupied with the lack of effective guidance from Paris, spoke with much violence.[32]

But Leclerc was perhaps crediting those with the authority to give such guidance with holding views attuned to his own. This was hardly the case. The political leadership of France for the greater part of the war in Indo-China was mostly that of the non-Communist left. However, with notable exceptions, their views on Indo-China belonged to the right rather than the left. And among the many personal tragedies of Indo-China, must be counted the fact that Léon Blum became Prime Minister of France at almost the moment the war broke out.

While Blum's own views on colonial issues were forward and liberal, the weight of the left still reflected traditional attitudes on policy toward the dependent territories. Perhaps this reflected in turn the politicians assessment of the views of the electorate. Whatever the reason, the French parties of the left cannot fairly disclaim responsibility for their country's Indo-China war.

[1] Devillers, p. 240.

[2] Devillers, pp. 242–3.

[3] Hammer, p. 159.

[4] Devillers, p. 297.

[5] Duncanson, p. 164.

[6] Devillers, p. 267.

[7] Salan, p. 17.

[8] Devillers, p. 300.

[9] Sainteny: *Ho Chi Minh and his Vietnam,* p. 71.

[10] Hammer, p. 190. *(Le Monde of 29 August)*

[11] Sainteny, pp. 80–82.

[12] *Ibid.* p. 87.

[13] Buttinger: *Vietnam: A political history,* p. 262.

[14] *Ibid.* p. 263.

[15] Salan: *Mémoirs,* p. 57.

[16] Duncanson, p. 165.

[17] Devillers, p. 331.

[18] *Ibid.* p. 331.

[19] Buttinger, p. 264.

[20] *Ibid.* p. 265.

[21] Hammer: *Struggle for Indo-China*, p. 183.

[22] Sainteny, p. 216. Hammer, p. 183.

[23] Buttinger, p. 266.

[24] Devillers, pp. 341 and 352.

[25] *Ibid.* p. 351.

[26] *Ibid.* p. 352.

[27] *Ibid.* p. 354.

[28] Sainteny, pp. 95–97.

[29] Salan, p. 28.

[30] Devillers, p. 357.

[31] Fall: *Indo-China 1946–62,* p. 12.

[32] Salan: *Mémoirs,* pp. 34, 35.

7 1946 – 1950 The French War: The National Phase

THE years of French War in Indo-China divide into two distinct periods. The first, essentially domestic, up to the end of 1949, when the Chinese Communists achieved final success on the mainland, and their forces reached the Indo-China border. The second, a period which culminated in the Geneva Conference of the summer of 1954. These later years were dominated by the re-emergence of China as an effective military power, and by growing United States effort to counter the Chinese position. A major Asian development, with special implications for Indo-China, was the Korean War, from June 1950 to July 1953; in particular, the forceful and effective intervention there, in November 1950, of very large numbers of Chinese "volunteers".

The 1949 watershed was clearly noted by General Navarre, who was to be the French Commander-in-Chief in Indo-China at the time of Dien Bien Phu: "As victorious Chinese Communists reached the frontier of Tonkin, a great decision faced us: either to win the war by investing heavily before Chinese aid changed the position, or to end by agreement. No intermediate solution was possible."[1] Likewise, M. Mendès France: "Our Indo-China concept is false: the military effort is too weak to achieve success: the political effort too weak to achieve a settlement: the alternatives are massive military expansion and sacrifice — or negotiation and concession, probably far greater than those which once would have sufficed."[2]

In February 1947, Ho Chi Minh wrote to Sainteny in the following terms:[3]

Dear Friend,

I have just learned that you are returning to France. I send you and Madame Sainteny my best wishes for a safe journey and good health.

I am sure that, like me, you regret that our efforts for peace have been demolished by this fratricidal war. I know you well enough to say you are not responsible for this policy of force and reconquest, and that is why we remain friends. And I can declare that our two peoples also remain friends.

There has been enough death and destruction. What should we do? France has only to recognise the independence and unity of Vietnam for

hostilities to cease immediately and, with peace and confidence restored,
we can work on reconstruction for the common good of our two countries.
For my part I am ready to work for a just and honourable peace. I
hope you will do the same. May God grant us success.

Devotedly Yours,
Ho Chi Minh.

In Sainteny's view, Ho Chi Minh was as much a Nationalist as a Communist, and France should have taken the risk of negotiation and a transfer of power on the basis of a referendum. Despite various other overtures by the Viet Minh, notably in letters[4] from Ho Chi Minh to General Salan, whom he had got to know well during 1945 and who was now the French Military Commander in Tonkin, and to M. Blum, negotiation was not, however, the mood of the French colonial establishment in the immediate aftermath of the events of December 1946. The one direct contact which there was between the two sides amounted in effect to a French requirement for unconditional surrender.[5] This was the case even though M. Blum himself while briefly in power was inclined personally toward negotiation, and General Leclerc was counselling wholehearted recognition of nationalism "to provide a fulcrum against communism".[6]

General Leclerc had been sent specially to Indo-China at the end of 1946 in the wake of M. Moutet, the French Minister for Overseas Affairs, who had been on his way to Indo-China when the events of 19th December took place. Despite contrary advice from Admiral d'Argenlieu, Moutet had tentatively sought contact with Ho Chi Minh, and there had been some response before Moutet received instructions from Paris to "terminate his mission".[7]

In his place, Leclerc assessed the dimension of the problem and, on his return to Paris early in January, was sounded on the possibility of going back to Indo-China as Commander-in-Chief. He consulted General de Gaulle, who observed that the policy of d'Argenlieu was the correct one, and counselled Leclerc against "compromising himself."[8]

Salan, whose testimony on matters concerning de Gaulle must of course take account of his own conflict with de Gaulle over Algeria and of his leadership of the Organisation Armee Sécrète (OAS), also recounts a later conversation between Leclerc and de Gaulle in February 1947. It was apparently a very stormy interview.[9] De Gaulle accused Leclerc of casting away Indo-China. Leclerc apparently replied: "Whose policy cost us Syria and the Lebanon?" Perhaps Leclerc may not have been quite so blunt toward his patron. What there is no doubt about, however, is that Leclerc, who was not blind to the atrocities of the Viet Minh, sensed the tide of nationalism in South East Asia, and realised that the clock could not be put back. His own final report and the associated memorandum of Colonel Repiton-Preneuf, his intelligence chief, spelt this out.[10] Leclerc's views were summed up in the famous phrase which has already been mentioned: "L'anticommunisme restera un levier sans point d'appui entre nos mains tant que le problème du nationalisme n'aura pas été résolu" — Anticommunism will be a lever without support until the problem of nationalism is resolved. But, as already mentioned, there were political objections to Leclerc's concepts for association.

One rationale, according to M. Maurice Schumann, was that the French Union would be undermined from the start if it accepted a Communist partner: the worm would be in the apple.[11] At the same time, and at first glance somewhat more surprisingly, the French Communist leaders were still, in 1947, against independence for Vietnam. In their case, and their policy changed not long after, one suggested reason was that they had to campaign on a nationalistic platform to gain electoral support outside of the party.[12] The fact that the Soviet Union did not recognise the government of Ho Chi Minh until 1950 also suggests that until then Moscow may have seen its objectives in France itself.

The French internal scene and M. Blum's fall from power was very relevant to the lack of response from the Government in Paris to Ho Chi Minh's letters, both reproduced below in full: their message, the cost of conflict between the two parties, and the need for peace on a basis of friendship and confidence within a structure of independence and partnership provided by the French Union. Their tone is as important as their actual content. The letter from President Ho Chi Minh to General Salan reads:

My Dear General,

I have just heard of your return to my country. Last year, when we travelled so much together, appears at the same time as yesterday and as centuries ago. We spoke a great deal together. On many questions concerning both people and affairs we were in agreement. In a word, we were great friends.

Circumstances which are not at all of our own making have now made us enemies. It is very sad indeed.

I know you well enough to be sure that if you had been here, and if you had possessed the necessary powers, the tragic events could and would have been avoided.

I know you well enough to appreciate that deep in your heart you are not a partisan of this fratricidal war which cannot settle anything, and will only damage the friendship and retard the course of constructive co-operation between our two countries.

But there it is. It is my duty as a patriot which compels me to fight for my country and for my fellow countrymen. For you, it is your duty as a soldier which requires you to act though your heart may disapprove.

Yet where is the glory in fighting a country which has extended a welcome? What is the glory in fighting a people who seek peace? What is the glory for France in fighting a Vietnam which asks only for unity and independence within the French Union?

Can the French Union really be founded on a basis of force on one side and of hate on the other? Can it truly go forward with its member countries in pieces and ruined, stained in blood and deep mourning? Of course not. If the French Union is to be realised, it must be based on friendship and reciprocal confidence.

Yet all this is politics. It is not your fault if things turn out otherwise.

Even so, although we have to meet as enemies, let us be chivalrous and honest enemies while awaiting to become friends once again. We have been friends — and personally we remain friends. Is that not so?

In the name of humanity, and in the name of our own personal friendship, may I ask you to prevent any further action by French troops against innocent villages and villagers and their temples?

I assure you that the French soldiers and civilians with us are being very well treated. I hope that ours are being similarly treated. The good Captain Cartier; is he still with you?

Please give me very best wishes to Madame Salan; and mes bons baisers to your boy and to the baby.

Je vous prie de croire mon cher Général à mes sentiments les plus distingués.

Ho Chi Minh
10th June 1947

P.S.   I should also be very grateful if you would forward the enclosed letter to Monsieur le President Léon Blum.

Letter from President Ho Chi Minh to M. Léon Blum.

"President Léon Blum: Monsieur Le President et Vénéré Camarade"

It is now more than three months since the war has engulfed my country, and there are the following matters concerning the war which I should like to draw to your attention.

(a)   *It is usually the case that before an outbreak of war the two sides have ideas and objectives and interests which are in conflict. There are no such differences between the French and the Vietnamese peoples. The Vietnamese people seek only to achieve the ideals of the French people: Liberty, Equality, Fraternity. The Vietnamese people wish to co-operate fraternally with the French people, and the French people for their part also wish to co-operate with the Vietnamese people. The Vietnamese people seek their unity and independence within the French Union, and the French people approve of this. What then is the cause of the war?*

(b)   *It is very painful to me to observe:*

(i)   *The war was launched immediately after the vote on the new French Constitution, which solemnly declared that France*

*condemned imperialism and the use of force against another
people.*

*(ii) The war was launched and has been continued under a
Socialist Government, and the French Socialist Party has
unanimously voted the credits for this war.*

*(c) To be strong, France wants to create a French Union, a union in
which, according to President (Prime Minister) Ramadier "all the
peoples understand each other and care for each other". Now this
war with its massacres, pillages, rapes and destruction and
barbarism can only sap the very foundations of this mutual understanding. Our friends, Eugene Thomas and Doctor Boutbrein, have
probably reported to you what they have seen in Indo-China. I can
therefore spare myself having to tell you of all the sufferings of my
country.*

*(d) France wishes that her economic interests in Vietnam should be
respected and developed. This is something on which the Vietnamese people are in entire agreement. Yet here is the balance
sheet after twenty months (of conflict) in Cochin China, and five
months in all Vietnam:*

*(i) tens of thousands of young French and Vietnamese killed and
wounded;*
(ii) millions of francs expended;
(iii) French businesses ruined;
(iv) French trade fallen to zero;
(v) towns, villages, roads and railways destroyed.

*If the war lasts another two years, the French economy in Indo-
China, as well as the Vietnamese economy, will be destroyed. But
the Vietnamese will have the men and the land and, as you know,
the guerilla can hold out for years and years.*

*(e) How then can this homicidal war be terminated? How can peace be
brought back? In my view the only possible policy is the one you
yourself announced in "Le Populaire" of 12.12.1946, a policy of
friendship and confidence based upon the unity and independence
of Vietnam within the French Union.*

*In the common interest, and for the common future of our two
peoples, I pray that you will be able to achieve the acceptance of your
wise and generous policies.*

*Please give my respects to Madame Blum, and my good wishes to our
friends the Brecks, the Luccys and the Rosenfields.*

En terminant je vous embrasse fraternellement.

Ho Chi Minh
10th June 1947

After the bloodshed of December 1946, and prior to these letters,
there had been the single brief contact previously referred to between
the two sides. It took place during May 1947 and was unsuccessful.
Following some feelers from the Viet Minh, Paul Mus, a distinguished

academic, who had also served as an officer on Leclerc's staff, was charged with conveying French terms to Ho Chi Minh. Mus travelled on foot from a French outpost, ten kilometres North of Hanoi, to Ho Chi Minh's headquarters, nearly one hundred kilometres distant, and delivered the terms which, effectively, amounted to unconditional surrender.[13] Ho Chi Minh flatly rejected the French position, saying that "they were terms for cowards, and there should be no place in the French Union for cowards".

In Ho Chi Minh's public statement to his followers after this meeting, he explained that his government had proposed negotiation. But the French terms demanded surrender, and this could not be accepted.[14] The public statement made by M. Paul Coste-Floret, the French Minister of War suggested, however, that the real stumbling block had been the French requirement that all the foreign advisers serving the Viet Minh should be handed over at once.[15] These advisers were mostly Foreign Legion deserters, and the French naturally felt strongly about them. No doubt Ho Chi Minh also felt strongly on the matter. His own statement does not suggest though that this was the single critical issue. Ho Chi Minh referred only to the French requirements that the Viet Minh surrender their arms, and that the French forces be given full freedom of movement. "This means that they want us to surrender: ... therefore, on behalf of the Government, I call on all my compatriots to make every effort for the Resistance".

The opportunity for negotiation had now passed, and it would be nearly seven years before another comparable opportunity would arise. The next time would be on the eve of the battle of Dien Bien Phu and, once again, an offer from Ho Chi Minh would be rejected. At this later stage, the final upshot would be French withdrawal. However at May 1947 the aftermath on the French side was a two pronged French policy.

One prong was military, but disturbances in Madagascar in 1947[16] prevented the full and timely deployment of all the French strike forces intended to surround and close in on the Viet Minh command stronghold in the hills of Thai Nguyen province, about fifty miles north of Hanoi. There were two main operations. The first, codenamed Lea, to establish an outer ring: the second, codenamed Ceinture, to tighten the ring. The top leaders of the Viet Minh were not caught, although a hoax by a member of General Salan's own communications staff briefly led the French to believe that Ho Chi Minh had been netted.

Although French casualties during the two months of the operation (October–November 1947) totalled nearly 700, the Viet Minh left some thousands dead and lost their main radio transmitter and upward of a thousand rifles. Much of the Viet Minh Treasury was also captured, and the Finance Minister killed. At the same time, General

Salan was conscious of the "hearts and minds" aspect. When heavy rains in the middle of 1947 threatened the dyke system of the North, there was an element of contact. General Salan broadcast that he was doing his best to contain the floods: he hoped that Ho Chi Minh was doing the same. Ho Chi Minh's broadcast reply was: "I understand your humanitarian intenion. You can be assured that I will do my best".[17]

Gradually, however, limitation of manpower confined French military policy to one of providing security in key areas of the North (despite terrorist attacks, Viet Minh political strength was weaker around Saigon and their pressure was less heavy in the South); and to attempts to entice the well armed regular army of the Viet Minh to pitched battle. The limitations of manpower itself stemmed from two political considerations: the first, that French conscripts should not be required to serve in Indo-China; the second, an element of reserve about training Vietnamese to combat the Viet Minh.

The other prong of French policy was political: to seek an alternative nationalist force with whom negotiation might be possible, and, as a first step, Admiral d'Argenlieu was replaced as High Commissioner by M. Bollaert, a radical Socialist parliamentarian. The next step was to select the alternative nationalist force, and the chosen instrument was the former Emperor Bao Dai. But the French political effort suffered perhaps from excessive colonialist influence. During eight years of war, no Prime Minister of France visited Indo-China, and a number of observers believe that Paris was hamstrung by imperfect appreciation of the nationalist forces at play. "There was a basic conflict inherent in the French Bao Dai policy: Bao Dai was valuable to the French only while he insisted on less than Ho Chi Minh: they supported him, counting on him not being too intransigently nationalistic: but the only hope for Bao Dai's success lay in his being able to offer himself to his people as a genuine nationalist".[18]

French contact with Bao Dai, by now away from Vietnam and living in Hong Kong, continued from the middle of 1947 to early 1949, with Bao Dai consistently seeking improved terms for any administration he might lead. In July 1947, Bao Dai said publicly: "I am neither for the Viet Minh nor against them: I belong to no party: peace will only return when the French realise that the spirit of our people today is not what it was ten years ago".[19] Eventually, in March 1949, an agreement was achieved which recognised Bao Dai as the Head of an independent state within the French Union.

But, in establishing Bao Dai as an alternative national focus to Ho Chi Minh, France had not yet offered the trump cards required by Bao Dai to play an effective hand. These cards were independence, international standing, and effective Vietnamese armed forces. Indeed, the late development of the last was subsequently to be propounded by

General Ely, the last French High Commissioner, as among the principal causes of the French reverse. "If only we had Vietnamised earlier".[20]

Internal political motive power was also absent. Ngo Dinh Diem declined to accept office under Bao Dai, saying, "The national aspirations of the Vietnamese people will only be satisfied when our nation enjoys the same political status as India and Pakistan."[21] But this was hardly being fair to Bao Dai's patriotism, and perhaps merely cloaked Diem's own ambition to rule.

The qualified independence as Associated States, agreed to by France in 1949 and 1950 in respect of Laos and Cambodia with their Kings, and with Vietnam, where Bao Dai was recognised as Head of State, was a long way from the example of the Commonwealth. By this time, M. Pignon, a former deputy to d'Argenlieu, had replaced Bollaert as High Commissioner, and, whatever his personal concept, his brief was one of maintenance of French supremacy. Defence and Foreign Affairs would remain the responsibility of France: law for French citizens in Vietnam would be French law: the courts to hear cases involving French nationals would also have a French content. To many Vietnamese, their new 'independence' did not seem very real.[22]

To borrow from the analysis which belongs later, it will never be known if Ho Chi Minh, for all his Marxist origins, might not have turned out a Tito if the French had played their hand differently. General Gavin, a distinguished American soldier during the Second World War, and later Ambassador in France, certainly believed that this would have proved the case: "Ho tends toward the combination of nationalism and communism associated with Marshal Tito."[23] Likewise, another former U.S. Ambassador and one time State Department expert on Asia, Edwin Reischauer: "Ho and his associates were ardent nationalists, and probably had deeper fears of the Chinese than the Yugoslavs had of the Russians."[24] Mr. Malcolm MacDonald, the British Commissioner General in South East Asia throughout the crucial period of the French War, also believed that while Ho Chi Minh was a Communist, he was even more a nationalist and that, if left alone, he would have been a Tito in relation to China.

In much the same way, opinion within the Kennedy administration leaned toward a view of Ho Chi Minh as a leader of nationalist Communism, historically mistrustful of the Chinese, and eager to preserve his own freedom of action rather than be the obedient servant of a questionably homogeneous international Communism.[25] On this view, if there had not already been commitment, it might have been possible to take a more relaxed view toward the evaluation of Vietnam. But the commitment, which also related to the global credibility of

United States power was, of course, already in existence, and this was the crucial factor. Although Kennedy might resent 'overcommitment' to South East Asia, the Dulles legacy of this commitment was the current reality which he had to face.[26]

Equally, there is a strong body of opinion which would dispute the view that Ho Chi Minh was a nationalist even more than a Communist. This judgment sees Ho Chi Minh as an international plotter, making use of nationalism as an important weapon in an international Marxist-Leninist armoury.[27] In support of this view, the fact is adduced that Ho Chi Minh stood consistently on the side of the Soviet Union against Tito and other nationalist movements in Eastern Europe. "The Soviet Union constantly shows loyalty to international solidarity and supports struggle for liberation of all oppressed nations." The writings of Ho Chi Minh do reveal an enthusiasm for Moscow and Marxist-Leninism extending over nearly fifty years.[28] Insurance against China may, however, have been an element in this.

Similarly, it will never be known what success might have been achieved if the French had given full scope to Bao Dai and the latent anti-Communist nationalism in the South in the late 1940s and early 1950s. Likewise, if American "Vietnamisation" had come earlier. Yet another "might have been", is the very effect of nearly thirty years of war. How might North Vietnam have developed without this hardening factor?

[1] Navarre: *Agonie de l'Indo Chine*, pp. 18–19.

[2] Devillers/Lacouture: *End of a War*. Mendés France: *Journal des débats parlamentaires*, 1950, p. 7002.

[3] Sainteny, p. 99.

[4] Salan: *Memoirs*, pp. 76–79.

[5] Hammer, p. 206.

[6] Devillers/Lecouture: *End of a War*, p. 13.

[7] Salan, p. 47.

[8] *Ibid*: p. 48.

[9] Salan: *Memoirs*, p. 48.

[10] Tournoux: *Sécrets d'état*, documents pp. 454–456.

[11] Devillers/Lacouture, p. 12., quoting a personal conversation with M. Schumann.

[12] Ellen J. Hammer: *Struggle for Indo-China*, pp. 190–191.

[13] Hammer, p. 206.

[14] Fall: *Ho Chi Minh,* p. 172.

[15] Hammer, p. 206.

[16] Fall: *Indo-China,* p. 29.

[17] Salan, p. 72.

[18] Hammer, p. 217.

[19] Lancaster, p. 179.

[20] Ely: *L'Indo Chine dans la Tourmente.*

[21] C.O.I., Vietnam Reference Book.

[22] Hammer, p. 234.

[23] *South East Asian Perspectives, Sept. 1972,* p. 8 (quoting pp. 62—63 of General Gavin's *Crisis Now).*

[24] *Ibid.* p. 11 (quoting p. 30 of Reischauer's *Beyond Vietnam. The U.S. and Asia).*

[25] Schlesinger: *Thousand Days,* p. 467.

[26] *Ibid.* p. 468.

[27] *Conflict Studies:* October 1973. *Indo-China:* The conflict analysed by Dennis J. Duncanson.

[28] *Ho Chi Minh on Revolution: 1920-66:* Bernard Fall.

8 1950—1954 The French War: The International Phase

BY 1950, the exclusive French nature of the Indo-China conflict was becoming subordinate to the international scene which, by the middle of the year, was dominated by the Korean War. In January 1950, the Chinese Communists, who by that time were firmly established as the government in Peking, had recognised the government of the Viet Minh. The Soviet Union can have had little option when it followed suit a few days later. Within Indo-China, the Viet Minh, always well armed, and commanded by General Giap, a ruthless and determined leader of considerable military accomplishment, and now in possession of modern anti-aircraft weapons, had opened up direct communication with China in a series of engagements on the frontier. These engagements provided a foretaste of the tragedy to French arms at Dien Bien Phu four years later (once again the name of Langson was associated with heavy French casualties). As for Giap himself, his own personal background may perhaps have added an extra dimension to his unrelenting conduct of the war. According to the late Professor Bernard Fall, one of the leading authorities on Indo-China, Giap's wife, a revolutionary like Giap himself, had been arrested in 1941 and subsequently sentenced to forced labour and had died in prison. Giap's wife's sister, also involved as a revolutionary, had been guillotined in Saigon.[1] To the French, Giap was a 'vrai dur'. Bitter and full scale war was now involved, and the United States responded to the new situation by agreeing to massive economic assistance to back the French military effort, and before long this assistance was underwriting three quarters of the monetary cost of the war.

At this early stage, United States' opinion in the Far East was by no means unanimous however as to the implications if Northern Indo-China were to fall to the Viet Minh. During the course of discussions in Singapore, General Willoughby, who at that time was General MacArthur's Intelligence Chief in Tokyo, said that he saw the situation in terms of the 'domino theory', that as one piece fell it would knock over the next and so on, and advocated a high degree of Western involvement. General MacArthur himself was, however, considerably more cautious as to the wisdom of such direct involvement on the ground in

Indo-China, and pinned faith on local nationalist sentiment as a bulwark against external communist expansion and the evolution of the 'domino situation'.[2]

An even more important American view was, of course, that of the Administration. In the pre-Korea phase, Mr. Dean Acheson, the then Secretary of State, had seen the American role as "help toward solving the colonial-nationalist conflict in a way that would satisfy nationalist aims and minimise the strain on our Western European allies."[3] In his memoirs, Acheson says that he did not find this an easy or popular role. "The French baulked with all the stubbornness I later knew so well, at moving swiftly, where they could move, in transferring authority over internal affairs". But, early in 1950, after the French National Assembly had ratified the Elysée Agreements, which recognised Vietnam, Cambodia and Laos as (in theory) independent states within the French Union, American policy took a step forward. Acheson says that, "with some hesitancy, we in the Department, recommended aid to France in combating Ho's insurgency".[4] This aid was limited to economic and military supplies and, compared to later American help, was relatively small scale.

Then came Korea, and, almost at once, American aid to the French increased hugely. In 1951 its cost exceeded five hundred million dollars. Powerful and persuasive pressure came from Paris for yet more help. But Acheson noted that Paris, and the French leadership in Indo-China, "resented enquiries about French intentions regarding transfer of authority to the three States."[5] Within the State Department, says Acheson, "there was a perceptive warning" from John Ohly urging that the appearance of the Chinese in Korea required the United States to take a second look at its rôle in Indo China.[6] We could, said Ohly, "be moving into a position where our responsibilities will tend to supplant rather than complement those of the French". And, in August 1951, Acheson records a warning from the Joint Chiefs of Staff against "any statement that would commit — or seem to the French under future eventualities to commit — U.S. armed forces to Indo-China."

But the money commitment remained, and with it some increased American exasperation about French political intentions. In Acheson's words, "I insisted that when we were contributing more than a third of the cost of the war it did not seem unreasonable to expect that we should be given the information to explain to our people why we were doing so, and the progress being made: furthermore, friendly suggestions on the conduct of affairs from an ally so strongly supporting them would not seem to be officious meddling."[7] Perhaps there was some failure of communication. The French may not have seen it that way.

As the international phase developed in Indo-China, the man chosen to lead the French effort was General de Lattre de Tassigny, a very senior officer of the highest reputation and a Free French hero of the Second World War. De Lattre was appointed Commander-in-Chief and High Commissioner, taking in political as well as military responsibility. His military assessment ran somewhat counter to the French Chiefs of Staff, who were inclined toward a concentration of effort in South Vietnam where French interests were greatest. De Lattre's judgement was that 'Tonkin was the bolt to the door' of South East Asia as a whole and, within a few weeks of his appointment, he had countered major offensives in the Red River Delta by regular Viet Minh divisions, and had re-established an effective perimeter. He inspired his troops with the famous phrase: "Désormais, vous serez commandés,"[8] — From now on you will be led. At Vinh Yen, about 20 miles North of Hanoi, de Lattre took personal command of the French forces against a very strong attack mounted by Giap with 24 battalions and supporting artillery. De Lattre's conduct of the battle was vigorous and determined and won the day. The French suffered six hundred casualties. The Viet Minh about five times as many. The French also took about five hundred prisoners.[9] The Viet Minh tide was held. But how to turn it back? De Lattre asked for considerable reinforcement. But conscripts were not to be employed in Indo-China. The result was the use of a large number of French Moroccan and Algerian units and, in the subsequent years of French war in North Africa, it was a commonplace to observe that the seeds of this later conflict were sown in Indo-China.

The French revival under de Lattre did not however last long. De Lattre was in Indo-China far less than a year, and early in 1952 he died of cancer. Yet his span was crucial. De Lattre, with the same qualities of realism shown by Leclerc five years before, plus an extra and exacting quality of capriciousness left as his legacy a Vietnamese Army which in the years ahead fought bravely to hold the line against the Communists. The two generals, both of them to lose sons in Indo-China, both of them posthumously to be named Marshals of France, sensed the importance of building up national forces and a national spirit to fight the Communist Viet Minh.

General Salan, once more back in Indo-China as military deputy to de Lattre, stresses the immense effort made by his Chief, within weeks of the death in battle of his son, the young Lieutenant Bernard de Lattre, to give a sense of cause to the young Vietnamese free to make a choice. Lieutenant de Lattre had been killed by mortar fire (the special expertise of the Viet Minh) while leading a Vietnamese platoon near Nam Dinh. The father's famous words at the prize-giving at the Lycée

Chasseloup-Laubat on 11th July 1951 were heart to heart. "Soyez des hommes":

"Be men. If you are Communist join the Viet Minh. Over there are men who fight bravely for a bad cause. But if you are patriots, fight for your country, for this is your war. Build a national army to take over from the French army. Young men of Vietnam, I feel for you as for the young men of my native country: The moment is come to defend your country: Vietnam will be saved by you."[10]

De Lattre also realised to the full the importance of American support, and in September 1951 he visited Washington to press his cause personally. It was a successful visit. He was received at the White House by President Truman, and was asked to address the cadets at the U.S. Army Academy at West Point. Shortly afterwards, General Lawton Collins, the U.S. Army Chief of Staff, visited Saigon to assess in person the material requirements of the French forces in Indo-China, and to see what might be done to hasten the arrival of U.S. supplies.

De Lattre's other preoccupation was perhaps less characteristic, but in the situation as it was in Indo-China it was military soundness itself. He sought the greatest possible effort to establish a framework of mutually supporting blockhouses in the Delta area of the North and, in particular, in the all-important sector between Hanoi and Haiphong. He sensed the absolute requirement to protect the population, and to demonstrate the French presence. To General Salan, who was by no means in full accord, almost his last words were: "I have two key enterprises which you must pursue: Vietnamisation and concrete".[11]

During 1952, Giap extended Viet Minh main force operations to Laos and[12] Cambodia, by-passing de Lattre's 'bolt to the door', established in the Red River delta area. At the same time, Viet Minh guerilla operations and terrorism behind the French lines were intensified. In a particularly hideous incident at the beach resort of Cap St. Jaques, 25 women and children were butchered by the Communist guerillas. Despite the effort made by de Lattre, and followed up by Salan who took over from him, the weight of numbers still lay against France. The greatest strength of the Corps Expéditionnaire was just under 200,000, with an equal number of local forces. Against this, the well armed main force units of Giap were of the same order as the French expeditionary force, with a total guerilla element of perhaps 250,000 men. Even the supremacy of French air power was threatened by a growing Viet Minh anti-aircraft capability, part of the steadily increasing flow of Chinese war material into Viet Minh held territory.

According to the book, a crucial phase of 'People's War' was now being entered. The laws of revolutionary warfare, as laid down by Mao

Tse-tung, and developed in Vietnam by Giap, outline three phases in a successful 'People's War'. Within Vietnam, these three phases had in fact been publicised in the late 1940s in a pamphlet by Truong Chinh, one of the leading Communist Vietnamese theoreticians.[13] "To begin with, the Viet Minh are weak and the enemy strong. At this stage, the Viet Minh withdraw to safe territory, and preserve their strength and content themselves with occasional harassing. In the second phase, there is equilibrium — neither side can gain to hold the territory of the other. At this stage, the military task of the Viet Minh is to tie down enemy units and sabotage communications and economic activities. This phase ends when the Viet Minh have sufficient strength to pass to the offensive, and conduct a war of manoeuvre to lead to Victory". For the Viet Minh, the third phase had now been reached.

Meanwhile, there were also the beginnings of difficulty for the French in Cambodia. During 1951, Son Ngoc Thanh, who had briefly headed the Government at Phnom Penh during the last days of the Japanese occupation, before being given short shrift by Leclerc, had been permitted to return to Cambodia. At once, he began to campaign for immediate and complete independence for the country. Early in 1952, his nationalist newspaper in Phnom Penh was closed down by the French and, shortly afterwards, he fled to the jungle area of the North West to join the Khmer Issarak, at that time the Cambodian equivalent of the Viet Minh. Within weeks, the Khmer Issarak accorded him the title of President of the Cambodian Committee of National Liberation. The next step was contact with the Viet Minh.

Sihanouk shrewdly recognised that he had to catch the nationalist tide to retain power. More than that, he had to do better than the Khmer Issarak. From now on, his objectives, vis-a-vis France, became those of the nationalists in the jungle: — and to get there first. Independence and Order were his watchwords. On the one hand, he now pressed the French harder than ever for immediate and full independence; and, on the other, he took personal command of his country's armed forces against the invading Viet Minh and their Khmer Issarak allies. Mr. Malcolm MacDonald has described this period of Sihanouk's activity as follows: "Sihanouk showed himself the champion of his people's freedom from both the old French Colonialism and the new Communist imperialism".[14]

Increasingly, it became clear that in Indo-China time was no longer running for France — if it ever had. M. Blum had sensed this when he was briefly Prime Minister in 1946 and 1947. In June 1953, it was openly recognised by M. Laniel, when he became Prime Minister. Within the Laniel Government, M. Reynaud provided a driving force. "This war must stop being a French war supported by Vietnam and must become a Vietnam war supported by France."[15]

On 3rd July, M. Laniel's government, spurred not merely by the Vietnam situation, but also by a dramatic and quickly effective gesture of self exile on the part of Sihanouk took a major step forward.

The episode involving Sihanouk is described in detail in Mr. Malcolm MacDonald's book *Titans and Others*.[16] "While the French hesitated, Sihanouk revealed his determination in an extraordinary way. A hitherto mostly hidden trait in his temperament suddenly appeared. An emotional impulsive streak exploded. Feeling frustrated, he jumped into a car one dark night, sped hundreds of miles across the Thai frontier to Bangkok, and settled in an hotel there. Declaring himself a voluntary exile from his country, he announced that he would not return unless the French conceded full national sovereignty to Cambodia". MacDonald goes on to comment: "friends and foes alike were astonished by his conduct, many of them thinking it as politically injudicious as it was regally unorthodox. Professional diplomats judged it stupidly amateurish, whilst intellectual nationalists called it puerile: I (MacDonald) confess I felt it imprudently risky; almost everyone assumed that Sihanouk had miscalculated, and that such behaviour could only result in his losing personal prestige without gaining advantage for his subjects."

The critics were proved wrong. Sihanouk's journey and his subsequent world travel had forced the issue. The governments in Saigon, Vientiane and Phnom Penh were informed of the French view, that the development of civil institutions and national armies in the three Associated States now enabled their independence and sovereignty to be 'perfected'. In particular, it should now be possible to conclude agreements for the transfer of responsibilities hitherto retained by France. In November 1953, President Auriol of France announced a concept for the French Union, somewhat akin to the free association of the Commonwealth.

The international climate was also right for settlement. Some elements of détente had set in after Stalin's death the previous March, and an armistice in Korea seemed close. What was now important for France, was to get the right climate in Indo-China for a settlement of the conflict. In a speech to the National Assembly, M. Laniel referred to a statement made at the Kremlin on 19th September by Mr. Malenkov, then the Soviet leader. Malenkov had expressed the wish to see the armistice in Korea "become the point of departure for new efforts aimed at lessening international tension in the entire world, and notably in the Far East." An analogous declaration had been made on 24th August by Chou En-lai.

Laniel announced that the French Government, for its part, "was ready to seize all occasions to make peace, whether in Indo-China or at the international level:". "I must repeat in the clearest and most categorical fashion that the French Government does not consider the Indo-Chinese problem as necessarily requiring a military solution." Events had moved a long way since January, when M. Letourneau, the then Minister for the Associated States, had told the British Ambassador in Paris that there could be no question of negotiations with Ho Chi Minh since even to talk of this had a damaging effect on Vietnamese morale.[17]

On the military side, the instructions now given to General Navarre, the newly appointed French Commander-in-Chief, were "to create the military conditions for an honourable political solution to be adopted when the time was ripe."[18] In turn, Navarre developed his plan. It involved two stages. The first, from mid 1953 to mid 1954, a period of strategic defensive within which local tactical offensives would sharpen the French forces. Then would follow an offensive to improve the French Government's negotiating position. "The upshot of the Navarre plan was the reverse of what was intended: the battle when it took place at Dien Bien Phu went entirely to the enemy."[19]

Yet, in fairness to Navarre, certain tactical offensive operations undertaken shortly after he took command were very successful. And the defeat at Dien Bien Phu may perhaps have stemmed from excessive projection by others, besides Navarre, of the factors which produced this success. One of the most notable of the early Navarre operations bore the code name "Hirondelle". It involved the occupation by three battalions of airborne troops of Langson, on the Sino-Tonkin border. Surprise was achieved, and more than 5000 tons of the Viet Minh stockpile of arms and supplies were destroyed. The evacuation of the French garrison from Na-San, about 200 kilometres North West of Hanoi, was also rated a success. But, in neither of these cases was the air supply distance as great as that for Dien Bien Phu from Hanoi. And, in both cases, elements of direct support were nearer to hand.[20]

Meanwhile, the net effect was some increase in military confidence which spread also to the political field.

In parallel with the military action, there would be a major diplomatic effort. France would seek as part of an overall Asian settlement to "hitch the Indo-China wagon" to the Korean peace talks, to be held in the wake of the signing of the Korean armistice on 27th July.

At this stage, there was an element of response from Ho Chi Minh. On 29th September, the Swedish newspaper *Expressen*, published a reply from Ho Chi Minh to questions put to him by their Paris correspondent, Sven Löfgren. The key words, re-broadcast several times by the Viet Minh, and confirmed personally by Ho Chi Minh himself on 18th December in a speech marking the seventh anniversary of the national resistance, were as follows:

"If the French Government want to negotiate an armistice in Vietnam, and to solve the problem of Vietnam by peaceful means, the people and government of the Democratic Republic of Vietnam are ready to meet this desire."[21]

By now, Dulles was the U.S. Secretary of State, and an anti-American view, and a wider political call to the French people from Ho Chi Minh also came through:

"Today, not only is the independence of Vietnam seriously jeopardised, but the independence of France is also gravely threatened. On the one hand, the U.S. imperialists egg on the French colonialists to continue and expand the aggressive war in Vietnam, thus weakening them more and more through fighting in the hope of replacing France in Indo-China; on the other, they oblige France to ratify the European Defence Treaty, that is, to revive German militarism.

Therefore, the struggle of the French people to gain independence, democracy and peace for France, and to end the war in Vietnam, constitutes one of the important factors to settle the Vietnam question by peaceful means".

Sadly, the pattern of the last months of 1946 was repeated. Once again, a message from Ho Chi Minh was apparently shunted into a siding by elements within the administration in Paris. M. Mendès France stood a powerful force for negotiation. But some members of the government, notably M. Bidault, the Foreign Minister, a 'hawk' since 1946, were hostile.

However, M. Pleven, the Defence Minister, urged that Alain Savary, a Socialist Deputy, might "sound the *DRV*" (the Democratic Republic of Vietnam, Ho Chi Minh's government). M. Laniel the French Prime Minister approved. The French Foreign Ministry shuffled. The matter dragged on for three months, and Bidault did not receive Savary until the beginning of March, just before the battle of Dien Bien Phu, which Bidault presumably awaited as a victory for France. "Ho Chi Minh is giving in", were Bidault's words. "Do not support him by this contact."[22] Unhappily for France, the full reality was not yet appreciated by her Foreign Minister. By the time Laniel and Pleven had persuaded Bidault, the inevitable had begun to happen at Dien Bien Phu.

Meanwhile, the British view was that the French should do no more than hold their ground militarily. Mr. Anthony Eden, then Foreign Secretary, did not consider that it would be in the best interest of France that the scale of the fighting should be increased. The Americans took a different view. Early in 1954, the British Ambassador in Washington was told by the State Department that the U.S. government were perturbed by the fact that Paris was not aiming to win the war, but was merely seeking a position from which to negotiate.[23] The American Chiefs-of-Staff were aware in detail of the battle being planned by General Navarre at Dien Bien Phu, and it was perhaps natural that they would not wish to see this offensive move put into reverse. The French Chiefs-of-Staff, although they had delegated a virtually free hand to Navarre, saw the situation somewhat more cautiously as General Navarre's plans moved towards their culmination at Dien Bien Phu.

[1] Fall: *Le Viet Minh*, p. 183.

[2] Conversation: Mr. Malcolm MacDonald − General MacArthur, recounted by Mr. MacDonald.

[3] Dean Acheson: *Present at the Creation*, p. 671.

[4] *Ibid*. p. 672.

[5] *Ibid*. p. 675.

[6] *Ibid*. p. 674.

[7] *Ibid*. p. 676.

[8] Salan: *Memoirs*, p. 187.

[9] *Ibid*. p. 206.

[10] Salan, p. 236.

[11] *Ibid*. p. 236.

[12] Giap, pp. 117–119.

[13] Buttinger: *Vietnam Political History*, p. 326.

[14] MacDonald: *Angkor*, p. 138.

[15] Devillers/Lacouture, pp. 35–7. Reynaud as reported in *Le Monde*, 27th June.

[16] MacDonald: *Titans and Others*, p. 172.

[17] Eden: *Full Circle*, p. 85.

[18] Navarre, p. 72.

[19] Duncanson, p. 200.

[20] Salan, p. 417.

[21] Devillers/Lacouture, pp. 45–48; *Ho Chi Minh, Selected Articles*, pp. 70–71.

[22] *Ibid*. p. 49.

[23] Eden: *Memoirs: Full Circle*, p. 90.

9   Dien Bien Phu

THE battle of Dien Bien Phu, where a French force of about 16,000 men was overwhelmed by the Viet Minh army under General Giap, is central both to the French War and, also, to the subsequent American War in Indo-China. The fall of Dien Bien Phu on 7th May 1954, after bitter fighting and a siege lasting 56 days, gave the coup de grâce to French will to continue their war. It also provided inspiration for the future to the Communist Vietnamese. Even the United States could be vulnerable in Indo-China. Bernard Fall, comparing the battle to the Marne and Stalingrad, depicts it as one "which changed the tone" of the conflict in Vietnam.[1] Even before the battle it was injudicious to underestimate Giap and his army. In the aftermath, doubly so.

The story begins on the ground with the French re-occupation of Dien Bien Phu on 20th November 1953 by an airborne operation; they at once re-established a *base aéro-terrestre,* a fortified position behind the enemy lines dependent on air supply. The position had been in Viet Minh hands for about a year since 30th November 1952, when a battalion size garrison had been withdrawn. The French re-occupation took place effectively, and with relatively light casualties. The area, close to the Laos border, and a centre of communication with China, Laos and into Tonkin, was one of the largest and richest valleys of North West Tonkin.

The plain within which the airfield was sited, measured roughly nine miles long by five across. Unhappily, this plain was overlooked by certain hills, which were to fall to the Viet Minh at the commencement of the siege on 13th March 1954. The area was also more than 300 kilometres from the Hanoi airfield complex on which it depended for supply and support. After brave resistance by the garrison, the flag of the Viet Minh was raised at Dien Bien Phu nearly two months later. In the aftermath, controversy was to focus on the why and wherefore of the occupation, as well as on the nature of the defence. The recrimination would also take in the United States and Britain, as well as the French forces and personalities directly concerned. And Dien Bien Phu, like Suez, would in later years be in the minds of some French leaders in their assessment of the reliability of the United States as an ally.

Navarre's own reason for choosing to establish the French strong-point at Dien Bien Phu was that he considered it vital for the defence of Laos. The Treaty proclaiming the Independence of Laos and its adherence to the French Union had been signed on 22nd October. Almost at once, it seemed that a major Viet Minh thrust would develop against Laos. At this stage, General Navarre's assessment ran as follows. The Laos agreement was a model for agreements to follow with Cambodia and Vietnam. For political reasons, therefore, Laos had to be defended.[2] This, despite his earlier military assessment that the Viet Minh main force could not be engaged with reasonable chance of success until 1954, when a large-scale French operation, Operation ATLANTE, was envisaged against the Viet Minh in the coastal area south of Danang (Tourane).

Within days, General Navarre issued orders as follows:

(a) On 3rd December, concerning Dien Bien Phu.[3]

"I have decided to accept battle in the North West under the following general conditions.

"The defence of the North West shall be centred on the air land base at Dien Bien Phu which must be held at all cost ....

"In view of the remoteness of the North West Theatre of operations from the Viet Minh main bases, and their logistical obligations, it is probable that the battle will be fought according to the following scenario:

(i) *The movement phase,* characterised by the arrival of the Viet Minh units and their supplies to the North West; the duration may extend over several weeks.

(ii) *An approach and reconnaissance phase,* in the course of which enemy intelligence units will make efforts to determine the quality and weaknesses of our defences, and where the enemy combat units will proceed with the positioning of their attacking forces. This phase may last from six to ten days.

(iii) *An attack phase,* lasting several days (according to the means employed), and which must end with failure of the Viet Minh offensive."

(b) On 12th December, concerning the coastal operation.[4]

"The essential objective which I expect to achieve is the disappearance of the Viet Minh zone which spreads south of Danang (Tourane).

In view of the considerable strategic and political results which can be expected from the complete execution of this operation, I have decided to subordinate to it the conduct of the whole Indo-China campaign during the first semester of 1954."

In his understanding book on Dien Bien Phu, General Catroux, who directed the confidential French enquiry into the disaster, stressed the importance to a Commander-in-Chief of clear directions from his government. This was something which Navarre lacked. But at the same time Catroux observes, in connection with the twin and conflicting objectives which Navarre had set for himself:

(a) The principal military strategic interest for the French lay in the central coastal zone (Atlante).
(b) But that once battle in the North West was accepted on 3rd December, all priority should have rested there and the ATLANTE operation should have been deferred.
(c) The tactical concept at Dien Bien Phu was, however, an intellectual view resting on insufficient information of the physical conditions of the region.

For his part, General Navarre would later point to the procession of senior French and American personalities who visited Dien Bien Phu during the weeks before the Viet Minh assault. Few of them at that time spoke strongly against the operational concept and the tactical deployment at Dien Bien Phu itself.[5] This tactical deployment, embodying 12 infantry battalions plus artillery and some tanks, being as follows:[6]

(a) A central position, covering the airstrip, and comprising five strongpoints.
(b) About two miles to the North and North East of the airstrip, on higher ground, two more strongpoints BEATRICE and GABRIELLE to cover the central position.
(c) About five miles to the South, another covering strongpoint, ISABELLE.
(d) Each defended position protected by barbed wire entanglements fifty yards wide plus minefields and other obstacles.

Although General Blanc, the French Army Chief-of-Staff, may have had some reservation about the terrain, and some Air Force anxieties were expressed by General Fay, the French Air Force Chief-of-Staff,[7] General O'Daniel, the Head of the U.S. Military Mission in Vietnam, was particularly enthusiastic;[8] and by this time the American influence in the Indo-China situation had become very considerable indeed. The very fact that such a senior general as O'Daniel, a former U.S. Army Commander in the Pacific, was the head of the U.S. Military Mission was a pointer in itself. Once the die was cast, however, the

General Leclerc and Ho Chi Minh — Hanoi, 1946. (Taken from *Histoire du Vietnam 1940—1952* by P. Devillers; published by Editions du Seuil, Paris.)

President Ngo Dinh Diem with U.S. Ambassador General Maxwell Taylor. (Taken from *The Last of the Mandarins: Diem of Vietnam* by A.T. Bouscaron; published by Duquesne University Press Pennsylvania, U.S.A.).

French had to fight the battle on their own, despite some powerful U.S. military lobbying in favour of massive intervention by U.S. air power.

At the same time as the French were consolidating their position at Dien Bien Phu, the Viet Minh were proceeding systematically toward its investment with forces well superior in number; and with artillery which both in quantity and in quality was far more than the French and their U.S. advisers had anticipated. On 13th March, the first day of the assault, the position BEATRICE, two miles north east of the airstrip was taken by the Viet Minh. A human wave attack engulfed the post which had been entrusted to a Foreign Legion battalion. The battalion commander, Colonel Gaucher, had been killed in the heavy artillery barrage which preceded the assault, and almost all his officers were also casualties. Next day, the hill position GABRIELLE, two miles north of the airstrip, was similarly overrun. From 15th March, the airstrip was directly exposed to enemy artillery:[9] Colonel Piroth, the artillery commander at Dien Bien Phu, was also a casualty. The failure of his twenty-four 105 mm. howitzers to smother the enemy batteries broke his spirit. During the night of 14th—15th March, the one-armed colonel committed suicide by blowing himself up with a hand grenade. The artillery situation was central to the defence of Dien Bien Phu — and within two days the advantage had gone overwhelmingly to the Viet Minh. French resources alone were now insufficient, and French hope was concentrated on a massive intervention by U.S. air power. This intervention was not however to materialise.

The intervention concept, given the code name VULTURE, which was developed jointly by General Ely, the French armed forces Chief-of-Staff, and Admiral Radford, his American counterpart, involved raids by a force of sixty B.29 bombers on the Communist position around Dien Bien Phu; fighter escort and ground attack operations being provided by carrier based aircraft of the U.S. Seventh Fleet. However, despite Radford's advocacy and the backing of Dulles, the U.S. Secretary of State, and of the then Vice President, Richard Nixon, the U.S. administration as a whole was reserved. President Eisenhower, in particular, was cautious, and inclined toward the views of General Ridgeway, the U.S. Army Chief of Staff and a former Commander in Korea, who doubted the value of heavy bombing in a close tactical situation, and sensed the risk of being drawn into another war on the ground in Asia.

M. Bidault recounts an interesting conversation at this stage with Mr. Dulles.[10] Bidault was still pressing for tactical help from the Seventh Fleet, but found Dulles 'glum'. "Foster Dulles obviously realised how difficult it would be to make the President and Congress accept this, so he merely looked glum and did not even promise to back my request in Washington: what he did, however, was to ask me if we would like the United States to give us two atomic bombs." Bidault goes on to say that he refused the offer: "however they were used, the Dien Bien Phu garrison would be worse off than before". Presumably Dulles had expected this response, and had made the 'offer' as a gesture, knowing it could not be accepted. It seems inconceivable that President Eisenhower would have approved the use of nuclear weapons.

As the siege at Dien Bien Phu continued, and the French peri-meter at Dien Bien Phu contracted, international attention focussed increasingly on the intervention aspect and the coming Geneva Conference. Mr. Dulles pressed Mr. Anthony Eden for British support. The reply from the British Foreign Secretary was that he did not believe that outside military intervention would now be able to remedy the Indo-China situation. This view would seem to have been well founded. On 18th September, during the course of a press interview on his return from captivity, General de Castries, the Dien Bien Phu garrison commander, sadly observed that massive U.S. intervention could only have been helpful at the very beginning of the siege; thereafter, the two sides were too closely locked for this help to have been a practical proposition.[11] On 24th April, there were further U.S.—U.K. discus-sions. Mr. Dulles and Admiral Radford now requested British military participation in Indo-China "so that although Dien Bien Phu might fall it would be demonstrated that France had powerful allies in the fight" [12]

Eden consulted the Prime Minister. Sir Winston Churchill's response was to the point: "Britain was being asked to assist in misleading the United States Congress into approving a military opera-tion which would in itself be ineffective and might well bring the world to the verge of a major war: this could not be accepted".[13] The British position remained one of achieving agreement at the imminent Geneva Conference. The British Foreign Secretary passed a memorandum to Mr. Dulles giving the British view on the outlook for South East Asia. Its first paragraph read as follows: "Communism in Asia cannot be checked by military means alone. The problem is as much political as military: if any military combination is to be effective it must enjoy the widest possible measure of Asian support." Dulles was disappointed, and within two years would be speaking in almost the same terms to Eden about Suez!

On 29th April, President Eisenhower wrote the epilogue. In a public statement, he said that the United States government would await the result of the Geneva meeting before taking further action. In his book, 'Mandate for Change', Eisenhower's own words on this episode were: "Under the conditions then existing, we would probably get not what we liked by way of settlement in Geneva, but rather a modus vivendi, a workable rather than a desirable arrangement. There was no plausible reason for the United States to intervene. We could not even be sure that the Vietnamese population wanted us to do so."[14]

Meanwhile, at Dien Bien Phu, the tragedy was drawing to its end. By 7th May, more than half the garrison were casualties. The air support had also been very costly. At this stage, General Cogny, the French Commander in Tonkin and the immediate superior of de Castries, the French Commander at Dien Bien Phu told de Castries: "You are going to be submerged, but no surrender: no white flag." Within the post, de Castries had made it clear that, from 17.00 that day, his forces would cease fire. Whether or not any white flags appeared (a matter on which there was subsequent French controversy) it seems clear that the Viet Minh understood the position.[15] At 17.30 a Viet Minh Section commanded by Captain Ta Quang Luat were at de Castries' command bunker. The central position had fallen. According to de Castries, the Viet Minh officer said: "ça va, il y a la conférence de Geneve, tout va s'arranger". A few hours later, the outpost at ISABELLE was also in Viet Minh hands.[16]

General Navarre's own assessment of the lessons of Dien Bien Phu was unrepentant. The Viet Minh concentration against Laos had been the real thing, and not a feint to draw him in. Dien Bien Phu had saved Laos, and thereby French honour. After the battle, the situation was in hand, and there was no need for hasty concessions.[17] On the military side Navarre did, however, concede four general factors, the majority of long standing, which in his view had contributed to the overall French reverse in Indo-China:[18]

(a) Underestimation of the enemy: — in particular in relation to his logistic capability (an underestimation to arise again in the later American war in Vietnam).

(b) Too much use of conventional military techniques and unsuitable military material in a guerilla situation. Flexibility, mobility and *ruse,* supported by positive political action should have been the watchword. Instead, there was 'immobilisme' and damaging dependence on cumbersome support. (Navarre believed this stemmed partly from leaving too much to American aid which, in his view, was altogether too frequently what the Americans chose to provide, and was often ill suited to the war on the ground.)

(c) French lack of numbers: the winning of a guerilla war required a numerical superiority which did not exist.

(d) A command structure which most of the time was unsound: the military and civil could not be separated. "It was only during the years when de Lattre combined the military and political leadership in Indo-China that the two effectively came together".

But, above all, Navarre blamed the French political leadership. The government — and this went for them all — had not 'involved the nation.'[19] The government had never indicated its objectives. Was the war for French influence? If so, that was one thing. Or was it a war on behalf of the United States supporting the anti-Communist politics of Mr. Dulles: another thing entirely?[20]

In Navarre's view, the years of French war in Indo-China were marked by a gulf between the French government, irrespective of party, and the French nation: between the 'pays legal' and the 'pays réel.' Navarre believed the 'pays réel' would have been prepared to offer more for Indo-China.[21] It is difficult not to think he was somewhat out of touch. History offers its examples of glory plus profit as a useful political formula in a democratic state. But, between 1946 and 1954, the war cannot have seemed very profitable to many French people. The reports reaching the British Foreign Secretary from the British Ambassador in Paris were to the effect that there was almost unanimous desire in France that the war should be ended.[22]

It certainly could not be said of the Viet Minh that their government did not involve the nation. In Giap's own words, "The Party Central Committee and the government decided that the whole people and party should concentrate their forces for the service of the front in order to ensure victory at Dien Bien Phu".[23] This meant everyone, whether they liked it or not. Giap also underlines the logistic effort, "The supply of food and munitions was as important as tactics: logistics constantly posed problems as urgent as the armed struggle. These were the difficulties the enemy thought insuperable for us: the slogan was all for the front: all for victory: in revolutionary war a strong rear is always the decisive factor for victory."[24]

Ho Chi Minh's victory proclamation read as follows:[25]

"Let me first express affectionate solicitude for the wounded and you all. The government and I have decided to reward you. But how? We will distribute insignia 'Combatant of Dien Bien Phu'. *What do you think? Once more let me advise you to be modest in victory. Do not underestimate the enemy. Remain ready to do all the government and party may ask of you. I embrace you all.*

Your Uncle,
Ho Chi Minh"

Giap's own order of the day, which included a special tribute to the porters and carriers who then, as later, contributed so much to the success of the Communist Vietnamese,[26] was very much in his own personal style. Giap's order read as follows:

"The Dien Bien Phu victory is the most prestigious we have ever achieved. We have struck a heavy blow at the French colonialist warmongers and the American imperialists seeking to expand the war. Victory is due to the guidance of President Ho Chi Minh, the Party Central Committee and the Government. It is also due to the heroism of all combatants, their spirit of sacrifice and will to win. Especially it is due to the people's porters. In the name of the Army I thank you.

Vo Nguyen Giap
General Commander-in-Chief"

On 8th May, the day after the fall of Dien Bien Phu, the Asian conference opened at Geneva. Giap's sense of timing could hardly be faulted. As for the motivation of Giap's army during the costly and bitter siege, a valid judgment is perhaps that of de Castries himself. In answer to a question at his press conference on 18th September, de Castries, who had also been able to form some views during captivity, merely commented: "The enemy soldiers seemed less animated by Communist ideology than by a fierce nationalism".[27]

[1] Fall, "Hell is a very small place," Preface.

[2] Navarre, pp. 188–206.

[3] Catroux, pp. 153–157. Fall, pp. 44–45.

[4] Catroux, pp. 166–172.

[5] Navarre, p. 217.

[6] *Ibid.* pp. 213–217.

[7] *Ibid.* p. 197.

[8] *Ibid.* p. 217.

[9] *Ibid.* p. 222.

[10] Bidault: Autobiography *Resistance*, p. 196.

[11] Roy: *La Bataille de Dien Bien Phu*, p. 588.

[12] Eden: *Full Circle*, p. 103.

[13] *Ibid.* p. 106.

[14] Eisenhower: *Mandate for Change*, p. 353.

[15] Roy: *La bataille de Dien Bien Phu*, pp. 320–331.

[16] Fall, p. 408.

[17] Navarre, pp. 261–266.

[18] *Ibid.* pp. 324–326.

[19] *Ibid.* p. 327.

[20] *Ibid.* pp. 95–100.

[21] *Ibid.* pp. 333–335.

[22] Eden: *Full Circle,* p. 82.

[23] Giap, p. 158.

[24] *Ibid.* pp. 159–160.

[25] Fall, pp. 422.

[26] *Ibid.* p. 422; Giap; p. 158.

[27] Roy, p. 588.

10   The 1954 Geneva Conference

"T HE restoration of peace in Indo-China was the most dangerous and acute of the problems with which I had to deal during my last four years as Foreign Secretary."[1] The words come from the third volume of the memoirs of Lord Avon (then Mr. Anthony Eden). The achievement of a period of peace in Indo-China in 1954, as a result of the Geneva Agreements, owed much to Eden's constancy in the face of what he himself described as "the ambushes of diplomacy";[2] and, in October of that year, he received the honour of a Knighthood of the Order of the Garter.

At the beginning of 1954, the Great Power Berlin Conference, mainly on German business, provided an opening. At this conference, Mr. Molotov, the Soviet Foreign Minister, proposed "discussion of the convening of a Five Power Conference, including China, to seek measures for reducing tension in international relations".[3] By mid-February arrangements were in hand for France, the U.S., Russia, China and Britain, as well as certain Asian countries concerned, to meet at Geneva on 26th April under the joint chairmanship of Russia and Britain. The months between were marked by the battle of Dien Bien Phu, and by discussions on the Western side of the possibility of intervention. By the time of the first formal session on 8th May, Dien Bien Phu had, however, already fallen to the Communist Vietnamese.

It was against the background of the fall of Dien Bien Phu, the previous day, that M. Bidault, for so long a 'hawk' on Indo-China, had to address the opening session on 8th May at which the British Foreign Secretary was in the chair. Bidault called for a cease fire, but in terms of such coolness toward political negotiation as to cause anxiety in France as well as at the conference. "If the party that has organized armed forces to battle the State of Vietnam (meaning the totality of the State within the French Union) has been admitted to the conference in order to reach agreement on the cessation of hostilities, this should not be interpreted as recognition."[4] His historical outline referred to the civilising role of France in Indo-China, and portrayed the war as "this conflict which was imposed upon us."[5] A few days later Mr. Eden was noting that M. Bidault's 'noises off', in tune with activity in Washington by the interventionist lobby, 'had their danger'.[6]

The second plenary session, chaired this time by the Soviet Foreign Minister, convened on 10th May. The conference now heard the Viet Minh version of the background of the war. M. Pham Van Dong, speaking as the representative of the Democratic Republic of Vietnam, (recognised by Moscow and Peking and other communist countries), asserted, unsurprisingly, that the French proposals proceeded from an outworn imperialistic colonial conception: any settlement must include military and *political* matters. He also accused the United States of seeking to convert Indo-China into an American colony after the French had been ousted.[7]

Pham Van Dong then came to the point, and gave the conference the Viet Minh terms for a settlement. There were eight conditions:[8]

(a) Recognition of the independence, territorial integrity and sovereignty of Vietnam, Laos and Cambodia.

(b) Conclusion of an agreement concerning the withdrawal of all foreign troops from the territory of the three countries, in accordance with timetables agreed by the belligerent parties. Before troop withdrawal, the stationing of French forces in certain limited sectors of Vietnam would be arranged: these troops were not however to interfere with the local administration.

(c) Free general elections in Vietnam, Cambodia and Laos, supervised by commissions representing the belligerent parties: prior to the election, parties would administer the areas under their control.

(d) The Viet Minh would examine the question of free association within the French Union. Likewise the Pathet Lao and the Khmer Issarak (respectively the militant left in Laos and Cambodia).

(e) Readiness to recognise French cultural and economic interest.

(f) Belligerents would take no action against collaborators.

(g) Prisoner of War exchange.

(h) Cease fire.

At its third plenary session, the Conference heard the case of the State of Vietnam. (At that time, this was the formal title accepted by France, the United States, Britain and others, in respect of the Bao Dai State within the French Union.) Bao Dai's representative, Nguyen Quon Dinh, put forward proposals which, in effect, presumed the virtual surrender of the very real military and political gains already achieved by the Viet Minh. Professor Randle's comprehensive account of the Geneva Conference suggests that Dinh's speech could justifiably be considered a fantasy — except that its content had been endorsed by the United States.[9] In fairness though, the speech did not seem fantasy at the Conference at the time when it was delivered. It was more or less what the Conference expected.

On the issue of the relationship between the Viet Minh and the Saigon administration Randle observes:[10]

(a) "The Viet Minh was a military force. It had fought as an independent and disciplined army for several years, and had won several victories. In contrast, the South Vietnam army was not an independent entity and had virtually no independence of action: its troops had little dedication to the government."

(b) "The Viet Minh had no capital city and occupied no important coastal cities, but the Viet Minh occupied a size-able portion of rural Vietnam. It was a government independent of France, disciplined and not given to schism. The State of Vietnam Government was neither united, disciplined nor truly independent. The French constantly interfered in its operations. Its Premiers, who did not meet with the approval of the French (usually because they were ardent nationalists), were forced to resign."

(c) "While the Viet Minh leaders exercised real independence in the Tonkin hills, the Vietnamese leaders of the South enjoyed neither independence in fact nor even equivocal inde-pendence. Indeed, the de jure independence of the Viet Minh was no more questionable than that of the Vietnam Government in Saigon. The de facto independence of the Viet Minh, coupled with military victory, rendered the claims of the Saigon delegate overly ambitious, were it not for the possibility that U.S. action might make them more plausible."

Between the Viet Minh position, and that of the French and the Saigon administration, the gap was certainly considerable. In addition, deep suspicion abounded. Lord Avon says that because of the uncertain attitude of the French and the Americans, it fell to him towards the end of May to undertake much exploratory diplomacy.[11] In particular, he played a major part in the establishment of a military sub-committee to study armistice possibilities.[12] "By mid-June, French reluctance, American apprehension and Chinese suspicion (and presumably Viet Minh suspicion also) were all combining to bring the conference to a standstill."[13]

What perhaps most concerned Eden was the lack of response by M. Bidault to an important statement on 25th May by Pham Van Dong. This statement concerned *demarcation* of zones of control, *representing a single holding* on which a cease fire might be based.[14] This important statement opening a door to settlement, quickly found favour with Casey (Australia), Lester Pearson (Canada), and Krishna Menon of India, (well known for his leftist sympathies), as well as with Eden, but brought no reaction from Bidault.

At this stage, the internal political situation in France provided the breakthrough. Pressure developed for a government headed by the Radical Socialist, Pierre Mendès France and, on 18th June, the French National Assembly massively gave a mandate to Mendès France by 419 votes to 47, with 143 abstentions. Mendès France had been a critic of the war for many years, and was determined now to end it. The Bidault policies were swept aside, and Mendès France publicly addressed an ultimatum to himself to resign if there were no settlement within thirty days. Partition of Vietnam now became the French objective,[15] and direct talks began with the Viet Minh.

Meanwhile, at the military sub-committee talks, the Viet Minh had responded to the French proposal for *regrouping* each side of the eighteenth parallel, with a suggestion that the thirteenth parallel would be a more appropriate demarcation line. Then, in mid July, Dulles flew to Europe, and met with Eden and Mendès France. This pressure no doubt helped. The Viet Minh could not be sure of the upshot if the Conference were to fail; and Mendès France continued to hold firm on partition at the eighteenth parallel, and two years before elections; while the Viet Minh position moved toward a demarcation line on the sixteenth parallel and elections within one year.[16] On the sidelines, Bao Dai, the Vietnamese Head of State, seems once again to have sought to serve the interest of his fellow countrymen. "Bao Dai showed great restraint, accepting the principle of partition, dwelling mainly on the safeguards required for South Vietnam."[17]

As Mendès France's thirty days closed in, Anthony Eden maintained his close contact with Chou En-lai and Molotov. In turn, their influence operated on the Viet Minh. On 18th July, Chou En-lai proposed to Eden that the supervisory machinery should comprise India, Canada and Poland. Eden says that from then on the tangled ends of the negotiations became clear.[18] He himself suggested to Mendès France the value of some contact with Chou En-lai; and the French Prime Minister met Chou En-lai in Berne. The London 'Times' reported the occasion as a 'frank and friendly exchange'; and the contact was sufficient to cause misgiving among those in Washington who viewed it as supping with the devil. On 20th July, Mendès France

and the Viet Minh were agreed on a demarcation line close to the
seventeenth parallel. Armistice agreements in respect of Vietnam, Laos
and Cambodia were initialled the same day. Those covering Vietnam
and Laos were signed by General Deltiel, for France, and by Ta Quang
Buu, Deputy Defence Minister, for the Viet Minh. The agreement
covering Cambodia was signed by the country's Foreign Minister, Tep
Phan. Sihanouk wished it to be abundantly clear that, as far as
Cambodia was concerned, the country had *already* achieved its
Independence.

The main points of the three military agreements were:[19]

(a) FOR VIETNAM

    I. Cease fire instructions should be issued at once.

    II. There would be 'demarcation' along the Song Ben Hat
       River (roughly the 17th parallel).

    III. Each side would withdraw within 300 days from the
        zone of the other.

    IV. Free population movement would be permitted within
        the 300 day period.

    V. General all-Vietnam elections would be held in July
       1956.

    VI. The 'zones' would not adhere to any alliance and new
        'bases' would not be established.

    VII. Supervision would rest with an International Control
         Commission (India, Poland, Canada).

(b) FOR CAMBODIA

    I. Cease fire instructions would be issued at once.

    II. There would be demobilisation of the 'Khmer Resis-
       tance', and no hostile action.

    III. All foreign armed forces (including the French and
        Viet Minh) should leave Cambodia within 90 days.

    IV. Elections during 1955.

    V. No foreign bases.

    VI. Acceptance of international supervision as above.

(c) FOR LAOS

    I. Cease fire instructions would be issued at once.

    II. Withdrawal of non-Lao military forces within 120
       days: the French being permitted however to retain
       two bases and a garrison not exceeding 3500 men.

    III. Pending 'political settlement,' the 'Pathet Lao' to hold
        the North Eastern provinces of Phong Saly and Sam
        Neua.

    IV. Acceptance of international supervision as above.

On 21st July, Mr. Eden took the chair at a final plenary session to put the seal of the conference on what had been achieved. Apart from the three military agreements, covering Vietnam, Laos and Cambodia, nothing was however signed. The other documents comprised unilateral declarations from France, Cambodia and Laos — two from each, and a 'final declaration', of uncertain juridical standing, but widely regarded as "an act of the conference", which took note of the various agreements and underlined the July 1956, all Vietnam election target.[20]

The two year delay in elections also reflected a U.S. view. General Eisenhower relates in his memoirs that he "never talked or corresponded with anyone knowledgeable in Indo-Chinese affairs who did not agree that in any election, while the fighting was on, possibly eighty per cent of the population would have voted for Ho Chi Minh as their leader, rather than Chief of State Bao Dai."[21]

But, ominously, neither the United States, nor the Saigon Government, now headed by Ngo Dinh Diem, subscribed fully to the final declaration. The text of this declaration is at Appendix C. South Vietnam said it would not seek to oppose the cease fire agreement but doubted if free elections would be possible in the Communist areas: the United States merely 'took note'[22] and stated that the U.S. would not use force to disturb the agreements. The text of the U.S. declaration at Geneva is also at Appendix C. At his news conference on 21st July, President Eisenhower made it clear that the "U.S. were not a party to or bound by the decision taken at the conference but hoped they would lead to peace."[23] For the U.S., their war in Indo-China was still some way off.

Meanwhile, Britain and the Soviet Union had incurred certain special responsibilities for Indo-China by virtue of their Foreign Secretaries' co-chairmanship of the Geneva Conference. At the end of the conference, the two Foreign Secretaries undertook to organise the finances of the three International Control Commissions set up by the Cease Fire Agreements on Cambodia, Laos and Vietnam. From this, stemmed their practice of receiving and circulating reports from the Commissions. This in turn led to a sense of distinctive involvement over and above responsibility as a member of the Security Council; and, in 1961 and 1962, for example, the two co-Chairmen played a major part in defusing a dangerous situation which had arisen in Laos. This special involvement lasted indeed until the Paris Conference in 1973 passed the responsibilities elsewhere.

As Geneva 1954 came to an end, the individual national reactions were much as to be expected. Tran Van Do, the Foreign Minister of the State, which in practical terms had now become South Vietnam, reported to Saigon: "We fought desperately against partition and for a neutral zone in the Catholic area of North Vietnam: absolutely impossible to surmount hostility of enemy and perfidy of false friends".[24] As for the Viet Minh, they felt that with or without elections the unification of Vietnam was now close. China and the Soviet Union can hardly have failed to feel pleasure at the anti-imperialist plus achieved by the Viet Minh. Laos and Cambodia were satisfied. In France, there was a sense of relief that the long war was at last over. Britain felt a good job done in helping to achieve this for France.

But the U.S. reaction, like that of South Vietnam, was reserved. Dulles told a news conference on 23rd July that "military developments in Indo-China and the disinclination of the French people to prolong the war led to a settlement containing many features we do not like". But the important thing, he said, "was not to mourn the past but to seize the future opportunity to prevent the loss of Northern Vietnam from leading to the extension of Communism throughout South East Asia and the South West Pacific".[25] This was a significant announcement of the 'domino theory', and from it would stem almost twenty years of even more direct and costly American involvement in the affairs of Indo-China. As so often, however, the penalties of a course of action actually taken are obvious. What can never be told is the penalties there might have been if the course of action had not been taken. This is the other side of the coin, and is one which, in fairness, needs to be considered by the critics of U.S. policy in South East Asia. It is difficult, though, not to have some feeling that the crusading tone adopted by Dulles may have sharpened rather than eased the tension of the times.

[1] Eden: *Full Circle,* p. 77.

[2] *Ibid.* p. 107.

[3] *Ibid.* p. 87.

[4] Devillers/Lacouture, p. 153. (The full text of M. Bidault's statement may be found in *Le Monde,* 11 May 1954.)

[5] *Ibid.* p. 157.

[6] Eden, p. 120.

[7] Randle: *Geneva 1954.* p. 207.

[8] Randle, p. 208; Devillers/Lacouture, p. 156.

[9] *Ibid.* p. 212.

[10] *Ibid.* p. 213.

[11] Eden, p. 120.

[12] *Ibid.* p. 125.

[13] *Ibid.* p. 128.

[14] Devillers/Lacouture, pp. 206–8.

[15] *Ibid.* pp. 244–258.

[16] Eden, pp. 139–141.

[17] Devillers/Lacouture, p. 264.

[18] Eden, p. 141.

[19] Randle, pp. 346, 349.

[20] Randle, pp. 339–345.

[21] Eisenhower, p. 372.

[22] Randle, p. 344.

[23] Eisenhower: *Mandate for change,* p. 371.

[24] Buttinger, p. 380.

[25] *Ibid.* p. 381.

11   1954 – 1956: Downhill from Geneva

T HE developments in the immediate aftermath of the Geneva
Conference divide into those predominantly international, and
those more domestic to Indo-China. Mr. Dulles continued to
work strongly for a Security Treaty covering South East Asia, from
which he appeared anxious to exclude India. Britain, on the other
hand, sought the greatest possible Asian association.[1] At Geneva, Eden
sought to allay the apprehension of Chou En-lai during the course of a
conversation on 17th July.[2] Elsewhere, British diplomacy worked hard
to reassure Asian suspicion before the final signing in Manila on 8th
September 1954 of the South East Asia Collective Defence Treaty
(SEATO).

The countries bound by this treaty were France, the United
States, Thailand, the Philippines, Pakistan, Australia, New Zealand
and Britain. Their agreement was to *act* in the event of a direct attack
on any member: in the event of an attack on a third party in the treaty
area (notably Indo-China) the agreement was to *consult*[3]. At much the
same time, decisions were also being taken in the United States to
assume greater direct responsibility in Indo-China. Decisions screened
from publicity were also no doubt being taken in Peking and Moscow
as to Communist objectives in Indo-China. The range of memoirs out of
Britain, France and the United States are not paralleled by Chinese
and Russian volumes.

Within Indo-China itself, the direct upshot of Geneva differed as
between Cambodia, Laos and Vietnam — a difference reflecting the
degree of previous Communist penetration and also the facility of
prospective penetration. Happily for Cambodia, it had been somewhat
on the margin during the eight years of the French War and,
fortunately for its immediate future, the demarcation of Vietnam along
the seventeenth parallel preserved this relative insulation. Prince
Sihanouk's policies also played their part in bringing peace and relative
stability to his country.

Within Cambodia, it was a point of honour to regard the
country's independence as of pre-Geneva origin, dating from 9th
November 1953 (M. Laniel's 'perfection' of independence). After

Geneva, Sihanouk worked vigorously to achieve the withdrawal of Viet Minh forces and the surrender of the Khmer Issarak insurgents, fore-runner of the Khmer Serai (whom he would later claim were receiving support from Bangkok and Saigon). There was, however, the explicit election requirement of the Geneva settlement. To begin with, Sihanouk sought to resolve this by a referendum on the "Royal Mission": in essence a vote of confidence in himself as a ruling King. The International Supervisory Commission now established in Cambodia did not however welcome this initiative. Not for the first or last time Sihanouk now opted for the dramatic gesture. On 2nd March 1955, while still continuing to exert practical authority, he formally abdicated as King in favour of his father, Norodom Suramarit.[4]

At once, Sihanouk formed a political movement (he was always anxious that it should not be seen as just another political party) which pledged itself to guard the interests of the peasants.[5] This well directed movement, the SANGKUM REASTR NIYUM (People's Socialist Com-munity) contested elections held in Cambodia in September 1955, and, against a disparate opposition, won a clean sweep of the seats in the Assembly. In October 1955, the International Supervisory Commission for Cambodia was able to report: "With the completion of general elections in Cambodia, a general political settlement may be said to have been achieved. The Commission's responsibility with regard to political matters concerning former resistants may therefore be regarded as concluded."[6]

While passing through Singapore during 1955, Sihanouk explained to Mr. Malcolm MacDonald the reasoning which had led him to abdicate as King (while continuing, though, to have a special place as Head of State). "Sihanouk explained that the nature of Cambodia's problem had changed: until recently Cambodia's greatest need was in the field of international affairs, seeking independence from France. As King he could lead the nation to this objective. But now the problem had turned to a range of internal affairs, and it had been difficult for him as King to deal with such matters."[7] Hence Sihanouk's act of abdication while still retaining authority.

Externally, the former Cambodian stance on neutrality was increasingly stressed. Cambodia ceased to regard itself as a member of the French Union, and announced that it rejected the consideration of its affairs automatically offered under the South East Asian Treaty. At the same time, the country sought and obtained aid from all the great powers, and, for the next fifteen years, achieved a relative peace. For Cambodia, Geneva 1954 was a considerable plus.

For Laos and South Vietnam, however, matters turned out less well. Some partial elections took place in Laos in 1955, but invariably the problem of the reintegration and control of the strategic North Eastern provinces bordering North Vietnam and China was the rock on which any overall national settlement would come to grief. In addition, the North Vietnamese military withdrawal was incomplete. The areas through Laos, which later on would be their all-important communications to the South, the Ho Chi Minh trail, were never given up. Their presence could never be ignored. In general though, while the Government of Laos was in the hands of Prince Souvanna Phouma, who accepted contact with Hanoi and Peking as well as with Washington, there was an element of modus vivendi.

Unfortunately, there were a number of occasions when certain Lao military leaders sought a more extreme anti-Communist position than the geographical situation of the country could safely afford. It was perhaps especially unfortunate for Laos that Prince Souvanna Phouma could not enjoy the same authority there as Sihanouk in Cambodia, where Sihanouk enjoyed an extra dimension of authority as Head of State and descendant of a thousand year dynasty of Kings of Cambodia. Yet, although the upshot of the 1954 Geneva Conference was less happy for Laos than for Cambodia, enough mutual confidence persisted within the country for there to be a further Geneva Conference, between May 1961 and August 1962, to seek to achieve peace, unity and neutrality in Laos.

But Vietnam was of course the country which mattered the most, and the responsibility for carrying out the conference terms in Vietnam was, in the first instance, generally recognised as falling to the French and the Viet Minh, the latter, now sovereign in their own right North of the 17th parallel, and solidly on the international scene as the Democratic Republic of Vietnam, a nation recognised by a number of non-Communist countries as well as by the Communist World. For the French, their responsibility did however involve an element of contradiction. It was one thing to leave the North, and the French were away from Hanoi by October 1954, and from Haiphong by May 1955. The real problem lay in the South, where the French had to seek to reconcile their treaty obligations to Hanoi under the Geneva Agreement, with their obligations toward the Government of Bao Dai in Saigon.

It might be possible to secure the transfer to the North of certain regular Viet Minh units. It was virtually impossible to achieve the dismantling of the clandestine Communist network in the South. Given the American policy now developing in South East Asia, it was also impossible for the French to act as the agent in the South for the implementation of the Geneva terms — even if they had wished to do so. In 1954 and 1955 the French faced the same basic political problem

as the Americans had to face nearly twenty years later. A condition of
peace was that the North Vietnamese expected them to bring a non-
Communist Government in Saigon to terms.

Meanwhile, Washington was also in an anomalous position. It
had assumed a political responsibility for the survival of a non-
Communist Government in the South, but Vietnamese National forces
were not yet strong enough to sustain its defence. The country still
depended on the French expeditionary force now regrouped in the
South under General Ely, who combined the function of Commander
in Chief and Commissioner General. An inherently complicated
situation was, however, eased by Ely's 'Atlantic' concepts and his
Washington experience, where he had got on well with General Collins
and others high in the American military hierarchy. Ely himself
apparently managed to stay on friendly terms with the American
authorities in Saigon despite the differences in policy between France
and the United States.[8]

At the beginning of August, the National Security Council in
Washington, had concluded that the Geneva settlement was a 'disaster'.[9]
There was no firm conclusion, however, as to what should be done. This
conclusion developed during the month. A memorandum from the
Joint Chiefs-of-Staff to the Secretary of Defence expressed the view that
there should be a complete withdrawal of French forces, French
officials and the French advisers "so as to provide motivation and a sound
base for the establishment of national armed forces." ... "It is absolutely essential that there be a reasonably strong stable government in
control: it is hopeless to expect a U.S. military mission to be successful
unless the nation concerned performs the governmental function
essential to the successful raising and maintenance of armed forces."[10]

On 20th August, President Eisenhower approved a National
Security Council paper on the situation. Its main points were:[11]

(a) Politically, the United States should work with Prime
    Minister Ngo Dinh Diem (who had taken over from Prince
    Buu Loc midway through the Geneva Conference) but would
    encourage him to broaden his Government and establish
    more democratic institutions.

(b) Militarily, the United States would work with France only so
    far as it was necessary to build up indigenous forces capable
    of providing internal security.

(c) Economically, the United States would begin giving aid
    directly to the Vietnamese Government in Saigon: not, as
    before, through the French: "the French were to be
    dissociated from the levers of power."

At about the same time, a CIA team had been introduced into Vietnam as the 'Saigon Military Mission'. Its leader, Colonel Lansdale, came with a considerable reputation after success against insurgency in the Philippines, and his Mission's objective, as stated in its own report, was "to assist the Vietnamese rather than the French."[12] The exploits of this mission were widely regarded as providing the model for two later novels, *The Quiet American* by Graham Greene, and *The Ugly American* by William Lederer. The Pentagon Papers reveal some of the Mission's activities: these included operations in the North involving Civil Air Transport, the Formosa based airline run by General Chennault, the former commander of the U.S. Air Force in China, who was well known as an active supporter of Chiang Kai-shek: their most important activity however seems to have related to the support and protection of Ngo Dinh Diem himself, not only in Saigon, but also in Washington, where Lansdale's influence operated strongly on behalf of the South Vietnamese Prime Minister. There were indeed some very special inner lines of communication. The Head of the CIA at this important period was Allen Dulles, the brother of John Foster Dulles, the Secretary of State.

There was also some spin off from Ngo Dinh Diem's earlier contact with influential Senators in Washington.[13] A report submitted on October 15th to the Senate Foreign Relations Committee by Senator Mansfield sharply objected to any plans to replace Diem, whose anti-French views were increasingly apparent. Mansfield said plainly that if Diem should be overthrown "The United States should consider an immediate suspension of all aid to Vietnam and the French Union forces there, except for aid of a humanitarian nature".

From now on events moved quickly. During October, the State Department announced that as from 1st January 1955, American financial support for the armies of Vietnam, Laos and Cambodia would be given directly rather than through the French. This information was indeed conveyed to Diem in an encouraging letter of support from President Eisenhower which contained the following words: "The purpose of this offer is to assist the Government of Vietnam in developing and maintaining a strong, viable State, capable of resisting attempted subversion or aggression through military means." During November, M. Mendès France visited Washington, and there was agreement that although General Ely would retain nominal command, the forces of the Saigon Government would be American trained. Despite some further internal American debate toward the end of 1954, the course was now set toward close United States involvement.

Meanwhile in Saigon, Ngo Dinh Diem was making it abundantly clear that for his part he would prefer this United States involvement to any further French tutelage. He made the point continuously that France had spoken only for herself at Geneva, and not in any way for his government in the basic Conference document which spelt out the requirement for elections during 1956. His own aim in the immediate aftermath of the conference was to consolidate his own power base. "There were two objectives: the first to win over Washington completely: the second to recruit reliable and blindly loyal supporters who would meet with the approval of American officialdom."[14]

As for the first objective, a new Vietnamese Ambassador to Washington, Tran Van Cheung was appointed from within the family circle. This was a link on which Diem could count. A more important link, however, was the one through the American Embassy in Saigon, where General Lawton Collins, who had just ceased to be Chief of Staff of the United States Army, was appointed as a special envoy of President Eisenhower. General Collins, who may possibly have also been reflecting some French views, was unimpressed with Diem and, in December 1954, advised re-evaluation of United States plans for South East Asia in the light of the reservation he had about Diem. However Mr. Dulles thought otherwise, and Collins was told that the United States now had no option but to back Diem and continue its aid to South Vietnam. On the internal front, Diem's objective in the after-math of Geneva, was to consolidate his own power base. His brother, Ngo Dinh Nhu, had already built up a useful labour organisation and, for reliable individuals to work on his behalf within the country, Diem also turned to the Catholic community.[15] Here he received welcome reinforcements from the North. The military regroupment under the Geneva Agreement also permitted population transfer, and Diem understandably sought to achieve the maximum movement South. Nearly a million Catholics had moved to the South by the middle of 1955. The corresponding movement to the North was about one hundred thousand.[16]

The obstacles to the consolidation of personal power by Diem were by no means just those of the Communist North. The army and the sects remained loyal to Bao Dai and the monarchy, on whose abolition Diem was widely known to be intent. But here the U.S. influence played its part. In August 1954, the French Government under U.S. pressure, frustrated the return of Bao Dai to Vietnam.[17] Shortly afterward, Diem engineered the disposal of the South Vietnam army commander, General Nguyen Van Hinh, an officer whose loyalty lay toward Bao Dai rather than himself. This left just the sects to be cracked and, during 1955, Diem moved vigorously and successfully against them. Despite urgent appeals for an armistice from the Emperor Bao Dai, who at this time was at his villa near Cannes, Diem still went ahead. In turn the 'Cao Dai', the Binh Xuyen and the Hoa Hao were all defeated.[18]

In a sense the sects had represented not merely subordinate armies, but also approached the status of subordinate Governments operating what could be considered as their own protection rackets over substantial areas of South Vietnam. They were no charge on Diem's Exchequer, and to a considerable extent they were self-supporting. They were also a significant force against the Communists. But, as far as Ngo Dinh Diem was concerned, the sects were unacceptable, not least because they were a source of French influence. By the spring of 1955, he was determined that they should be eliminated. Diem called on General Ely to order the necessary action, but Ely declined to be answerable for battles in the streets of Saigon.

In particular, Diem had sought the earliest possible elimination of the Binh Xuyen who controlled both the Saigon police and the gambling and prostitution business of the town. Diem wished their headquarters to be taken over, and gave orders to a Colonel Tri to storm the building. These orders were countermanded by Ely. In addition, the French refused to meet the national army's demands for ammunition and transport. In both these instances General Collins, the American Ambassador Extraordinary, whose views on Diem were very different from Lansdale's, was widely regarded as approving the line taken by Ely.[19]

But the episode was only a temporary setback for Diem. A few weeks later, he again ordered action against the Binh Xuyen. This time, he made sure that Ely's objections were disregarded, and the attack successfully went forward. Among its leaders was Colonel Duong Van Minh who, eight years later, would also be among the leaders of the coup which overthrew Diem himself.

Whatever the merits in relation to the internal scene, and some observers saw significance in the support given to Diem by Cochin Chinese elements in the army, the success certainly achieved international impact. It signalled to the French that it was time to go, and their final withdrawal took place shortly after. It also gave Diem status in Washington, where, after further representations from General Collins, Mr. Dulles was once again seriously considering whether the United States should seek some other horse to back in South Vietnam. On 28th April 1955, when the crisis with the sects was approaching its peak, Diem told Lansdale that he had just received word from Washington that the United States were about to withdraw their support. Lansdale, whose "Saigon Military Mission" had been helping Diem in his counter-measures against the sects (and had also been pressing the Embassy as a whole for support), offered Diem encouragement. At this stage, Diem ordered the decisive action against the sects. Thereafter, American support was confirmed.

On 29th April, the day following the battle in Saigon, in which civilian casualties had run into hundreds, M. Faure, the French Prime Minister had spoken critically of Diem. On the same day, Mr. Dulles called in M. Couve de Murville, the French Ambassador in Washington, to warn him against any further French moves to unseat Diem.[20] In Paris, Mr. Dillon, the American Ambassador, spoke in the same terms to Faure himself. And, to rub it in, the French were reminded that the military stores which were required by Diem came from American aid. On 30th April, Diem received a cable from the Administration in Washington assuring him of continued U.S. support.

All was now set for Diem to move against the monarchy, and the culmination of a well orchestrated 'spontaneous' campaign came toward the end of 1955. In October 1955 a referendum was arranged to decide the issue, monarchy or republic. "The referendum was so contrived as to give nearly six million votes to Diem and a mere sixty thousand to Bao Dai; the ballot papers had been printed to portray Diem in lucky red, Bao Dai in unlucky green, while in Saigon, according to French reports, the returning officers returned 605,000 votes by 450,000 voters. The Republic of Vietnam was proclaimed on 20th October 1955, and six days later (and recognised at once by the U.S. government) Diem proclaimed himself President".[21] It is difficult to be sure if this episode was entirely in the best interest of Diem's fellow citizens. Whatever his faults, Bao Dai, who in 1975 was still alive and resident in the South of France, had more than once shown a capacity to bridge the hostilities which infected his realm.

Throughout this period, Hanoi watched with growing anxiety this elimination of French influence in the South in favour of a U.S. presence. Ho Chi Minh expressed these anxieties personally to Sainteny, back once again in Hanoi as the French representative.[22] Sainteny, whose path would cross that of Ho Chi Minh yet again, could reasonably regard himself as a man with considerable knowledge of Ho Chi Minh. Certainly no one else from the West ever achieved his degree of contact. Yet at the same time, Sainteny had been cautious of taking up the appointment and, before its acceptance, had sought and obtained the blessing of General de Gaulle. Perhaps the General already sensed the new tide to be caught.

In 1955 and 1956, Paris seems however to have minimised their Mission in Hanoi. In Sainteny's view, this was because of American pressure, both direct and through SEATO, of which France was at that time an active member. After a meeting with Ho Chi Minh in March 1955, Sainteny telegraphed Paris: "The DRV is worried about

French enterprises forsaking North Vietnam. The leaders see in this abandonment a desire on our part to back the South and leave the North to confront its problems alone with its Socialist allies". Even more, the government in Hanoi was concerned at what they regarded as French back-sliding on the Geneva Agreement clause on country wide elections.

Between 1954 and 1956, the holding of the elections throughout Vietnam, which they were confident of winning, remained the dominant objective of Communist policy. Presumably, Diem thought that whatever the international supervision on which he might insist, the Communists would win, and he set his face against even the preparatory electoral discussion, referred to in the principal document of the Geneva Conference.[23] In fairness, however, Diem, like others before and later, may have seen divided Vietnam as the true reality. He must also have appreciated the numerical voting superiority of the North.

While Diem was stressing that his government was not bound by the Geneva Conference, consultation continued between the Geneva co-chairmen in an attempt to solve the impasse on the elections conceived at Geneva. A Hanoi proposal for a new international conference received backing only from the Chinese and Russian governments. However, on 8th May, the British and Soviet Foreign Ministers urged both Hanoi and Saigon to try to implement the Geneva agreements, and expressed concern that electoral discussions had not taken place.[24]

The month of July 1956, during which elections were to have been held throughout Vietnam, came and went. There were no elections. For the Communists in the South, it was a period of disarray. An American intelligence report, referred to in the Pentagon Papers, states that Le Duan, one of the most important of the Vietnamese Communist leaders, returned to the North at about this time: "He informed the politburo that it was wasting its time with orders for political struggle and urged military pressure."[25] A war phase, which would last seven years, and would largely be fought by Vietnamese, was about to begin.

---

[1] Eden, pp. 96–110.

[2] *Ibid.* p. 140.

[3] Eisenhower, p. 374.

[4] Randle, p. 499.

5. *B.I.S. The Khmer Republic*, p. 18.

6. Cmd. 9671.

7. MacDonald: *Titans and Others*, p. 179.

8. Hammer, p. 355.

9. *Pentagon Papers*, p. 14.

10. *Ibid.* p. 15.

11. *Ibid.* p. 15.

12. *Ibid.* p. 54.

13. Lancaster, p. 396.

14. Devillers/Lacouture, p. 333.

15. Duncanson, p. 215.

16. *C.O.I. Vietnam*, p. 17.

17. Devillers/Lacouture, p. 321.

18. Duncanson, pp. 220–21.

19. Lancaster, p. 386.

20. Buttinger, p. 407, quoting *Christian Science Monitor* of 30.4.1955.

21. Duncanson, p. 223 — partially referring to Lancaster's *The Emancipation of Indo-China*, p. 899.

22. Devillers/Lacouture, p. 388; and Sainteny, pp. 135–140.

23. Duncanson, pp. 223–224; Randle, pp. 470–474.

24. *C.O.I. Vietnam*, p. 18.

25. *Pentagon Papers* (New York Times), p. 75.

12   1956 – 1963: A Conflict Just Contained

FOR South Vietnam, the years from 1956 to 1963 belong without question to Ngo Dinh Diem. "In two years (1954 – 56) Diem had transformed himself from the powerless and expendable local Chancellor of an absentee monarch into the executive Head of State of a sovereign republic. The new state was his personal creation."[1] In his lifetime, this remained true.

The central philosophy of this new state was Diem's creed of 'Personalism,' which seems to have had the message that, for the wider social good, men should accept their lot. The major instrument of this creed was Diem's own family circle. "In a Communal Personalist State, the person would enjoy the human dignity, and liberty of living under regulations and controls reminiscent of totalitarian regimes, but differing from them, because, in the latter, unity and enthusiasm are brought about artificially and by lies .... The Personalists took a view of the family and of relations between the sexes in accordance with the conventions of French Catholic Society."[2] Ho Chi Minh and his colleagues could have been forgiven if they felt they were now up against another of their own authoritarian ilk.

The personal politburo for Diem was the family circle. One brother, Ngo Dinh Nhu, husband of the Madame Nhu, who later became known for her observations about "barbecued monks", was the Political Adviser to the President — the party manager. Another brother was Ngo Dinh Thuc, Catholic Archbishop of Hué. A third brother, Ngo Dinh Can, was the Province Chief of Lowland Annam. The youngest brother, Ngo Dinh Luyen, was employed as a diplomat and served for a while as Ambassador in London. Although Diem himself was a bachelor, there were, in addition, certain relations through marriage to add to the team and, for nearly seven years, this small group ran South Vietnam.

In many ways this was a considerable management achievement. From 1957 onward, there was Communist military activity against the Diem government in which Hanoi played an expanding rôle. To begin with, this activity took the form of the assassination of local leaders and supporters of the régime. In 1960, nearly 1400 such persons were killed.[3] The military arm responsible for this activity were the Viet Cong, (abbreviation for the Vietnam Cong San) the Vietnam Communists, who, increasingly used the Ho Chi Minh trail for infiltration and supply. (The Ho Chi Minh trail being, as mentioned previously, a number of trails running through Eastern Laos from North to South Vietnam, a network rather than a main road.)

The Diem administration reacted with some vigour toward this Communist activity and not without a measure of success. A "strategic hamlet" scheme whose effectiveness (or not) aroused much controversy, was initiated to improve security in the countryside. Although by 1961, the United States military mission in Vietnam numbered about 700 and there was also a small British advisory mission, led by Sir Robert Thompson who had previously done well in Malaya, the weight of the anti-Communist effort lay with the Saigon authorities. Despite pressure by Mr. Dulles, President Eisenhower had been cautious of excessive United States involvement. 1961 was however the year of the famous inaugural speech of President Kennedy. *"Let every nation know, whether it wishes us well or ill, that we shall pay any price, bear any burden, meet any hardship, support any friend, oppose any foe, to ensure the survival and the success of liberty."* The mood of the day, and it is not so long ago, should be recalled. It needs to be remembered that at the time the words were spoken, President Kennedy's commitment to liberty fired the imagination of young people in America and elsewhere in the world. The green beret of the Special Forces stood alongside the Peace Corps as the symbol of President Kennedy's 'new frontier'. And there was not the slightest doubt whom President Kennedy saw as the enemy of liberty. In West Berlin he spelt it out — "there are many people in the world who really do not understand, or say they do not, what is the great issue between the free world and the Communist world. Let them come to Berlin. In the world of freedom, the proudest boast is — 'ich bin ein Berliner' ".

The Kennedy message must have been music for President Ngo Dinh Diem, who at about this time was in the midst of his own re-election effort, in which, unsurprisingly, he gained about six million of the seven million votes cast. Once it was over, Walt Rostow, who was the Deputy Presidential Assistant for National Security, advised President Kennedy on 12th April 1961, "I believe we must turn to gearing up the whole Vietnam operation."[4] The memorandum ranged widely and, as well as touching on an increase in the strength of the U.S. military mission, it discussed the problem of persuading Diem to "broaden the base of his government." Previously, Elbridge Durbrow the U.S. Ambassador in Saigon in a report which commented adversely on "Mr. and Mrs. Nhu" had concluded:[5] "if Diem's position continues to deteriorate ... it may become necessary for the U.S. government to consider alternative courses and leaders to achieve our objective" (denial of South Vietnam to the Communists).

The 'tilt' was now toward increased U.S. intervention and, in the spring of 1961 in the light of Rostow's counsel, President Kennedy authorised the deployment of 400 Special Forces troops in Vietnam. At the time, this deployment was not publicly disclosed.[6] A visit to Vietnam by Vice President Lyndon Johnson was also arranged, and this took place in May 1961. Johnson's subsequent report to the President, which contained much of significance, included the following points which were perhaps to be expected:[7]

(a) "There is no alternative to U.S. leadership in South East Asia."

(b) "SEATO is not now and never will be the answer because of British and French reluctance to support decisive action."

(c) "Diem is a complex figure beset by many problems. He has admirable personal qualities but he is remote from the people, and is surrounded by persons less admirable and capable than he. The country can be saved if we move quickly and wisely. We must decide whether to support Diem or let Vietnam fall ... in this case we would say to the world we don't stand by our friends ... this is not my concept."

(d) "The most important thing is creative American management of our military aid program."

(e) "The fundamental decision required of the United States is whether we are to attempt to meet the challenge of Communist expansion in South East Asia or throw in the towel."

In addition, however, the report included the very important observation that American combat troop involvement was not only not required: it was undesirable. There were also the following imaginative words: "The greatest danger South East Asia offers the United States is not the momentary threat of Communism itself, but the danger which stems from hunger, ignorance, poverty and disease. Whatever strategies we evolve we must keep these enemies the point of our attack."[8]

Vice President Johnson's report briefly held the tide against the direct American combat troop deployment now being urged by the top leadership of the American armed forces. Then, on 13th October, possibly spontaneously, but perhaps as a result of some local U.S. military suggestion, the Saigon Government formally changed its mind on U.S. military participation.[9] That day, on Diem's specific authority,

South Vietnam submitted to the Americans a request that "U.S. combat units be introduced into South Vietnam as combat trainer units: part, as a symbolic strength to be stationed near the 17th parallel in the North, which would also free ARVN (Army of the Republic of Vietnam) forces there for anti-guerilla action, also "similar purposes station U.S. units in several provincial seats in the Central Vietnam highlands." In putting this requirement to the Americans, Nguyen Dinh Thuan, the Vietnamese Acting Defence Minister, said that "token forces would suffice." The South Vietnamese also requested a view on accepting possible Chinese Nationalist military help.

These requests from Saigon came on the eve of a visit there by General Maxwell Taylor, a former U.S. Army Chief-of-Staff, who acted as a military adviser to President Kennedy. The instructions given to General Taylor were to study the three alternative courses:

(a) Bold U.S. intervention, to defeat the Viet Cong using up to three U.S. divisions.

(b) Lesser U.S. intervention, involving the sending of a smaller combat element with the essential task of establishing a U.S. military presence.

(c) No U.S. combat intervention, but an increase in equipment and munitions assistance.

General Taylor's recommendation was for the middle course, with emphasis on the provision of relatively small support and training elements possessing combat capability. This recommendation was broadly accepted in Washington, despite some State Department reservation. The State Department members of General Taylor's mission had observed that, since it was an open question if Saigon could succeed, even with U.S. help, it would be a mistake for the U.S. to commit itself irrevocably to the defeat of the Communists in Vietnam.[10] At this stage, Mr. Rusk, the Secretary of State, also expressed reluctance about "American prestige being committed too deeply to a losing cause."[11]

Shortly afterwards, Rusk was associated with Mr. McNamara, the Defence Secretary, in a very important memorandum, which the President adopted almost in full as American policy.[12] This document recommended that the U.S. should commit itself to "preventing the fall of South Vietnam to the Communists." On the method of achieving this objective, it was, however, more cautious: — "The commitment of U.S. forces to South Vietnam involves two different categories:

(a) Units of modest size required for the direct support of South Vietnamese military effort, such as communications, helicopters and other airlift, reconnaissance aircraft, naval patrols, intelligence units, etc; and

(b) larger organised units, with actual or potential direct military missions.

Category A should be introduced as speedily as possible.

Category B units pose more serious problems."

The reasons for caution on major combat commitment were threefold:[13]

(a) "The 1962 conference on Laos was in the offing. It would be a pity to damage its prospects."

(b) "It would be well if forces from other nations could also be associated — as they had been in Korea."

(c) "Once U.S. troops are engaged will it be possible to count on strong South Vietnamese effort?" (Shades here of General Ely's words, at the end of the day for France, that Vietnamisation was the key.)

The final U.S. government decision, almost completely in line with the Rusk/McNamara recommendations, was announced on 14th December, 1961, in a public exchange of letters between President Kennedy and President Diem.[14] President Kennedy's letter minced no words: "our information has convincingly shown that the campaign of force and terror now being waged against your people and your government is supported and directed from the outside by the authorities in Hanoi" ... "if the Communist authorities in North Vietnam will stop their campaign to destroy the Republic of Vietnam, the measures we are taking to assist your defence effort will no longer be necessary. We shall seek to persuade the Communists to give up their attempts of force and subversion".

Certainly, the American action was an all-important first step. Even so, the American military build up was very small scale by comparison with later standards. In November 1961, there were 1000 U.S. servicemen in Vietnam; two months later, 3000; six months later, nearly 6000; and by the end of 1962, about 11,000. Casualties mounted proportionately — 14 in 1961, 109 in 1962.[15] The commitment was still contained: the hazard lay in its open ended nature, and the perhaps understandable pressure of the United States Joint Chiefs-of-Staff for an increase in the American military effort.

In some degree these military views reflected those of the French more than a decade before. The U.S. Chiefs-of-Staff asserted:[16]

(a) "any South East Asian war will be a peninsular campaign in which the U.S. has a wealth of experience." (In the aftermath of Korea this was an understandable view.)

(b) "study of the problem indicates that the Communists are limited in the forces they can sustain in war in that area because of natural logistic and transportation problems." (This was less understandable: General Navarre had thought exactly the same before the battle of Dien Bien Phu, and this previous error of judgment might have been expected to have had a larger place in U.S. military thinking.)

In certain ways, 1962 was indeed a year of lull, and in Laos a potentially dangerous international moment was weathered. On 23rd July, the 14 Power Conference on Laos finally reached agreement on the neutralisation of that country; a signpost for peace, despite setbacks which followed. As the 14 Nations were Burma, Cambodia, Canada, the Peoples Republic of China, the Democratic Republic of Vietnam (Hanoi), the Republic of Vietnam (Saigon), France, India, Poland, Thailand, the Soviet Union, the United States and Britain, as well as three Laotian groups, the agreement represented a very considerable diplomatic achievement.

The Laos conference had its origins in the events of late 1960, when right wing forces under General Phoumi Nosavan threatened the recently formed neutralist government of Prince Souvanna Phouma. Within Laos, political leadership rested largely with the three princes; Souvanna Phouma, the neutralist; Souphannouvong, the leader of the Pathet Lao left; and Boun Oum, the leader of the right. But their authority was not exclusive. In August 1960, a Captain Kong Lae, who eschewed advancement in rank, but who effectively commanded the loyalty of a parachute battalion, mounted a coup in Vientiane to buttress the authority of the existing neutralist government. Shortly afterwards, General Phoumi Nosavan, a military leader of the Lao right, who was related to the Thai Prime Minister, Sarit Thanarat, commenced to threaten the neutralist government from his base in Southern Laos. The neutralist government claimed that Nosavan's artillery, firing from positions on the Thai side of the Mekong, had bombarded areas close to Vientiane.[17]

It may well have been a campaign where the sound effects were greater than the action. But an international echo was already being struck. Broadcasts from Phoumi's headquarters at Savannakhet stressed the aid being given by the Communists to the Pathet Lao. For their part, the Pathet Lao, entrenched in their stronghold close to the border with North Vietnam, asserted that Phoumi was merely an agent of Thailand and of the United States. At the end of November, Prince Souvanna Phouma asked Moscow for assistance. On 4th December, Soviet aircraft commenced to fly in petrol and foodstuffs. On 11th December, it was reported that they had brought in military supplies.[18]

But, by this time, Souvanna Phouma was close to a temporary eclipse and, shortly afterwards, a government of the right, with Phoumi as Defence Minister, was established in Vientiane.

At this stage, the neutralist forces of Captain Kong Lae, made common cause with the Pathet Lao in an area North of Vientiane, and commenced to regain ground. They were helped by a Soviet air lift. In Washington, the level of concern mounted. On 19th February 1961, from Luang Prabang, the Royal Capital, the King of Laos, who was tacitly recognised by all three contenders for power in his kingdom, made an international appeal for the neutralisation of Laos. Prince Sihanouk helped the course of settlement by sponsoring some initial talks in Phnom Penh and, during March, Britain proposed to the Soviet Union that, as co-chairmen of the 1954 Geneva Conference on Indo-China, they might now launch a conference to seek to achieve a settlement on Laos.

These events took place during the very first months of President Kennedy's Presidency, in the immediate aftermath of his famous inauguration speech announcing American readiness to go anywhere to defend the cause of freedom. On 24th March 1961, the President affirmed United States support for the goal of a neutral independent Laos while, in relation to previous American support for Phoumi, he also added that "if in the past there has been any possible ground for misunderstanding of our desire for a truly neutral Laos, there should be none now."[19] Within the official circle, Kennedy expressed the view that "Laos was not a land worthy of attention by the Great Powers," and, that "the effort to transform it into a pro-Western redoubt had been ridiculous, and that neutralisation was the correct policy. But, at the same time, Kennedy realised that the effort he referred to had been made, and that American prestige was now engaged.[20]

In public, Kennedy repeated that "every American will want his country to honour its obligations to the point that freedom and security may be achieved", and this public statement was backed up by precautionary military action to ensure that the seriousness of United States purpose was clearly understood by the Soviet Union. The Seventh Fleet was put on alert, and a battalion of U.S. marines was airlifted into Vientiane from Thailand. There was also action in SEATO. Mr. Dean Rusk, the recently appointed Secretary of State in the Kennedy administration, flew to Bangkok for a meeting of the SEATO Council (the Foreign Ministers of the SEATO powers). On 29th March, the SEATO Council announced that, while approving efforts for peace in Laos, it was to be noted that "if these efforts fail, and there continue to be active military attempts to obtain control of Laos, members of SEATO are prepared, within the terms of the treaty, to take whatever action may be appropriate."[21] At the same time, President Kennedy put his personal backing into a strong diplomatic effort to make sure that the Soviet Union understood that with the new administration there had been a change in United States policy. The previous policy of putting pressure on Souvanna Phouma to forsake neutralism, accept Phoumi Nosavan, and create a right wing government in Laos was not the policy of the Kennedy administration. Now, the American objective was a neutral Laos, and British and Indian diplomatic support was sought to this end.

During April, the Soviet Union replied favourably to the British suggestions on Laos and, on 24th April, joint communications from Britain and the Soviet Union were publicly calling for a cease fire in Laos, and issuing invitations to a 14 power conference in Geneva. Meanwhile, there was direct contact between the United States and the Soviet Union, and the communiqué issued on 4th June 1961, following the meeting at Vienna between President Kennedy and Mr. Kruschev, recorded that "the President and the Chairman reaffirmed their support of a neutral and independent Laos under a government chosen by the Laotians themselves, and of international agreements for ensuring that neutrality and independence ..." Subsequently, in a broadcast to the American people on 6th June, President Kennedy spoke of the discussions on Laos as being the only ones in his encounter with Mr. Kruschev which offered some immediate prospect of accord.

The President's personal and effective drive for a more modest American stance on Laos was carrying the day, despite certain powerful American military pressures for intervention. The President had sensed the importance of easing the direct great power confrontation in an area he did not consider to be vital to the United States. His own words sum up this policy: "After all, India is more directly threatened than we are, and if they are not wildly excited why should we be?"[22]

The auguries were therefore good for the 14 nation conference on Laos, under the co-chairmanship of Britain and the Soviet Union, as it was formally opened by Prince Sihanouk in the middle of 1961. As so often, however, in international discussions concerning Indo-China, an initial log jam developed, with the Communists seeking priority for a general declaration on neutrality, while the Western side pressed for control arrangements. The agreement which was eventually reached represented a considerable diplomatic achievement.

The British and Soviet Foreign Secretaries were the formal Conference co-chairmen. For almost the whole of the Conference, however, the British representative and acting co-chairman was Mr. Malcolm MacDonald who, after ten years of responsibility in South East Asia, had recently served as British High Commissioner in India. Likewise, for the Soviet and American delegations, Mr. Pushkin acted most of the time for Mr. Gromyko, and Mr. Averell Harriman for Mr.

Dean Rusk. However, the Chinese Foreign Minister, Marshal Chen Yi, was personally present for most of the Conference, which took place at a time when the split in the Communist world between Peking and Moscow was becoming increasingly apparent.

Alongside the considerable differences of substance which the Conference had to face, there was also a major procedural problem in relation to the Laotian delegations. The three contending factions, the right led by General Phoumi Nosavan, the neutralists led by Prince Souvanna Phouma, and the left under Prince Souphannouvong each claimed to represent Laos, and refused to sit at the conference table with their rivals. This particular deadlock was broken by an Anglo-Soviet initiative. Mr. MacDonald and Mr. Pushkin invited the three Lao leaders to tea. After some initial courtesies, the two acting Co-Chairmen announced that while they themselves had appointments, they hoped their Laotian friends would finish their tea. Pushkin observed to MacDonald, as they left the room, that it was a pity the doors could not be locked until those inside had reached agreement.[23] In fact, the occasion turned out well, and the contact established over the tea cups was subsequently built on and contributed toward the agreement reached several months later.

Before this agreement was reached, there had, however, been an upsurge in fighting in the North West, close to the Thai border, between Pathet Lao elements and the forces of General Phoumi. This development caused much concern to the Thais and, on 17th May 1962, Thailand appealed to SEATO. On the same day, President Kennedy announced the despatch of some additional forces to Thailand, reaffirming, however, that there was no change in U.S. policy toward Laos. On 24th May, it was announced that some British forces would also be sent to Thailand — in this case a squadron of Hunter jet fighters.

But the flurry quickly subsided. At the beginning of June, direct negotiations between the three Laotian leaders were resumed, and agreement came surprisingly soon. The neutralist, Prince Souvanna Phouma, would be Prime Minister and would also hold the Defence portfolio. The right wing group and the Pathet Lao received four portfolios each, and there was general agreement that the government would seek unanimity as its modus operandi. This happy upshot was quickly blessed by the Geneva Conference as a whole in a 14 Power declaration issued on 23rd July 1962.

Unhappily, the full provisions of the Geneva Agreement on Laos proved short lived within the country itself. But this does not detract from its success. On the South East Asian scene as a whole, its achievement was that it defused a dangerous moment of great power confrontation.

On the wider world stage, there was perhaps an even greater achievement. The problem of Laos had been the principal foreign affairs preoccupation of the first one hundred days of the Kennedy administration, looming even larger than the Bay of Pigs fiasco in Cuba. Kennedy's handling of Laos had been characterised by a blend of realistic military preparation with quiet and effective diplomacy. The Soviet Union had been kept aware of American intentions, and every opportunity had been offered for an honourable settlement. There had been none of the menacing talk from official elements in Washington, which had characterised the 1954 Dien Bien Phu crisis. Within weeks of his own famous inaugural speech, Kennedy was keeping a firm grip on official words as well as deeds. With power there was great responsibility and, in October 1962, the lessons learnt in the handling of the Laos episode were applied to the altogether graver Cuban missile crisis. Once again, Kennedy acted with quiet firmness while seeking a settlement and leaving a way out for his opponent. It has more than once been suggested that Laos in 1961 was a dress rehearsal for Cuba in 1962.

Meanwhile, in Vietnam in 1962, General Harkins, one of the most senior officers of the U.S. army, had arrived in Saigon to set up the Military Advisory Command Vietnam, (MACV), a title which survived to the end ten years later. The American presence expanded, and with it the problem of establishing satisfactory operational relationships with the South Vietnamese. Diem frowned on those of his officials in the countryside who "got on too well with their American advisers."[24] In turn, many Americans grew exasperated with Diem, doubting his belief that the tide was now turning against the Viet Cong.[25] Even so, for official America, the months at the turn of the year were a season of bullish public pronouncements about the war.[26] Admiral Felt, the U.S. Commander-in-Chief in the Pacific, predicted victory within three years, and President Kennedy, during the course of his State of the Union address on 14th January 1963, asserted that "the spearpoint of aggression has been blunted in Vietnam."

[1] Duncanson, pp. 225.

[2] *Ibid.* p. 216, quoting from Grevillot's *Les grands courants de la pensée contemporaine: Existensialisme, Marxisme, Personalisme Chrètien.*

[3] *C.O.I. Vietnam*, p. 20.

[4] *Pentagon Papers* (N.Y.T.), p. 119.

[5] *Ibid.* p. 118.

[6] *Ibid.* p. 91.

[7] *Ibid.* pp. 127–131.

[8] *Pentagon Papers*, p. 129.

[9] *Ibid.* p. 140.

[10] *Ibid.*, p. 102.

[11] *Ibid.*, p. 102.

[12] *Ibid.* p. 106.

[13] *Ibid.* p. 108.

[14] *Pentagon Papers*, p. 109, and Department of State Bulletin XXXVII (January 1962) pp. 13–14.

[15] *Pentagon Papers*, p. 110.

[16] *Ibid.* p. 153, 1962 memorandum from Joint Chiefs-of-Staff to Mr. McNamara.

[17] *Central Office of Information: Laos*, p. 22.

[18] *Ibid.* p. 23.

[19] *Central Office of Information: Laos*, p. 25.

[20] Schlesinger: *One Thousand Days: Kennedy*, p. 299.

[21] *C.O.I.*, p. 26.

[22] Schlesinger, p. 301.

[23] Recounted by Mr. MacDonald.

[24] Duncanson, p. 325.

[25] *Pentagon Papers*, p. 155 (State Department Memorandum to Mr. Rusk).

[26] *Ibid.* p. 164.

13 *The Downfall of Ngo Dinh Diem*

A T this stage, the Americans estimated that against ARVN numbers of about 250,000, the Viet Cong had a main force strength of about 23,000, plus 100,000 irregulars, and an unknown number of sympathisers.[1] The Viet Cong power, then as later, was in the countryside, above all when darkness fell. They were not, however, the only element in the country hostile to the Diem administration, and, in the end, the fuse which blew was that of the Buddhist opposition. The event which set the fuse, was Buddhist reaction to the considerable jubilee celebration in Hué during April 1963 of Diem's brother, Ngo Dinh Thuc, the Catholic Archbishop.

Opinions differ on the nature of the Buddhist unrest, led by a politically minded monk called Thich Tri Quang, and the extent to which it was "neutralist". On one view, it may be represented as an orchestrated minority movement serving the Communist cause.[2] On another, it was an explosion of popular feeling with a wider base than that of the Buddhist community.[3] Whatever the truth, Diem was ill served by his family circle. On 8th May, the anniversary of Buddha's birthday, police opened fire during the course of a Buddhist demonstration in which, contrary to regulations, the Buddhist flag flew alone without the National flag (as the Vatican flag had done a month before during the Archbishop's jubilee celebrations). Nine people were killed. Thereafter, came the public suicide by fire on 11th June of an elderly Buddhist monk, Thich Quang Duc.

The photographs of this suicide, in protest against the Diem régime, reached all over the world. Now, if ever, the situation needed cool handling. Instead, Madame Nhu foolishly ridiculed the "barbecued monks", and Nhu himself sent troops to storm certain Buddhist pagodas. Thich Tri Quang went into hiding and, at one stage, was accorded sanctuary in the American Embassy. For Ngo Dinh Diem, time was running out. On 24th August, Henry Cabot Lodge, the new U.S. Ambassador in Saigon and a very special appointee of President Kennedy, received a State Department cable with the ominous message:[4] "Diem must be given chance to rid himself of Nhu and his coterie, and replace them with best political and military personalities available. If, in spite of your efforts, Diem remains obdurate and

114

refuses, then we must face the possibility that Diem himself cannot be preserved."

The reply sent by Lodge next day, on the eve of presenting his credentials to Diem, was shiveringly blunt.[5] "Believe chances of Diem meeting our demands are virtually nil. And, by making them, we give Nhu a chance to forestall or block action by military. Propose therefore we go straight to Generals with our demands without informing Diem. Would tell them we prepared to have Diem without Nhus, but it is up to them whether to keep him. Would also insist Generals take steps to release Buddhist leaders and carry out June 16th agreement. Request immediate modification instructions. However, do not propose move until satisfied E and E plans. Harkins concurs. I present credentials President Diem tomorrow."

These telegrams pointed very directly at the Nhus. As always, more than one view is possible but, to a large number of observers, Ngo Dinh Nhu and his wife were the focal cause of disaffection against Diem's Administration in South Vietnam.[6] In their view, Nhu's general conduct of affairs in order to secure obedience was barely distinguishable from that of the Communists. His strong arm element, the so called 'Special Forces', aroused resentment, not least in the armed forces themselves. Yet, while Nhu himself may have been ill-regarded, his wife, who earned the sobriquet 'Dragon Lady', was even more widely detested.

In the name of a Women's Solidarity Movement, she sought to control public and private morality and, along with much else, dancing was forbidden.[7] At the same time, her personal take from the system was widely regarded as excessive. Within Vietnam, she made enemies for Diem's Government, and her remarks on the immolation of the Buddhist monks aroused strong feeling against her abroad. Not the least of her faults as a political person was that she had no touch with the press. Perhaps, more than any one individual, she bore responsibility for the storm clouds gathering against Diem.

However, at the end of August, the South Vietnamese Army conspiracy against Diem temporarily dissolved from within, apparently because of some doubt among the generals who were involved as to the extent of their U.S. backing. In particular, the generals feared that Mr. Richardson, the local CIA chief, might be undercutting them with the Diem administration. The U.S. impulse for a change of régime did not lapse. During the course of a television interview on 2nd September, President Kennedy applied some personal pressure. He said, "The South Vietnam government would have to take steps to bring back popular support: otherwise the war could not be won: but success was possible with changes in policy and perhaps with personnel."[8]

At the end of September, Mr. McNamara and General Taylor visited Saigon to assess the position and to seek to bridge the gap between Ambassador Lodge and General Harkins, who was less certain of the merit of moving against Diem. The final words of a telegram from Harkins to Taylor summed up Harkins's views, as the coup against Diem was being remounted. "After all, rightly or wrongly, we have backed Diem for eight long hard years. To me, it seems incongruous now to get him down, kick him around and get rid of him. The United States has been his mother superior and father confessor since he took office, and he has leaned heavily on us. Leaders of other undeveloped countries will take a dim view of us if they too were led to believe the same fate lies in store for them".[9]

By this time, the operation against Diem was however well in train. Basic judgments had been formed during the McNamara/Taylor visit to Saigon at the end of September. On 5th October, Richardson of the CIA was reassigned from Saigon, after what are described as behind the scenes efforts by Ambassador Lodge to obtain his transfer. Also on 5th October, Colonel Conein, the CIA contact man with the Vietnamese generals, held a key meeting with General Duong Van Minh (Big Minh) one of the most senior ARVN officers, and an old tennis playing acquaintance of General Taylor.

At this time, Minh was, however, in a staff appointment because Diem was not sure of him. Minh was able though to give the names of other generals who at that stage were associated with him: these names included Tran Van Don, Tran Thien Khiem and Tran Van Kim. Minh stressed the importance of knowing the U.S. position.[10]

The White House reply to Lodge's report of this meeting gave some guidance.[11] "While we would not wish to stimulate coup, we also do not want to leave the impression that U.S. would thwart a change of government or deny economic or military assistance to a new régime if it appeared capable of increasing effectiveness of military effort, ensuring popular support to win war, and improving relations with the United States".

The White House message also directed the CIA contact to obtain detailed information, so that Washington might be better able to assess Minh's prospects of success. Yet, at the same time, the message cautioned against "being drawn into reviewing or advising on operational plans or other actions which might tend to identify the United States too closely with a change of government."

For Diem the writing was now on the wall. During October, the Generals' coup was remounted and, despite Harkins' reservations, Ambassador Lodge counselled in the strongest terms against action to thwart it. The Washington reply from McGeorge Bundy, the

President's Special Assistant for National Security, merits quotation in full.[12]

"Your 1964 most helpful. We will continue to be grateful for all additional information giving increased clarity to prospects of action by Don or others, and look forward to discussing with you whole question of control and cut out on your return, always assuming one of the D Days does not turn out real. We are particularly concerned about hazard that unsuccessful coup, however carefully we avoid direct engagement, will be laid at our door by public opinion almost everywhere. Therefore, while sharing your view that we should not be in a position of thwarting coup, we should like to have option on judging and warning on any plan with poor prospects of success. We recognise that this is a large order; but the President wants you to know of our concern."

In Saigon, events moved toward their climax. Rumour of coup abounded. On 27th October, Lodge saw Diem: "a fruitless frustrating exchange".[13] On 28th October, Nhu is reported to have told foreign correspondents: "What about the coup: the generals haven't got a chance."[14] The Pentagon Papers suggest that Nhu was laying a trap, manoeuvering for a false coup, to lure the anti-Diem group into the open, when they could be crushed by the troops of the Saigon military commander, General Ton That Dinh, an officer on whom Nhu was sure he could count. But Dinh himself had now joined the conspiracy. By 29th October, Lodge clearly felt that the United States was committed to the coup, and that it was too late for second thoughts, and he communicated this view forcefully to Washington.[15]

The final message which issued from the White House to the Ambassador was stern; "Your thoughtful message leads us to believe that a significant area of shading exists on a crucial point ... we do not accept as a basis for U.S. policy that we have no power to delay or discourage a coup ... if you should conclude there is not clearly a high prospect of success you should communicate this doubt to generals in a way calculated to persuade them to desist at least until chances are better."[16]

On 30th October, Admiral Felt, the U.S. Commander-in-Chief, Pacific, was due to call on Diem. The call took place as planned, and Lodge and Felt presented themselves at the President's palace midway through the morning.[17] By this time, Lodge knew of the imminence of the coup against Diem. For his part, Diem was aware of the family plan to draw the generals into a trap. At noon, just before his departure from Saigon, Felt held a press conference. He praised the nation's leadership and said the war was going well.[18]

By this time, the troop movements for the coup were in train, and some journalists at the press conference, aware of the way the wind was blowing, observed that General Tran Van Don, who was with Felt, appeared impatient.[19]

But the coup ran like clockwork. At 1.30 p.m., coup forces seized the police headquarters, Saigon radio and airport, and other key points, and surrounded the President's palace.[20] The 'Special Forces' of Colonel Le Van Tung, on which Diem had counted, had already been partially neutralised by American insistence that they should not permanently be held in Saigon.[21] Their final emasculation was also timed for 1.30. Every Friday, the General Staff held a lunch, over which military problems were discussed. Tung, regarded by Colonel Conein, the CIA contact with the generals, as one of the most dangerous men on the board, was also invited to this luncheon on 30th October. At 1.30, General Don announced the coup and invited participation. All accepted willingly, except Tung, who was then shot.[22]

During the afternoon, the generals called on Diem and Nhu to surrender. The brothers replied by asking the generals to come to the palace for consultation, a tactic used in a previous coup attempt in 1960 to delay the coup long enough for loyal forces to take counter action. The generals refused.[23] Diem then called Lodge on the telephone. The following conversation ensued:[24]

Diem   Some units have made a rebellion and I want to know the attitude of the U.S.

Lodge   I do not feel well informed enough to tell you. I have heard the shooting but do not know all the facts. Also it is 4.30 a.m. in Washington, and the U.S. Government cannot possibly have a view.

Diem   But you must have some general ideas. After all I am a Chief of State. I have tried to do my duty. I want to know what duty and good sense require. I believe in duty above all.

Lodge   You have certainly done your duty. As I told you only this morning, I admire your courage and your great contributions to the country. No one can take away the credit for all you have done. Now I am worried about your physical safety. I have a report that those in charge of the current activity offer you and your brother safe conduct out of the country if you resign. Had you heard this?

Diem   No. (*Then pause*) You have my telephone number?

Lodge   Yes. If I can do anything for your physical safety, please call me.

Diem   I am trying to establish order.

The final act remained to be played out. While fighting continued around the palace, Diem and his brother escaped by a secret tunnel into Cholon, the Chinese quarter of Saigon. When the palace fell at dawn on 1st November, they were in the small Catholic Church of St. Francis Xavier in Cholon. At about 9 a.m., an army detachment took them into custody, and later the same day both men were reported dead. Two days later, their brother Ngo Dinh Canh, who had sought refuge in the U.S. consulate in Hué, passed into the custody of the generals, and he was later executed. Madam Nhu was in the United States. Monsignor Ngo Dinh Thuc was in Rome. After nine and a half years, the Ngo family rule of South Vietnam had come to an end.

History has yet to assess Ngo Dinh Diem. A wide range of observers credit him with qualities of honesty, courage and patriotism, alongside excessive reliance on a family circle of lesser quality. In a contribution to *The New Republic,* Graham Greene has written of Diem: "One pictured him sitting there in the Norodom Palace, sitting with his blank brown gaze, incorruptible, ill-advised, going to his weekly confession, bolstered up by his belief that God is always on the Catholic side, waiting for a miracle. The name I would put under his portrait is The Patriot ruined by the West."

As Diem's Administration was analysed, both at the time and later, it was common for observers to ask why Diem tolerated abuses which lay so clearly at the door of the Nhus. This was also a question asked by those politically hostile to Diem, since his personal honesty and good intentions were widely accepted, even by his enemies. On one view, the governing factor was family loyalty: that and nothing else. And it was a loyalty which held, even after it became clear to Diem that Washington sought a break with the Nhus. On another view, however, this loyalty was political: in essence, a realisation that the system depended on Nhus party organisation and his network of informers. As so often, the truth may lie somewhere between, with perhaps some nationalist credit due to Diem for not wishing to be too completely a creature of his U.S. allies.

Interesting American comment on the coup is contained in Arthur Schlesinger's memoir of the Kennedy Administration: *A Thousand Days: John F. Kennedy in the White House.* This memoir, published in 1965, is, however, somewhat at variance with the documentary evidence revealed in the Pentagon Papers some years later. Schlesinger, a very distinguished historian and a former Professor of History at Harvard, served as a Special Assistant to the President during the Kennedy administration and portrays the coup situation in the following terms: "It is important to state clearly that the coup of 1st November 1963 was entirely planned and carried out by the Vietnamese. Neither the American Embassy nor the CIA were involved in instigation or execution"[25] ... "what lay behind the coup was

not the meddling of Americans, quiet or ugly."[26] Clearly a great deal
hangs on the meaning ascribed to the word "involved".

Schlesinger adds that he saw the President soon after the latter
heard that Diem and Nhu were dead. He says he found President
Kennedy sombre and shaken. The President had clearly had his own
reservations, and it would be surprising if the final upshot had not been
upsetting for him. Although the Generals in Saigon were claiming that
the two Vietnamese leaders had committed suicide, Kennedy was
doubtful. Diem was too good a Catholic to have taken this way out.
Kennedy's insight and anxieties are further revealed by Schlesinger.
"With his (Kennedy's) memory of the French in Indo-China in 1951, he
had always believed there was a point at which our (American) intervention might turn Vietnamese nationalism against us."[27]

Perhaps it may turn out that American involvement in the
downfall of Diem will favour his reputation in Vietnam in years to come
and assure him a place among the well-remembered heroes of the
Vietnamese people. Already there are some signs of this. For the United
States, the death of President Diem would lead to large scale involvement and the longest war in American history. American dead in this
war would exceed 50,000, a figure to be measured against the 489
Americans killed and wounded in Vietnam in the year of Diem's
downfall.[28]

[1] *Pentagon Papers*, p. 155.

[2] Duncanson, p. 335.

[3] Halberstam: *Making of a Quagmire*, p. 207.

[4] *Pentagon Papers*, p. 194.

[5] *Ibid.* p. 195.

[6] Buttinger, p. 446.

[7] Malcolm Browne: *The New Faces of War*, p. 170.

[8] *Pentagon Papers*, p. 175.

[9] *Pentagon Papers*, p. 221.

[10] *Ibid.* p. 213; Telegram Ambassador Lodge to State Department of 5 October.

[11] *Ibid.* p. 216; Telegram White House to Ambassador Lodge of 6 October.

[12] *Ibid.* Telegram McGeorge Bundy to Ambassador Lodge of 25 Oct. 63.

[13] *Ibid.* p. 182.

[14] Lacouture: *Vietnam between Truces*, p. 84.

[15] *Pentagon Papers*, p. 182.

[16] *Ibid.* p. 230; Telegram McGeorge Bundy to Ambassador Lodge of 30 October 1963.

[17] *Ibid.* p. 187.

[18] Halberstam, pp. 288–289.

[19] *Ibid.* p. 289.

[20] *Pentagon Papers:* p. 187.

[21] *Ibid.* p. 212. (Paragraph 4c of McNamera/Taylor memorandum of 20 October for President Kennedy.)

[22] Halberstam, p. 290.

[23] *Pentagon Papers*, p. 187.

[24] *Ibid.* p. 212; Excerpt from telegram Ambassador Lodge to State Department 1 November 1963.

[25] Schlesinger: *One Thousand Days*, p. 847.

[26] *Ibid.* p. 848.

[27] *Ibid.* p. 848.

[28] *Pentagon Papers*, p. 110.

14   The Other Side

IT would be an unusual conflict where the good was all on one side, and the bad on the other. Few situations can possibly be so tidy. In any case, this begs the meaning of the words good and bad. But it does perhaps need to be borne in mind that the war in Indo-China was generally open and accessible to the press from only one side — and this was not the Communist Vietnamese side. In succession, the French and the Americans and the South Vietnamese opened the door to correspondents, and frequently had to suffer reporting disagreeable to their cause. Whatever the merits, this was not the case for the other side. During the twenty years from 1954 to 1974, relatively few journalists believed to be hostile were granted permission to visit North Vietnam.

Because of this, there was in the West some element of lacuna about what was happening "on the other side". What now follows is a somewhat sketchy outline to provide background to the developing pattern of events. It is true that certain non-Communist writers such as James Cameron, Bernard Fall, Jean Lacouture and others, were able to report briefly on North Vietnam on the basis of their own direct observation. But their reports often emphasised their difficulty in getting in and out with their material. And inevitably, it was the publicised views of Ho Chi Minh and his colleagues and successors and their international supporters, which governed the news out of Communist Vietnam.

Between 1954 and 1963, these views concentrated on attacking the government of Ngo Dinh Diem, "for contravening the Geneva Agreement". The Communist Vietnamese focussed, in particular, on the decision of the South against elections in the whole of Vietnam, and on the military association of the South with the United States. A talk which Bernard Fall had in Hanoi in 1962 with Ho Chi Minh and Pham Van Dong, the Prime Minister, showed the way the situation was seen in the North. Fall asked the North Vietnamese leaders for their current assessment of Ngo Dinh Diem's position.[1] Pham Van Dong's reply was as follows: "it is difficult. He (Diem) is unpopular, and the more unpopular he is, the more American aid he will need to have to remain in power. And the more American aid he receives, the more he will be seen as an American puppet and his popularity will decline further".

The North Vietnamese leaders clearly perceived that American "over weight" in the South would work to their (Hanoi's) benefit.

Again, during an interview at about this time with Lacouture, Pham Van Dong had this to say:[2] "There are after all three kinds of people in the South. The friends of the Americans such as Diem and others; they have already lost their game. The people; they are with us. The intellectuals and the bourgeoisie; they remain very attached to France. Thus the solution depends on an understanding that would permit joining the masses to the intelligentsia and middle class in order to establish democratic rule. If only France would play its rôle and contribute to peace." Subsequently, Ho Chi Minh spoke to Lacouture on his memories of France; of General Leclerc, to whom he seemed genuinely attached, and of General Salan, by this time in disgrace because of his action in Algeria: "he was so careful, and now!"

A feature of the interviews with Fall and Lacouture, as with a later visit by James Cameron, was the fashion in which Ho Chi Minh apparently dropped in on journalists' calls on Pham Van Dong. When Cameron called on Pham Van Dong in 1964 Ho Chi Minh "padded in" half way through.[3] Cameron had been hearing the Communist exposition from Pham Van Dong — insistence on the implementation of the 1954 Geneva Conference Agreement and so on. Ho Chi Minh, who spoke in rusty English, and poured out a beer, and lit one cigarette from the stub of another, said he preferred to chat rather than talk of serious things. To Cameron, he gave the genuine image of being "Uncle Ho".

Cameron observed; "the effect of this (Ho Chi Minh's personal presentation) is more important than his enemies understand. American politicians, who believe they are fighting any army of card-bearing Communists are continually baffled to find that at least half their foes are confused and exasperated peasants, who merely want to get back to their farms, who have never heard of Karl Marx, but are inclined to believe well of Communism just because Uncle Ho says so." For what it is worth, the creed of Communist Vietnamese prisoners taken in Cambodia, during the war there in the early seventies, appeared to have little to do with Communism. Their mission, so they said, was to free Indo-China from the Americans. Just as the attackers at Dien Bien Phu said their task was to liberate Vietnam from the French. The Communist mainspring clearly operated at the top. Lower down, however, nationalism and simply esprit de corps may have had greater weight.

There is one aspect, though, on which both the critics and the supporters of the Communist Vietnamese are agreed, and that is the extent of the mobilisation of the people under Communist rule. On the

Communist side this is recognised as the will of the people. By their critics, as something very different. To some, it is indistinguishable from slavery.

Even before the Communist success in the North, many of the peasants owned the land they worked. But Communist doctrine called for re-arrangement of land ownership and, in the early days of the new State, a very fierce policy of land reform was established. This policy was closely associated with Truong Chinh, the theoretician who at that time was the Secretary General of the Lao Dong, the Communist workers party of Vietnam.

Peasant resistance developed. Food production went down. General Giap's soldiers, the Vietnamese Peoples' Army, now found themselves engaged against peasant dissidents. Ho Chi Minh sensed that theory had gone too far, and intervened personally. In November 1956, Truong Chinh was dismissed from his key post, even though retaining status as a Politburo member. A new appointment was now made, which would also relate to the years of conflict soon to follow against the South. Le Duan, who had been a senior Communist Commander in the South during the years of conflict against the French, now took over as Secretary General (later to be retitled First Secretary) of the Lao Dong. This sharpened the Communist sword against the South, and led increasingly into the acts of terror referred to in the account of events in the South. The Communist leadership proclaimed this as liberation.

Without the proof of the secret ballot, and a real choice of alternative candidates to vote for, the truth is difficult to assess. The true patriotism has been questioned of a cause which condemned so many fellow countrymen to decades of war. A number of observers hostile to Hanoi have indeed drawn the parallel of the years of Nazi supremacy harnessed to German nationalism. The view persists that deep down there may be a powerful nationalist impulse for fulfilment, which is seeking expression. Plus other ingredients. Perhaps in its time scale also, the German comparison may not be wholly without relevance. It was some years before Nazi expansion, which may have commenced as redress against believed injustice, over reached itself. Certainly, Hanoi achieved victory in Vietnam in 1975, in spite of United States military effort and the bombing. But a great deal of this bombing took place in the countryside of South Vietnam, Cambodia and Laos. It is questionable, even taking account of the sharp American attacks immediately prior to the Paris Agreement and the cease fire of January 1973, if the weight of the war was felt as heavily in the North as in the South. A partial reason for this was the Hanoi campaign, which began in 1962, to promote migration from the towns. But the major reason was prolonged

U.S. hesitation, based in large measure on ethical and domestic considerations, against using its power to its full limits. Would another great power necessarily show this restraint?

Throughout the second Vietnam war, which commenced in 1956 and reached its crescendo in the period after the death of Ngo Dinh Diem, the North Vietnamese consistently denied the presence of their forces in the South, even when more than 100,000 of their army were generally regarded as engaged. For many years, the North Vietnamese negotiating positions stood on the following:

(a) The affairs of South Vietnam were for settlement by South Vietnamese.
(b) The peaceful reunification of Vietnam was for settlement by the people 'in both zones'.
(c) Pending reunification, the military provisions of the Geneva Agreement should be accepted.
(d) United States intervention must cease.

The North Vietnamese were also insistent that the political arm of the Viet Cong, first the National Liberation Front, later the Provisional Revolutionary Government, should be associated in any peace talks, and various peace programmes were published by these bodies. For a considerable time, this insistence on the political rôle of the Viet Cong proved a stumbling block. The Government in Saigon naturally had no wish to acquiesce in power-sharing in the South, and in what they regarded as a charade to benefit Hanoi. In due course, however, and after some light-hearted international press attention to the special shape of a conference table to suggest to those who sought it, but not to others, the four sided nature of talks, this difficult point was turned. Given the political direction from Hanoi, and their powerful military involvement, it would be surprising if the two Communist Vietnamese governments were not very close. Indeed, a number of observers saw the Communist Provisional Revolutionary Government in the South as a mere phantom serving the propaganda interest of the North: in effect a weapon in the armoury of the leadership in Hanoi.

Certainly, if there really were two genuinely independent governments, albeit allied, it would be surprising, given the traditional North/South divisions of Vietnam, if their interests were always completely identical. And, when the unification of Vietnam was proclaimed in Hanoi on 24th June 1976 (ratification took place on 2nd July), it was on the basis that the flag, the capital, the insignia and the national anthem be those of the North. The reward for the South was that Saigon would in the future be known as Ho Chi Minh City. Only the years to come will show how the new unity will develop.

During the conflict, the North Vietnamese leadership was much of an age and closely knit. When Ho Chi Minh died in 1969, he was nearly eighty years old. His successor as President, Ton Duc Thang, was even older. The Praesidium elected after Ho Chi Minh's death was far from young, the six leading members being Pham Van Dong, Vo Nguyen Giap, Le Duan, Ton Duc Thang, Truong Chinh and Hoang Van Hoong. It is usually a fact of life that changes in faces mean changes in policy. Almost ten years after the death of Ho Chi Minh, the Hanoi leadership is no younger. Before long, the new State is bound to have new men at the top. There can only be speculation about the effect this will have.

In the same way that Saigon depended upon American aid, the Viet Cong depended upon Hanoi. But much more so. The difference between the Viet Cong and Hanoi blurred. In any case, the unification of Vietnam was the announced aim of the government in Hanoi. The motive power was that of Hanoi. As for Hanoi, itself, its operations in the South and its "sinews of war", depended on help from the Communist countries. "South Vietnam's resources in manpower and material lie in the North", wrote Party Secretary, Le Duan, to General Thanh, the Communist commander in the South, "and can never be exhausted because we have on our side the Socialist bloc, and the full potential of the Chinese people". The Soviet Union provided North Vietnam with loans and grants for economic purposes, as well as considerable quantities of military equipment, notably for air defence. China also gave much aid, including military aid and, in the quarrel between China and the Soviet Union, Hanoi mostly appeared to seek the middle course. In the mid 1960s, journalists attempting to pin down the North Vietnamese position on this issue, received short shrift.[4] Ho Chi Minh's will, published shortly after his death in 1969, called for unity in the world Communist movement, and enjoined the party in North Vietnam to work to restore this unity; this was generally taken, however, as a vote for the Soviet view. Seven years later, on 2nd July 1976, the National Assembly of the New Socialist Republic of Vietnam endorsed the unification of the Nation proclaimed the week before. The policy enunciated on this occasion by Le Duan, also leaned more to the Soviet than the Chinese view of the international scene.

Sainteny, who attended the funeral of Ho Chi Minh as the representative of the French Government, had met the North Vietnamese leader three years previously. At that time, Sainteny was in South East Asia preparing the ground for de Gaulle's famous visit to Phnom Penh. Once again (as in his will) Ho Chi Minh stressed the imperative of the unification of Vietnam, and the capability of the Vietnamese people to resist foreign invasion: "invaders may destroy our towns but in the end we will wear them out". Sainteny observes: "for him (Ho Chi Minh), Vietnamese nationalism and communism were, respectively, goal and means to attain that goal: the two complemented each other, merged". At the same time, Ho Chi Minh never completely lost his interest in French affairs. Late in life, for an example, he asked Sainteny for an album of Maurice Chevalier records! China might be the powerful neighbour, but the Chinese was not the only external culture.[5] Vietnamese reserve toward the Chinese brand of Communism is clearly weighted by nationalist as well as by ideological factors.

It would have been very surprising indeed if Ho Chi Minh had not felt deeply satisfied by de Gaulle's speech in Phnom Penh in September 1966. In his biography of President de Gaulle, Lacouture describes the event in these words:[6] "The challenge he (de Gaulle) issues, a proud solitary old man against the greatest world power, right on the very fringe of the battle zone, from the soil of a weak country continually under the threat of war remains one of the great moments ... it was the nationalist who spoke, expressing himself in Gaullist fashion, teaching America a lesson ... it was the strategist, pointing out the advantages of a skilled retreat ... it was the intellectual asserting himself with well timed reference to American philosophy and history". Clearly de Gaulle had moved on from 1946. Yet, as Lacouture shrewdly observes, de Gaulle was only a decoloniser insofar as decolonisation, having become inevitable, could be harnessed to serve the interests and independence of France.

A number of other French observers stressed the strong nationalistic motivation of Ho Chi Minh. Some of them also saw similarities between Ho Chi Minh and Gandhi: what Bernard Fall described in his profile of Ho Chi Minh as "a certain deceptive simplicity, not often found in Communist leaders". Other observers would argue that Ho Chi Minh's Gandhi-like deportment was merely an act. There may not be so many Communist leaders, though, who have frankly and publicly admitted the shortcomings of their administration as Ho Chi Minh did in 1956 when the country's land reform programme had run into difficulty: "the leadership of the Party Central Committee and of the Government is sometimes lacking in correctness, and control and encouragement are disregarded: all this has caused us to commit errors".[7]

In the same way that Gandhi identified himself with traditional Indian values, so Ho Chi Minh appears to have avoided personal excess, and to have identified himself to the end of his days with the traditional values of Vietnam.

During the war years, economic information like other information out of the North, was sparse. Much effort was made to increase agricultural production, and harvests of four to five million tons were reported. There was also industrialisation, but after the mid-1960s this development was limited. This was a result of the threat and indeed the fact of United States bombing. The Thai Nguyen iron and steel complex was a frequent target for United States bombing. Such new industrial plants as were constructed were on the whole small and dispersed.

However, after the 1973 Paris Agreement, the North Vietnamese leadership began to make some forward looking economic statements. During March, Le Duan, the Party First Secretary argued in the Party magazine Hoc Tap that the country needed to take advantage of world technology to assist the building of the Socialist revolution. A little later, Truong Chinh, still a leading party ideologist, who usually stressed the predominance of the ideological revolution, said that the technical revolution would soon be the main one. In April, Pham Van Dong spoke in Sweden of his country's reconstruction needs.

Soon after the war ended, the economic guidelines for the new Vietnam were published. This came in advance of the formal unification of North and South. Although there were, in theory, two governments, there was only one party, the Lao Dong (Vietnam Workers Party), and the leadership of the party was in Hanoi. On 2nd September 1975, at the celebration of the thirtieth anniversary of Ho Chi Minh's Declaration of Independence in Hanoi's Ba Dinh Square, Pham Van Dong spoke on these terms. North Vietnam should display its courage and intelligence in rapidly expanding its heavy industry. The message to the South was to become a prosperous region for agricultural production, to meet the needs of the people and to provide export earnings.[8] The future will show how these and other directives will work out. The future will also clarify whatever the aims of Hanoi may be in relation to the whole of Indo-China. The party established under Ho Chi Minh's auspices in 1930 was a unified Communist Party of Indo-China and its objectives related to Indo-China as a whole.

At this point, the "view from the other side" suggests possible contradictions. The conjunction of Vietnamese nationalism and Communism is one thing: that of Cambodian nationalism and an acceptance of external Communist leadership would be another. The common factor of all the Cambodians engaged in their Civil War was reserve toward Vietnam. A later chapter touches on the tragic five years of Civil War in Cambodia, which culminated in the capitulation of Phnom Penh on 17th April 1975, and the events of human misery which followed. The point for emphasis at this stage is the antipathy which exists between the Khmer and Vietnamese peoples.

In the case of Cambodia, information "from the other side" was sparse, as far as the country itself was concerned, both during the war years and since. Across a river, or across a mile of paddy, there could be another world. But there was no lack of comment from Prince Sihanouk during his years in Peking: and, in his case, the view from the other side was very directly orientated toward China. It was with good reason that Sihanouk established his headquarters in Peking after his deposition. It was also significant that Khieu Samphan, a senior Red Khmer leader, visited Peking as the Cambodian war came to an end. Whatever the government of Cambodia, China would always seem a protection against further Thai or Vietnamese expansionism into Cambodia. The basic facts of geography would always impose a Chinese interest in South East Asia, and this would always help Cambodia. The same could not be said with certainty of the United States: nor of the Soviet Union.

Likewise, the geographical facts of life relate to Laos. In that country, the final days of 1975 were marked by the end of the Monarchy and the establishment of a Peoples Democratic Republic. But there was little bloodshed; and, recalling the past when Ho Chi Minh had appointed the former Emperor, Bao Dai, to be a Counsellor of Government, the former King of Laos was appointed a Counsellor to the new President.[9] Prince Souvanna Phouma was also appointed to a post of apparent honour as Counsellor to the Government. Only the future will show if these are merely gilded shackles. For a country like Laos, so close alongside Vietnam, the view toward Hanoi must loom large, especially in the North Eastern part of the country. Yet there must also be a Chinese dimension; and the considerable Chinese road building effort in North West Laos could also be a pointer toward the future. It would be very surprising indeed if China were not carefully observing developments in the areas bordering the new unified Socialist Republic of Vietnam.

[1] Fall: *Ho Chi Minh*, p. 321.

[2] Lacouture: *Vietnam between Truces*, p. 40.

[3] Cameron: *Here is your enemy*, p. 116.

[4] Lacouture, p. 41.

[5] Sainteny: *Ho Chi Minh*, p. 167.

[6] Lacouture: *de Gaulle*, p. 180.

[7] Fall: *Ho Chi Minh*, p. 275 (Ho Chi Minh's statement of 18 August 1956 on peasant resistance to certain land reform procedures).

[8] *Far Eastern Economic Review*, 12 September 1975 and *Asia '76 Yearbook*.

[9] *Far Eastern Economic Review*, 19 December 1975.

15 1964 – 1968: Crescendo

THE assassination of President Kennedy in Dallas came three weeks after the death of Diem. An early problem facing the new President of the United States was that of determining the nature of the involvement in Indo-China, into which the United States was increasingly being drawn. On the day of Kennedy's funeral, President Johnson issued the following memorandum to his senior advisers:[1] "it remains the central objective of the United States in South Vietnam to assist the Government and people of that country to win their contest against the externally directed Communist Conspiracy".

In January 1964, the U.S. Chiefs-of-Staff recommended bluntly: "The United States must be prepared to put aside many of the self imposed restrictions which now limit our efforts, and to undertake bolder action which may embody greater risks ... the failure of our program in South Vietnam would have a heavy influence on the judgments of Burma, India, Indonesia, Malaysia, Japan and the Philippines as to U.S. resolution. Finally, this being the first real test of our determination to defeat the Communist 'wars of national liberation' formula, it is not unreasonable to conclude there would be a corresponding unfavourable effect on our image in Africa and Latin America."[2] This was the domino theory in full flood.

The Central Intelligence Agency, so often cast as the villain by those hostile to the U.S. involvement in South Vietnam took a more measured view and questioned this assessment.[3] "With the possible exception of Cambodia, it is likely that no nation would quickly succumb to Communism as a result of the fall of Laos and South Vietnam. Furthermore, a continuation of the spread of Communism in the area would not be inexorable, and any spread which did occur would take time, time in which the total situation might change in any number of ways unfavourable to the Communist cause".

The C.I.A. analysis quoted in the Pentagon Papers does not enlarge on this factor of imponderability. But it is not too fanciful to conceive that their experts may have seen the development of tension and contradictions on the Communist side if and when the dominoes started to fall their way. Which Communists would take over? Would they all be in agreement — Moscow, Peking, Hanoi and the local leaders? Few projections stand up if taken too far and, looking back ten years, to the time when it was made, the C.I.A. reserve on the domino theory comes out well. However, the very considerable pressure on the President from his closest advisers tended to weigh toward increased U.S. involvement. One can only speculate on the advice the President might have received, had he accepted Robert Kennedy's June 1964 offer to serve as Ambassador in Saigon.[4]

Within the Defence Department in Washington, a view of U.S. aims was encapsulated in a memorandum to Mr. McNamara from Mr. John McNaughton, the Assistant Secretary for Defence, who headed the Pentagon foreign affairs planning staff. The memorandum read as follows:

"American Aims:
70% to avoid a humiliating U.S. defeat (to our reputation as guarantor).
20% to keep South Vietnam and adjoining territory from Chinese hands.
10% to permit the people of South Vietnam to enjoy a better, freer way of life.
Also, to emerge from the crisis without unacceptable taint from the methods used.
NOT 'to help a friend', although it would be hard to stay in if asked out."

Increased Viet Cong activity led to pressure for stronger U.S. reaction, notably, for the bombing of the North "to strike the serpent's head". Although the contingency planning for this was in train, President Johnson still held back however from ordering such major escalation. In June, Mr. Blair Seaborn, the new Canadian representative on the International Control Commission, was asked to apprise Hanoi of the risk in the situation, notwithstanding the U.S. wish for peace. Seaborn was also instructed to offer the carrot of aid if tension could be diminished. M. Pham Van Dong did not accept this proposition. Meanwhile, clandestine activity on a modest scale continued against the North, and this led indirectly toward major U.S. involvement.

The clandestine activity, known as operation Plan 34A, came under the direction of General Harkins in Saigon, although the operations were by no means all U.S. manned. It covered three principal elements:[5]

(a) Direct action in the North by sabotage and psychological warfare teams (with emphasis in the coastal areas), and intelligence overflights by U2 aircraft.

(b) Air operations in Laos (where the Ho Chi Minh trail was already much in use by the Communists) by a force of up to 40 T28 aircraft. (The T28 being a relatively unsophisticated machine, a development of the Harvard trainer familiar to aircrew of the Second World War.) Some of these T28s had Lao pilots, but most of the fliers were Thai. There were also a few American pilots.

(c) Destroyer patrols in the Gulf of Tonkin (the so-called 'de Soto patrols') to gather radar and coast defence intelligence as well as to show a resolute presence.

In June 1964, General Westmoreland succeeded General Harkins in Saigon. At the end of July 1964, South Vietnamese commandos, working within the Operation Plan 34A, staged an amphibious raid on the North Vietnamese islands of Han Me and Han Nieu in the Gulf of Tonkin. The North Vietnamese reacted vigorously against this raid. Separately, the U.S. destroyer Maddox was in the Gulf of Tonkin on intelligence gathering patrol, with strict instructions to remain at least eight miles offshore.

After dark on the night of 2nd/3rd August, when the Maddox was about twenty miles offshore, three North Vietnamese torpedo boats launched a torpedo attack. One of the craft was stopped dead in the water and sunk by gunfire from Maddox. The two other boats were damaged by supporting aircraft from the U.S. aircraft carrier, Ticonderoga, which was also in the area.[7]

About twenty-four hours later, during the night of 4th August, Maddox, now accompanied by a sister destroyer, Turner Joy, was once again ordered to close the coast of North Vietnam. This time the instructions were to cruise further North, and to keep at least eleven miles offshore. President Johnson's memoirs state that the object of these orders was to separate the de Soto patrol from any South Vietnamese commando activity, while reaffirming U.S. rights in international waters. The Voice of America broadcast a U.S. government message advising Hanoi "to be under no misapprehension as to the grave consequences of unprovoked military action against the United States".[8] The episode which followed has a number of elements of uncertainty. For reasons which are not entirely clear, perhaps political, perhaps relating to North Vietnamese naval inexperience and to the fact that another 34A operation was once again separately in train, the North Vietnamese apparently chose to attack the now re-inforced U.S. naval patrol. Once again, the U.S. destroyers seem to have played an effective part. There was also other military action. When news of the North Vietnamese attack reached Washington, President Johnson's first reaction was to seek detailed confirmation that it really had taken place. Once this was received, he gave orders for limited action by U.S. carrier borne aircraft against North Vietnamese naval installations and oil storage facilities.[9]

At the same time, President Johnson went on television to inform the U.S. people of the action in progress. He stated that the U.S. response was 'limited and fitting', and emphasised that Washington sought no wider war.[10] The message was also addressed to Peking, to ensure that the Chinese leaders realised that the retaliation was aimed only at North Vietnam and not at China.

The Administration also drafted the Congressional resolution, generally known as the Gulf of Tonkin resolution, for the men who would be its sponsors. These included Senator Fulbright, Chairman of the Senate Foreign Relations Committee, later to be a major critic of the Indo-China involvement, and Representative Morgan. President Johnson's book stresses the importance he attached to this Congressional support. It was in the line of the advice about the vital need for full Congressional backing, which he had himself given to President Eisenhower, when Eisenhower faced crises in the Middle East and the Formosa Strait.[11]

The key words of the resolution read as follows:[12]

"Resolved by the Senate and House of Representatives of the United States of America in Congress assembled, that Congress approve and support the determination of the President, as Commander-in-Chief, to take all necessary measures to repel any armed attack against the forces of the United States and to prevent further aggression.

The United States regards as vital to its national interest, and to world peace, the maintenance of international peace and security in South East Asia. Consonant with the Constitution of the United States, and the Charter of the United Nations and, in accordance with its obligations under the South East Asia Collective Defence Treaty, the United States is therefore, prepared, as the President determines, to take all necessary steps, including the use of armed force, to assist any member or protocol state of the South East Asia Collective Defence Treaty requesting assistance in defence of its freedom."

During the Congressional hearing, the U.S. Defence Secretary was questioned about the South Vietnamese operations in train at the time of the attacks on the U.S. destroyers. Mr. McNamara replied very definitely: "Our ships had no knowledge of it, were not connected with it and in no sense of the word can be considered to have back-stopped the effort."[13] These were plain words, although Senator Fulbright subsequently had this to say: "The Gulf of Tonkin incident, if I may say so, was a very vague one. We were briefed on it, but have no way of knowing, even to this day, what actually happened. I do not know if we provoked the attack in connection with supervising or helping a raid by the South Vietnamese or not."[14] This 1966 statement stands interestingly alongside a significant exchange between Senator Cooper and Senator Fulbright during the 1964 hearings. Cooper asked, "if, looking ahead, the President decided that it was necessary to use such force as could lead to war, do we give that authorisation by this resolution?" Senator Fulbright replied that this was his interpretation.[15] On 7th August, the congressional resolution was passed by a vote of 88 to 2 in the Senate, and 416 to 0 in the House of Representatives.[16] Later on, the circumstances of the Gulf of Tonkin incident were much questioned by the President's critics. What can never be known, is whether there would have been this questioning if the President's action had brought success.

It would have been surprising if at this time Hanoi was not taking the forthcoming American Presidential election into account. As previously mentioned, a basic feature of the policy of Ho Chi Minh and his colleagues, was their wide strategic outlook. Equally, it would have been very surprising if President Johnson did not also have the election in mind and, for his part, he still sought to communicate restraint.

Low risk interim measures were ordered "to assist morale and to show the Communists we still mean business."[17] In addition, a range of bombing studies were put in train. But there was still no heavy sustained bombing of the North and, in the November election, President Johnson won a massive victory against Senator Goldwater, whose campaign platform included full scale air attack on North Vietnam. As 1964 came to an end, U.S. bombing of North Vietnam still remained an option to be closed should events so warrant.

Within South Vietnam itself, 1964 had been a year of some confusion. The November 1963 coup may well have gone to the head of certain army officers. Within little more than a year it was repeated half a dozen times and the military situation went downhill. The price of the feuding within the South Vietnamese Army was a major deterioration in the campaign against the Communists.

An important aspect of the coup against Diem, was that most of the central personalities were men of the South from Cochin China.[18] It may be that such men did not look upon the North with the same intensity as the emigrés, or those with homes near the border. Certainly, there was nothing to dispose the Cochin Chinese military or civilian bourgeois to favour Communism in the South. Nevertheless, such men might merely feel "different" rather than intensely hostile. At his first press conference, General Minh emphasised "we have not the slightest intention of engaging in re-conquest or crusade: we want to be left in peace."[19]

Later, in answer to a question about relations with France he replied: "I am speaking French: So!" At the end of the press conference, one of Minh's colleagues said: "This neutralism talked of in Paris: what does it mean: a pause before Communisation: or a key to the reconciliation of the two Vietnams? General de Gaulle should be more explicit".

Whatever the reason, the first government of General Minh lasted only two months. On 30th January, the young general Nguyen Khanh, who was apparently widely regarded as a protegee of General Harkins, led the first coup. The aim of the coup was said to be to prevent the neutralists, supported by a foreign power (France), from taking power.[20] Nguyen Khanh lasted about six months. Then Nguyen Cao Ky came on stage. Ky, a colourful Air Force general, married to a glamorous wife, was an emigré from the North and could certainly not be regarded as minded toward neutralism. Almost at once, he told the press that he intended to take the war to the North.[21] Before the end of the year, there was yet another coup, the aftermath of which was described by General Maxwell Taylor, who had relieved Cabot Lodge as U.S. Ambassador in Saigon, in terms leaving little doubt as to who was who.

According to the Embassy cable, General Taylor summoned the "Young Turks", among them General Nguyen Van Thieu, later to become President of South Vietnam, and then spoke as follows:[22] "Do you understand English? (Vietnamese officers indicated they did ....) I told you at General Westmoreland's dinner we Americans are tired of coups. Apparently I wasted my words. Maybe this is because something is wrong with my French, because you evidently didn't understand. I made it clear that all military plans which I know you would like to carry out are dependent on government stability. Now you have made a real mess. We cannot carry you forever if you do things like this."

General Taylor must have been effective. After this, the coup tempo diminished. By the middle of 1965, General Nguyen Van Thieu became the man in the chair, and his authority was subsequently consolidated in two elections, generally regarded as unrigged; certainly they were held in the full glare of Western press attention. (For the 1967 election, President Johnson arranged for a special American delegation, representative of Congress, the Trade Unions, Radio, the Press and other elements to be present as observers.)[23]

In the wake of the political and military upheavals in Saigon, which had so much diminished the effectiveness of the South Vietnamese war effort, mid 1965 faced the American administration with a very difficult issue. A strong body of opinion considered that,

without some further large scale American help, it was probable that
the U.S. involvement inherited by President Johnson would be involvement in a débacle. At this stage, the views of the military were naturally
a major factor in the consideration of what might be done. And some
American commanders appear to have been very confident that, with
their methods and their leadership and using their own troops, things
would go better: the reverse of Vietnamisation.

General Westmoreland told Washington in July 1965 that, by
using his "Search and Destroy" strategy, he could defeat the enemy by
the end of 1967.[24] His command in Vietnam had already been considerably reinforced. Now he asked for a virtual doubling of his strength by 44
battalions, 100,000 men. General Taylor had some reservations about a
major build-up of U.S. ground forces[25], and Mr. George Ball, the
Under Secretary of State, believed "the U.S. was pouring its resources
down the drain in the wrong place". President Johnson relates that Mr.
Ball (as usual) spoke strongly in opposition, and that his views were
given a long and very careful hearing.[26] Johnson's wide consultations
also took in Congressional leaders. Most supported the proposed build
up, but Senator Mansfield, the Majority Leader, expressed reserve.
Mansfield spoke of deepening discontent in the country, and said he
thought the best hope was "quick stalemate and negotiation."[27]
Finally, President Johnson came to his decision. At a press conference
on 28th July 1965, President Johnson announced, "I have asked the
commanding general, General Westmoreland, what more he needs to
meet the mounting aggression. He has told me. We will meet his
needs." The President added a personal note: "I do not find it easy to
send our finest young men into battle ... this is the most agonising and
painful duty of your President."[28] By the end of 1965, U.S. forces in
South Vietnam numbered nearly 200,000.

By this time, the ground war in the South was in harness with an
air war "against the serpent's head" in the North. Contingency plans for
bombing North of the 17th parallel had been refined during 1964, and
there had been much domestic U.S. pressure for reprisal raids after a
Viet Cong attack in November on American aircraft at Bien Hoa air
base, near Saigon. On 7th February 1965, a further Viet Cong attack on
U.S. elements at another air base, this time at Pleiku, drew as response
reprisal raids, codenamed Flaming Dart. Shortly after this, an
altogether larger sustained air campaign, codenamed Rolling Thunder,
was put into effect. Even so, the programme approved by President
Johnson pulled some of its punch. As first put into operation, it
involved "limited action against military targets South of the 19th
parallel:" that is, South of Hanoi.

The dissenting memorandum, which Mr. Ball had put to the
President, had contained the following key passages:[29]

(a) "No one has demonstrated that a white ground force, of whatever size, can win a guerilla war which is at the same time a civil war between Asians, in a jungle terrain, in the midst of a population that refuses co-operation to the white forces, and this provides a great intelligence advantage to the other side."

(b) "Once we deploy substantial numbers of troops in combat, it will become a war between the U.S. and a large part of the population of South Vietnam, organised and directed from North Vietnam and backed by the resources of both Peking and Moscow".

(c) "Once large numbers of U.S. troops are committed to direct combat, they will begin to take heavy casualties in a war they are ill-equipped to fight in a non co-operative countryside".

(d) "The cost of a compromise solution involves judgment as to the cost to the U.S. in terms of our relations with countries in the area, the credibility of our commitments and our world prestige. In my view, if we act before we commit substantial U.S. troops in South Vietnam, we can, by accepting some short term costs, avoid what may be a long term catastrophe. I believe we tend grossly to exaggerate the costs involved in a compromise settlement".

Ball then gave his own appreciation of the costs of compromise. Overall, he thought reaction in Asia would be parochial. Thailand could contain a threat merely from Indo-China. Japan would prefer wisdom to valour. For some countries, special reassurances would be needed. Europe would welcome an easier U.S. relationship with the Soviet Union, even though de Gaulle might crow. Africa would probably not be interested. "On balance, I believe we more seriously undermine the effectiveness of our world leadership by continuing the war and deepening our involvement than by compromise: we cannot ignore the fact that the war is unpopular, and that our role in it is perceptively eroding the respect and confidence of other nations toward us".[30]

With the President's difficult decision made the other way, and with General Westmoreland's "Search and Destroy" strategy now coupled to an air war against the North running at about two hundred sorties a day, the U.S. casualties foreseen in Ball's memorandum became fact. Increasingly the load of the war rested on U.S. armed forces, and General Westmoreland's troop requests rose dramatically: from 175,000 men in June 1965 to 275,000 that July, to 440,000 in

December. All these requests for a war now being fought as an American war were loyally and rapidly approved by the President.

The desired victory was however to prove elusive. One expert view (that of Sir Robert Thompson who headed the British Advisory Mission, in Saigon from 1961 to 1965) was that American impatience operated against them. Given the situation, quick results were simply not to be had. Thompson's summing up, even before this, had been:[31] "if we plan for a long haul we may get quick results, but if we go in for quick results we may at best get a long haul." Again, to quote Thompson[32], "The Americans were strategically out-manoeuvred, and the doors were left wide open for the Tet offensive." (The Communist attack on Saigon and other cities in the South in January–February 1968.)

Some of Thompson's strongest criticisms were directed against General Westmoreland's "Search and Destroy" strategy:[33] Westmoreland's very distinguished combat record included experience at various levels of command in North Africa, Sicily, Normandy, Germany and Korea; the last in command of an airborne combat team: it did not however include experience of counter insurgency operations.

In Vietnam, General Westmoreland's major concept was to employ relatively large American forces to hunt the enemy in his (the enemy's) areas. From time to time, when there was contact, the Viet Cong suffered some killed: the Americans usually a lesser number. But, to the Communist commanders, their own casualties loomed less significantly than American casualties to Washington. Often too, the ordinary Vietnamese in their villages were victims of passing American "Search and Destroy" operations. The net gain lay with the Communists. Their central strategic objective was to weary the American people of the Vietnam involvement. By a ruthless and determined presence in the shadows, they also sought to win the immediate local battle "for hearts and minds". A traditional maxim sometimes seen in temples in Vietnam summed up the need:[34]

> "Hu kuo, pi min"
> (Defend the nation and protect the citizen)
>
> To be read backwards as,
>
> "Min pi, kuo hu"
> (The citizen protected, then the realm defended)

The military problem was familiar. The issue held reminders of anti-submarine war at sea, and the controversy over convoys. During both the World Wars against Germany, bitter experience had shown that destroyers and escort vessels were wasted if they hunted the enemy on the ocean. It was like looking for a needle in a haystack. Relatively few submarines were detected, and merchant ships on their own continued to be attacked. However, as soon as merchant ships were gathered in groups and given escort, the enemy had to pay a higher price if he sought to attack. There were, of course, special problems and skills involved in convoy at sea. Likewise, with protection against the Viet Cong or indeed against any similar force.

In the book *No Exit from Vietnam*, Sir Robert Thompson stresses the extent to which U.S. forces were tied down in a positional rather than a mobile role over the mainly unpopulated areas of the map. Khe Sanh, the American stronghold in the North West, (a "hedgehog", not completely dissimilar to what was intended at Dien Bien Phu), rates some of Thompson's harshest criticism:[35] "When the records are available, the absurdity of holding Khe Sanh will rate a book by itself. Holding it, relieving it, and evacuating it were all regarded as victories. A similar situation developed on the Cambodian border, where, as a result of chasing North Vietnamese and Viet Cong units into the jungle and across the border, American troops were tied down: fortunately, misgivings about security in the rear led to some of these troops being kept back nearer Saigon: this saved the city, at the time of the Tet offensive."

Thompson was also critical of the U.S. bombing effort against the North at this time.[36] "The bombing had a minimal effect on infiltration" ... "it enabled the North to organise the whole country with the full support of the people" ... "It justified, domestically and internationally, the despatch, still not officially admitted, of North Vietnamese units to the South" ... "it even gave Russia and China in the midst of their controversy a common bond in support of the North Vietnamese people" ... "it attracted to Hanoi great international sympathy and support, in addition to awakening the conscience of the U.S. itself".

What is not stressed in that passage, but is fact, is that, as far as centres of population were concerned, the bombing was not remotely of the same order of magnitude as was carried out by both sides during the Second World War. It is often quoted that the tonnage of bombs dropped by the Americans during the Indo-China conflict exceeded the total tonnage of bombs dropped by both sides in Europe during the Second World War. This may be so. But in Indo-China, huge tonnages fell, in fact, on virtually empty jungle. The results of the bombing would seem to have been exaggerated by both sides. It did not achieve the interdiction of supplies which the U.S. Air Force claimed for it. Nor were the civilian casualties as numerous as sometimes claimed. Hanoi did not get the treatment meted out to London, Berlin and Tokio.

Indeed, up to the middle of 1966, President Johnson had not only suspended bombing on several occasions, but had also maintained the

U.S. bombing line well south of Hanoi. The President was, however, receiving pressing advice from his Chiefs-of-Staff, and from Mr. Rostow,[37], his Assistant for National Security, to order attacks on the oil depots around Hanoi and Haiphong. The President was extremely anxious about civilian casualties.[38] The military predicted that 'casualties could be held under 50'.[39]

Against this background, the attacks were at last ordered. Raids commenced in June 1966. For a while, they appeared to be very successful. Then Mr. McNamara, a frequent advocate of bombing pause for diplomatic gain, expressed doubt on the effectiveness of the raids. On 14th October 1966, he submitted that "The Rolling Thunder program of bombing the North has neither significantly affected infiltration nor cracked the morale of Hanoi: there is agreement in the Intelligence Community on these facts".[40]

The Joint Chiefs-of-Staff, who on some subjects had for some time held certain views very different to those of the Defence Secretary, disputed this opinion, and requested that their dissenting opinion should be passed to the President.[41] The bombing went on, punctuated by pauses to help possible negotiation, one of them during the course of peace discussions in London between the British and Soviet Prime Ministers in February 1967.

The ground war also received an increasingly cool scrutiny from Mr. McNamara. In March 1967, General Westmoreland bid for a further 200,000 troops to achieve an 'optimum' force of 671,616 men.[42] General Westmoreland argued that this would obviate the requirements for a major expansion of South Vietnamese forces[43] — which hardly appears a vote for the cause of Vietnamisation.

The Joint Chiefs-of-Staff now leaned toward some mobilisation of reserves to achieve this target.[44] On 19th May 1967, Mr. McNamara advised against giving General Westmoreland the full reinforcement he had requested.[45] President Johnson described this 22-page document as one of the most detailed to come from his Defence Secretary. The weight now lay heavily on the shoulders of the President. At the beginning of July, he asked McNamara to visit Saigon to study the matter with the military. The upshot was a reduced reinforcement bid.[46] On 4th August, President Johnson approved a 55,000 troop increase to bring the strength of General Westmoreland's forces to a total of 525,000 men. While this was an 'agreed figure', it was the first time that a request for reinforcement in Vietnam had not been fully met.

During the late autumn of 1967, President Johnson received a further major memorandum from his Defence Secretary. It concluded with recommendations for:[47]

(a) A U.S. announcement that their efforts were stabilising, and that U.S. combat forces, and air operations would not be expanded.
(b) A bombing halt.
(c) A study of military operations in the South, aimed at reducing U.S. casualties, and giving the South Vietnamese greater responsibility for their own security.

The President sought the widest views on the memorandum. There was a mixed response. Military leaders expressed their doubts. Dean Rusk, the Secretary of State, agreed with *stabilisation* but was against *announcement*. He also fully agreed with what later came to be called *Vietnamisation*. On bombing, he was sceptical, though he did think "we should take the drama out of our bombing by cutting back on operations in the Hanoi-Haiphong area."[48] Finally, the President wrote a note for the file giving his views. He describes this in his memoirs as "a step I rarely made during my years at the White House." The main points were:[49]

(a) Stabilisation of U.S. force levels — Yes. Announcement — No.
(b) Progress toward Vietnamisation — Yes.
(c) A unilateral total bombing halt would be a mistake: it would be generally interpreted as weakness. But if there were real hopes for peace the position would be different.

There were a number of British efforts toward peace, notably through contact with Mr. Kosygin the Soviet Prime Minister, during the course of 1966 and 1967. During their visit to Moscow in February 1966, Mr. Wilson, the British Prime Minister, and Lord Chalfont, then a Minister of State at the Foreign Office with disarmament responsibilities, had lengthy discussions with the Soviet leadership about a peace formula for Vietnam. At this stage, however, they formed the impression that "The Soviet Government were unable to exercise any real pressure on Hanoi in the face of continuing militant Chinese pressure."[50] Lord Chalfont also spent six hours in discussion with an important North Vietnamese delegation which was in Moscow at the same time. Here too, there was "an absence of concrete result".[51]

But, almost exactly one year later, during a return visit to London by Mr. Kosygin, it appeared that the Soviet Union might now perhaps be more able to influence Hanoi toward peace. Mr. Wilson writes: "for the first time he (Mr. Kosygin) was prepared to talk business".[52]

On the British side, there was much contact with the Americans to make sure there would be no misunderstanding as to the American position. Mr. Kosygin indicated, in turn, that he was in contact with Hanoi. A possible formula began to emerge on the basis of the United States giving up bombing (temporarily halted during the London talks) provided North Vietnamese infiltration into the South "were to cease". It was a long shot. Given the background of deception and mistrust, it is difficult to know if this formula would have come to anything on the ground in Indo-China.

But, at a key moment during the Anglo-Soviet discussions, when hopes were high, a "clarification" arrived from Walt Rostow. The main points were:[53]

(a) The United States would stop the bombing once infiltration *had* stopped.

(b) Prior to this cessation of bombing, the United States would stop further augmentation of their forces in South Vietnam. But Hanoi itself would have to announce very soon after the bombing halt (which would be public) that its own infiltration was also halted.

This clarification embodied a reversal of the basis of the talks in London. Previously, it had been thought that A, (the bombing halt) would come before B, (the infiltration halt). It now appeared that things were the other way round, and the effect was to stymie the discussions between Mr. Wilson and Mr. Kosygin. Even so, a last minute effort was made to achieve a formula, following a message from the Prime Minister to the President on the Downing Street — White House teleprinter.[54] The President agreed that if a North Vietnamese *assurance* could be obtained within 24 hours that the infiltration *had* stopped, the United States would not resume its bombing. But time was too short. Mr. Kosygin's reaction to the Prime Minister was that the proposal was an ultimatum.[55] There was no response from Hanoi, and the bombing recommenced within a few hours.

There were perhaps more other efforts for peace than was generally realised at the time. President Johnson's memoirs detail the U.S. contacts with North Vietnam between 1964 and 1968; along with the various peace channels which were used. On much of this mediation Johnson's views were reserved. "There was never any shortage of self appointed "mediators" who, without our encouragement and, often, even our knowledge, tried to make their own contacts, I did not question the good intentions and sincerity of many of these free-lance "peacemakers", but I do think many of their spontaneous efforts may have harmed more than they helped. I know they often did more to confuse issues than to clarify them. We could never be sure if we were hearing accurate reports of what Hanoi had said or wanted us to hear, or whether we were hearing wishful thinking about what Hanoi might be willing to do in various circumstances."

Of all the published peace proposals, the direct correspondence between President Johnson and Ho Chi Minh, quoted in full at the end of this chapter, is perhaps the most revealing of the gulf there was to be bridged. On the North Vietnamese side, even the tone is different to what it had been to the French. The very important correspondence, which spells out the issues, also picks up the strong American wish for direct negotiation rather than contact through third parties.

The problem facing President Johnson as a Commander-in-Chief, conscious of the effort and sacrifice of the American troops in the field, can only arouse sympathy. If there is a fair criticism which can be levelled at President Johnson, it is that he was too much the Commander-in-Chief, relying on top military advisers who often were out of touch with the realities of Vietnam, instead of acting as President, taking account of broader considerations. With the Tet (Vietnamese New Year) offensive of 31st January 1968 these broader considerations would come to a head.

Letter from President Johnson to President Ho Chi Minh:

February 8, 1967

Dear Mr. President,

I am writing to you in the hope that the conflict in Vietnam can be brought to an end. That conflict has already taken a heavy toll — in lives lost, in wounds inflicted, in property destroyed, and in simple human misery. If we failed to find a just and peaceful solution, history will judge us harshly.

Therefore I believe that we both have a heavy obligation to seek earnestly the path to peace. It is in response to that obligation that I am writing directly to you.

We have tried over the past several years, in a variety of ways and through a number of channels, to convey to you and your colleagues our desire to achieve a peaceful settlement. For whatever reasons, these efforts have not achieved any results.

It may be that our thoughts and yours, our attitudes and yours, have been distorted or misinterpreted as they passed through these various channels. Certainly, that is always a danger in indirect communication.

There is one good way to overcome this problem and to move forward in the search for a peaceful settlement. That is for us to arrange for direct talks between trusted representatives in a secure setting and away from the glare of publicity. Such talks should not be used as a propaganda exercise, but should be a serious effort to find a workable and mutually acceptable solution.

In the past two weeks, I have noted public statements by representatives of your government, suggesting that you would be prepared to enter into direct bilateral talks with representatives of the U.S. Government, provided that we ceased unconditionally and permanently our bombing operations against your country and all military actions against it. In the last few days, serious and responsible parties have assured us, indirectly, that this is in fact your proposal.

Let me frankly state that I see two great difficulties with this proposal. In view of your public position, such action on our part would inevitably produce world-wide speculation that discussions were under way and would impair the privacy and secrecy of those discussions. Secondly, there would inevitably be grave concern on our part whether your Government would make use of such action by us to improve its military position.

With these problems in mind, I am prepared to move even further towards an ending of hostilities than your Government has proposed in either public statements or through private diplomatic channels. I am prepared to order a cessation of bombing against your country, and the stopping of further augmentation of U.S. forces in South Vietnam, as soon as I am assured that infiltration into South Vietnam by land and by sea has stopped. These acts of restraint on both sides would, I believe, make it possible for us to conduct serious and private discussions leading toward an early peace.

I make this proposal to you now, with a specific sense of urgency arising from the imminent New Year holidays in Vietnam. If you are able to accept this proposal I see no reason why it could not take effect at the end of the New Year, or Tet, holidays. The proposal I have made would be greatly strengthened if your military authorities and those of the Government of South Vietnam could promptly negotiate an extension of the Tet truce.

As to the site of the bilateral discussions I propose, there are several possibilities. We could, for example, have our representatives meet in Moscow, where contacts have already occurred. They could meet in some other country such as Burma. You may have other arrangements or sites in mind, and I would try to meet your suggestions.

The important thing is to end a conflict that has brought burdens to both our peoples, and, above all, to the people of South Vietnam. If you have any thoughts about the actions I propose, it would be most important that I receive them as soon as possible.

Sincerely,
Lyndon B. Johnson

Ho Chi Minh's reply:

February 15, 1967

Lyndon B. Johnson
President of the United States

Your Excellency:

On February 10, 1967, I received your message. Here is my reply:

Vietnam is thousands of miles from the United States. The Vietnamese people have never done any harm to the United States, but, contrary to the commitments made by its representative at the Geneva Conference of 1954, the United States Government has constantly intervened in Vietnam, has launched and intensified its aggression against South Vietnam for the purpose of prolonging the division of Vietnam and of transforming South Vietnam into an American colony and an American military base. For more than two years now, the American Government, using its military planes and its navy has been waging war against the sovereign and independent Democratic Republic of Vietnam.

The U.S. Government has committed war crimes and crimes against peace and against humanity. In South Vietnam, a half million American soldiers and soldiers from satellite countries have used the most inhuman and barbaric methods of warfare such as napalm, chemicals and toxic gases to massacre our compatriots, destroy their crops and level their villages. In North Vietnam, thousands of American planes have rained down hundreds of thousands of tons of bombs destroying towns, villages, factories, roads, bridges, dykes, dams and even churches, pagodas, hospitals and schools. In your message you seem to deplore the suffering and the destruction in Vietnam. Allow me to ask you: who is perpetrating these awful crimes? It is the American and satellite soldiers. The United States Government is entirely responsible for the critical situation in Vietnam.

American aggression against the Vietnamese people is a challenge to the countries of the Socialist camp, menaces the people's independence movement, and gravely endangers peace in Asia and the world.

The Vietnamese people deeply love independence, liberty and peace. But, in the face of American aggression, they stand as one man, unafraid of sacrifices, until they have gained real independence, full liberty and true peace. Our just cause is approved and supported strongly by all the people of the world, including large segments of the American people.

The Government of the United States is aggressing against Vietnam. It must stop this aggression as the only way leading toward the reestablishment of peace. The Government of the United States must stop the bombing, definitively and unconditionally, and all other acts of war against the Democratic Republic of Vietnam, withdraw from South Vietnam all its troops and those of its satellites, recognize the National Liberation Front of South Vietnam and allow the people of Vietnam to settle their problems by themselves. This is the essence of the Four Points of the Government of the Democratic Republic of Vietnam as well as the expression of the principles and essential provisions of the Geneva Accords of 1954 on Vietnam. It is the basis for a just political solution of the Vietnamese problem. In your message you suggested direct talks between the Democratic Republic of Vietnam and the United States. If the Government of the United States really wants such talks, it must first unconditionally halt the bombing as well as all other acts of war against the Democratic Republic of Vietnam. Only after the unconditional stopping of the bombing and all other American acts of war against the Democratic Republic of Vietnam, can the Democratic Republic of Vietnam and the United States enter into conversations and discuss the questions in which both parties are interested.

The Vietnamese people will never yield to force nor agree to talks under the menace of bombs.

Our cause is entirely just. It is our hope that the Government of the United States acts with reason.

Sincerely yours,
Ho Chi Minh

Second Letter to Ho Chi Minh:

April 6, 1967

Dear Mr. President,

I was, of course, disappointed that you did not feel able to respond positively to my letter to you of February 8.

But I would recall to you the words Abraham Lincoln addressed to his fellow Americans in 1861:

"Suppose you go to war, you cannot fight always: and when, after much loss on both sides, and no gain on either, you cease fighting, the identical old question as to terms of intercourse are again upon you."

In that spirit I wish to reaffirm the offers I made in my earlier letter. We remain prepared to talk quietly with your representatives to establish the terms of a peaceful settlement and then bring the fighting to a stop: or we are prepared to undertake steps of mutual de-escalation which might make it easier for discussions of a peaceful settlement to take place. Talks to either of these ends could take place in Moscow, Rangoon, or elsewhere.

Despite public discussion of our previous exchange of views, our responsibilities to our own peoples and to the world remain; and those responsibilities include bringing the war in South East Asia to an end at the earliest possible date.

It is surely clear that one day we must agree to reestablish and make effective the Geneva Accords of 1954 and 1962: let the people of South Vietnam determine in peace the kind of government they want: let the peoples of North and South Vietnam determine peacefully whether and how they should unite: and permit the peoples of South East Asia to turn all their energies to their economic and social development.

You and I will be judged in history by whether we worked to bring about this result sooner rather than later.

I venture to address you directly again, in the hope that we can find the way to rise above all other considerations and fulfill that common duty. I would be glad to receive your views on these matters.

Sincerely,
Lyndon B. Johnson

[1] President Johnson: *Vantage Point*, p. 45.

[2] *Pentagon Papers*, p. 274. Memorandum dated 22 January 1964 from U.S. Chiefs of Staff to U.S. Defence Secretary.

[3] Ibid. p. 254.

[4] Johnson, p. 99.

[5] *Pentagon Papers*, p. 255.

[6] *Ibid*. p. 238.

[7] *Ibid*. p. 259.

[8] Johnson, p. 113.

[9] *Ibid.* p. 115.

[10] *Ibid.* p. 117.

[11] *Ibid.* pp. 115–119.

[12] *Pentagon Papers,* p. 265.

[13] *Ibid.* p. 267.

[14] Buttinger, 484, quoting a *Look* interview with Senator Fulbright, 31 May 1966.

[15] Johnson, p. 119.

[16] *Ibid.* p. 118.

[17] *Pentagon Papers,* p. 315.

[18] Lacouture, p. 126.

[19] *Ibid.* p. 128.

[20] *Vietnam,* p. 24. Lacouture, p. 133.

[21] Lacouture, p. 141.

[22] *Pentagon Papers,* p. 337.

[23] Johnson, p. 264.

[24] *Pentagon Papers,* p. 462.

[25] *Ibid.* p. 412.

[26] *Ibid.* p. 414; Johnson, p. 147.

[27] Johnson, p. 151.

[28] *Ibid.* p. 153.

[29] *Pentagon Papers,* p. 449. Memorandum 'A compromise solution to South Vietnam from Under Secretary of State George Ball, 1 July 1965'. Johnson, pp. 147–148.

[30] *Pentagon Papers,* p. 459.

[31] Thompson: *No Exit from Vietnam,* p. 125.

[32] *Ibid.* p. 242.

[33] *Ibid.* p. 142.

[34] Duncanson, p. 403.

[35] Thompson, p. 142.

[36] *Ibid.* p. 140.

[37] *Pentagon Papers,* p. 499; Memorandum from Mr. Rostow dated 6 May 1966.

[38] Johnson, p. 240.

[39] *Pentagon Papers,* p. 449.

[40] *Ibid.* p. 543; Memorandum from Mr. McNamara, dated 14 October 1966.

[41] *Ibid.* p. 553; Memorandum from General Wheeler, Chairman Joint Chiefs-of-Staff, dated 14 October 1966.

[42] *Ibid.* p. 558; Memorandum by General Westmoreland on force requirements, 18 March 1967.

[43]*Ibid.* p. 528.

[44]*Ibid.* p. 528.

[45]Johnson, p. 369.

[46]*Ibid.* p. 370.

[47]*Ibid.* p. 372.

[48]*Ibid.* p. 377.

[49]*Ibid.* pp. 377–8.

[50]Wilson: *Labour Govt.,* 1966–70, p. 214.

[51]*Ibid.* p. 215.

[52]*Ibid.* p. 348.

[53]*Ibid.* p. 357.

[54]*Ibid.* p. 358.

[55]*Ibid.* p. 364.

16   1968: Climax

FOR the United States, 1968 was the year of climax in Vietnam: as 1954 had been for the French. It was the year of the Tet offensive, in which United States public opinion suffered the shock of learning that Communist Vietnamese main force units had penetrated into the heart of Saigon and a number of other large cities in the South. They were indeed able to see something of the battle on their own television sets. Perhaps less noticed at that time by much of the U.S. press — or at any rate less publicised — was the fact that the population of these cities did not appear to rally to these Communist units.

President Johnson described the weeks before and after Tet as "a period of activity as intense as any of my Presidency."[1] 1968 was the year in which he announced, on 31st March, that he would not accept his party's nomination for another term as President. In the same speech, he announced that he was stopping most of the bombing of the North, in the hope that it would lead to peace: also his intention that the expansion and modernisation of the armed forces of South Vietnam would now become a goal of the very highest priority.[2] It was a year when many established policies were stood on their head.

In President Johnson's memoirs, his personal feelings came through strongly:[3] "I warned a group of Congressmen in the summer of 1967 that Ho Chi Minh believed he could win in Washington as he did in Paris: I wish I could report that the enemy failed as decisively with that goal as it did with others." "... I did not expect the enemy effort to have the impact on American thinking that it achieved. I was not surprised that elements of the press, the academic community and Congress reacted as they did. I was surprised and disappointed that the enemy's efforts produced such a dismal effect on various people inside government, and others outside, whom I had always regarded as staunch and unflappable. Hanoi must have been delighted. It was exactly the reaction which they sought."

It was certainly a very testing time for President Johnson. Tension was already high in the Pacific area. Late in January 1968, the North Koreans seized the U.S.S. Pueblo, a small intelligence gathering ship attached to the Pacific Fleet and imprisoned its crew. At much the same time, an assassination squad of North Koreans penetrated into

Seoul, intending to murder President Park of South Korea, and their attempt came close to success.

Meanwhile in Vietnam, there had been intelligence reports of a major Communist operation in the offing. The likely target was thought to be Khe Sanh, where the American position bore some similarities to that of the French at Dien Bien Phu.[4] There were also some indications that the cities of Hué, Quang Tri and Danang in the North of the country might come under attack. The military problem was complicated, however, by the imminence of the Vietnamese holiday season of Tet, marking the lunar New Year. It was a season of truces, and the Viet Cong had claimed they would observe a seven day truce. For their part, the Americans planned a two day truce.[5]

The expected enemy offensive flared up in the North on 30th January. The main assault elsewhere began twenty-four hours later, in the middle of Tet. North Vietnamese and Viet Cong forces hit five of the six largest cities of South Vietnam; 36 of the country's 44 provincial capitals were attacked. In Saigon, a suicide squad penetrated the grounds of the United States Embassy and held out for a while. Indeed, had it not been for the resolute action of a small Embassy guard, who bought time by their resistance, the Embassy might even have fallen to the attackers. But a helicopter mounted counter attack by U.S. paratroopers restored the position. The Communist Vietnamese left nineteen dead, and the Embassy was saved. The greatest Communist success was at Hué, the old Imperial capital of the Emperors of Vietnam. Here, they held out for 26 days and, after their departure, more than 3,000 of the city's inhabitants were said to have been murdered during the course of the occupation.[6]

Overall, despite the shock and the publicity success, the direct military results of the Tet offensive may perhaps have been disappointing to General Giap and the Communist military leadership. General Westmoreland assessed the events in the following terms, in his[7] Report on the War in Vietnam: "The Tet offensive had the effect of Pearl Harbour. The South Vietnamese Government was intact and stronger: the armed forces were larger, more effective and more confident. The people had rejected the idea of a general uprising, and enemy forces, particularly those of the Viet Cong, were much weaker." Even some critics of the U.S. involvement recognised that General Westmoreland's assessment was not out of line within Vietnam itself.[8] But this was only part of the picture. Despite the importance of gains on the ground, these were less important to Giap than the bull's eye of American public opinion. This had been hit at the very centre.

The U.S. Chiefs-of-Staff sought permission to bomb close to the centre of Hanoi.[9] Mr. McNamara opposed this. The Chiefs-of-Staff also asked General Westmoreland what reinforcement he might require. He asked for another 200,000 men, and this request was blessed by the Chiefs of Staff. To achieve this, there would have to be some call up of reserves.[10] Mr. McNamara, about to give up the post of Defence Secretary to take the international post as head of the World Bank, said he did not think the proposed 200,000 increase would make a major difference: "The key was the South Vietnamese army."[11]

Meanwhile, on the diplomatic front, President Johnson received a call at the White House on 21st February from U. Thant, the U.N. Secretary General. U. Thant's message was that he had heard that Hanoi was ready to negotiate if the bombing was halted.[12] The President established the "Clifford Group" to report on the options which lay open; Clifford, a well known lawyer, and an old friend of the President, being McNamara's successor.[13] The President also decided to confer again with a very distinguished group of Americans with whom he had previously discussed the Vietnam situation.[14]

This group, popularly known as the Wise Men, included former Secretary of State, Dean Acheson, former Under Secretary, George Ball, McGeorge Bundy, Arthur Dean, Douglas Dillon, Henry Cabot Lodge and the retired diplomat, Robert Murphy. Its military component comprised three former Chiefs-of-Staff, General Bradley, General Ridgeway and General Maxwell Taylor, and Cyrus Vance a former Deputy Secretary of Defence. President Johnson was eventually to find that six of these special advisers favoured some form of disengagement, four were opposed, and one was in between.[15] Johnson wrote: "I had always regarded the majority of them as very steady and balanced. If they had been so deeply influenced by Tet, what must the average citizen be thinking." Vice President Humphrey, who had listened to the discussion with them, commented to the President, "Tet really set us back". Johnson observed, "I had to agree, but I remained convinced that the blow to morale was more of our own doing than anything the enemy had accomplished with its army. We were defeating ourselves."[16]

In addition to the external political strains, the President also now had to weigh up his political standing within his own Democratic party. The Presidential election was due at the end of the year, and the first Democratic primaries were now in train in New Hampshire. In this election, Senator Eugene McCarthy, who was campaigning against the President's war policy, was running very close. On 20th February, Senator Robert Kennedy, who had parted company with the President's Vietnam policy during the course of 1966, said in a speech in Chicago: "The United States is not winning the war and should no longer be trying to: the enemy has finally shattered the mask of illusion with which we have concealed our true circumstances even from ourselves." On 16th March, Kennedy announced that he would seek the Democratic nomination for the Presidency.[17] President Johnson's own words in his memoirs are descriptive: "We were moving down to the wire."

The President now had before him the report of General Wheeler, the Chairman of the U.S. Chiefs-of-Staff, who had visited South Vietnam at the end of February.[18] The report said that the Communist Vietnamese had committed 67,000 men in the Tet offensive. It also said that the Communists had lost over 40,000 dead. Official American figures of enemy dead, based partly on "body count", and partly on assessment of the casualties to be inferred from air attack, had often been doubted before this by American journalists and others in Vietnam. Now, they were questioned by Arthur Goldberg, the American representative at the United Nations who had been brought into the discussion. There was a basic non-sequitur. If the numbers claimed as killed in the bombing of the Ho Chi Minh trail were right, where did the numbers come from now being claimed as killed in South Vietnam itself? In the jungle, the results of air attack are not always easy to assess. It is difficult not to feel that there was much exaggeration in the results attributed to the interdiction bombing by the U.S. Air Force. Indeed this in turn may relate to a wider question mark against the direction of the U.S. military effort in Vietnam. Understanding must always go to those bearing the burden of responsibility. And the political constraints on the U.S. military were formidable. Even so, U.S. military policy sometimes appeared the captive of what can only be described as fallacious quantification. If x of something were good, then $10x$ of the same thing must be ten times as good. But, alongside much else, this presupposes an enemy lacking flexibility. This was not the case with the Viet Cong.

It is easy to be wise after the event. But there may also have been too much American faith in what could be achieved by technology; and a tendency to give attention to the moves of the American pieces on the chessboard of Indo-China without fully appraising the objectives and possible moves of the other side. The stresses of the situation enhanced human inclination toward self-deception. In the end the very weight of the American effort probably commenced to work against achievement of its aims. Certainly, quantitative projections of what could be achieved by air power on a "more of the same" basis, could only have been misleading, to the point of danger, if they had been taken seriously, The tonnage of explosives employed was sometimes used to calculate the casualties caused. If the enemy casualties as claimed daily and published were added up, there would have been no Viet Cong left.

General Wheeler's report to President Johnson made the assessment that, while the long term intention of the enemy was to destroy the Saigon government and its armed forces, its interim minimum objectives were to seize sufficient territory and to gain control of enough people to lead toward "an N.L.F. dominated government".[19] The report considered that, while the enemy had suffered heavily around Saigon, its capability elsewhere was largely intact. This was notably the case in the First Corps area in the North of the country; and the top U.S. objective in Vietnam remained that of being able to counter a Communist offensive from the North, a conventional military invasion across the frontier. Against this background, General Wheeler endorsed General Westmoreland's bid for a further 200,000 men.

Although some of the President's civilian advisers, notably Walt Rostow, were maintaining a hard line, the weight of the Clifford group was somewhat the other way.[20] Their initial draft memorandum cast doubt on the value of providing the additional 200,000 troops for Vietnam, and added that, if further escalation occurred, "it will be difficult to convince critics that we are not simply destroying South Vietnam in order to save it": ... moreover, "this growing disaffection, accompanied as it certainly will be, by increased defiance of the draft, and growing unrest in the cities because of the belief that we are neglecting domestic problems, runs great risks of provoking a domestic crisis of unprecedented proportions".

The draft memorandum concluded that the American presence in South Vietnam should be used to buy time for a South Vietnamese defence effort and, that General Westmoreland should be instructed that his principal mission was to provide security to populated areas, along what the memorandum described as the demographic frontier. In particular, General Westmoreland should be instructed that he was not to wage a war of attrition against enemy forces, or seek to drive them from the country.[21]

The Pentagon reacted against this "apparent repudiation of American military policy in South Vietnam", and disagreed profoundly with the proposed population security strategy.[22] In their view, this would enable the enemy to deploy its forces more easily for attacks of its own choice, and would in fact bring the war closer to the mass of the civilian community. The argument among the President's advisers swayed to and fro, but in a speech at Minneapolis, on 18th March, the President gave an indication of his own views at that moment: "Hanoi was seeking to win something in Washington that they can't win in Hué" ... "those of you who think that you can save lives by moving the battlefield in from the mountains to the cities have another think coming".

On 22nd March, it became known that General Westmoreland would be recalled to Washington as Army Chief-of-Staff. On 25th March, the President's close advisory group, the "Wise Men", met again, and the majority confirmed their turn about on the war. On 26th March, General Creighton Abrams, Westmoreland's Deputy in Vietnam reported to the President.[23] He spoke well of the South Vietnamese armed forces. As Westmoreland's successor in Saigon, the problems of Vietnamisation would rest significantly with him. On 31st March, the President spoke on television.[24] After announcing that he was now ready "to take the first step to de-escalate the war", he told the American people that he would not seek, and would not accept the nomination of the Democratic Party for another term as President.

This was the climax. But the business of Vietnam remained a major concern for the remainder of the Presidency. Within a few days of the 31st March speech there was a political response from Hanoi. Contact continued. The break came on 3rd May, when the North Vietnamese Embassy in Vientiane asked William Sullivan, the U.S. Ambassador, to call to receive a message for the President. Hanoi was suggesting peace talks in Paris. President Johnson liked the final words of Sullivan's *flash* telegram reporting this progress .... "Congratulations to those in Washington whose eyeballs are made of such sound stuff."[25]

American delegates, headed by Averill Harriman, who had led the U.S. delegation for most of the 1961/1962 Geneva Conference on Laos, reached Paris within seven days. But the talks began badly; the North Vietnamese had their eyes on the U.S. domestic scene, and made points accordingly. And before any "serious" talks could start, the North Vietnamese required that there should be a complete halt to bombing: the partial halt was insufficient. During October General Abrams, to whose commonsense military/political judgment tribute seems due, told the President the risk in a complete halt was one worth taking.[26] On 31st October, the President spoke once again to the American people on television.[27] He discussed events since March, and then said: "As a result of these developments I have now ordered that all air, naval and artillery bombing of North Vietnam cease".

President Johnson's final words on the Vietnam problem speak for themselves.[28] "I felt I was turning over to President Nixon a foreign policy problem that, although serious, was improving: an ally that was stronger than ever before" ... "all this we accomplished, but not without great cost at home" ... "a certain degree of violent disagreement with our Vietnam effort was inevitable: but I believe it passed the bounds of reasonable debate and fair dissension:" ... "this dissension prolonged the war, prevented a peaceful settlement on reasonable terms, encouraged our enemies, disheartened our friends and weakened us as a nation. These dissents were weighed inside the administration with a seriousness not generally understood: the war and the political and social currents in South East Asia are complex and difficult to describe in simple formulas, and there was certainly justification for debate and for differences in judgment in a free society of strong minded men and women dealing with unfamiliar problems on the other side of the world." The dissension existed not only in the United States. The central fact is that President Johnson altered course, in spite of the personal misgivings he felt about doing so.

[1] Johnson, p. 385.

[2] *Ibid.* p. 435.

[3] *Ibid.* pp. 383–384.

[4] *Ibid.* p. 384.

[5] *Ibid.* p. 381.

[6] Johnson, p. 382.

[7] General Westmoreland, Report on the War in Vietnam, p. 169.

[8] Frances Fitzgerald; *Fire in the Lake.*

[9] *Pentagon Papers,* p. 593. Johnson, p. 387.

[10] *Pentagon Papers,* p. 597.

[11] Johnson, p. 392.

[12] *Ibid.* p. 395.

[13] *Ibid.* p. 394.

[14] *Ibid.* p. 409.

[15] *Ibid.* p. 418.

[16] *Ibid.* p. 418.

[17] *Ibid.* p. 539.

[18] *Pentagon Papers,* p. 615 — Report of Chairman, Joint Chief-of-Staff on Situation in Vietnam and MACV requirements.

[19] *Pentagon Papers,* p. 619.

[20] *Ibid.* p. 610.

[21] *Ibid.* p. 603.

[22] *Ibid.* p. 602.

[23]*Ibid.* p. 417.

[24]*Ibid.* p. 435.

[25]Johnson, p. 504.

[26]*Ibid.* p. 521.

[27]*Ibid.* p. 528.

[28]*Ibid.* p. 529.

17 Cambodia: 1954 to 1970: Precarious Peace

WHEN the U.S. intervention in Cambodia took place at the end of April 1970, the Communist Vietnamese intervention against South Vietnam from Cambodia had already been in progress for at least four years. In President Johnson's own words: "early in 1966, Sihanouk became an active participant in the Chinese Communist program to supply Communist forces in South Vietnam. By the end of 1966, Cambodia's main port, Sihanoukville (later, Kompong Som) had become a principal supply point for Chinese military equipment going to the Viet Cong and North Vietnamese. Other supplies moving down from Laos (along the Ho Chi Minh trail) were also fed into Cambodia for trans-shipment to the Communist forces in Vietnam."[1] The Communist 1968 Tet offensive was indeed largely mounted from the Cambodian frontier region, at one point only about 40 miles from Saigon itself.

The anti-American trend in Cambodia had developed in the late 1950s and early 1960s. In the aftermath of the 1954 Geneva Conference, Prince Sihanouk had accepted military as well as economic aid from the United States. But at the same time Sihanouk emphasised Cambodian neutrality, notably during the 1955 Bandung Conference of non-aligned nations and, shortly afterwards, while visiting Peking in February 1956.[2] While in Peking, Sihanouk stressed his considerable reservations about SEATO: Cambodia had no wish to be a SEATO protectorate. What was sought by Sihanouk was the maximum recognition of his country's independence and neutrality, and of her territorial integrity within her existing frontiers. He found American policy on this disappointing. His own published account also suggests that he found the then American Ambassador patronising and familiar and lacking in taste.[3]

Sihanouk's reserve toward the United States was founded in personal as well as national political grounds. He believed there were influential American elements who wished to see him removed from power: in particular, Sihanouk believed there had been C.I.A. complicity in various plots against him during 1959.[4] Sihanouk's account, is that Colonel Lansdale, who had been so much involved in

157

clandestine activity in Saigon in the middle 1950s, had visited Angkor in February 1959 and contacted General Dap Chuon, the area military commander. Sihanouk already suspected Dap Chuon of conspiring against him. This visit by Lansdale decided him to take action. Orders were issued for Dap Chuon's arrest, but he was shot "while trying to escape". Subsequently, Sihanouk took a group of about 20 diplomats, including Western representatives, to Dap Chuon's villa to see "evidence of the conspiracy". Later on, Sihanouk said he believed that General Lon Nol was also involved in the plot, and had Dap Chuon shot to avoid his own incrimination. Other notable names involved were Sam Sary, a former Cambodian Ambassador in London, and Son Ngoc Thanh, Sihanouk's old adversary. The year also saw a more direct attempt against the régime. A gift box sent to the Palace in Phnom Penh turned out to be a bomb, and its explosion killed the Chief of Protocol.[5]

Sihanouk's political reserve concerned the extent of American support for Thailand and South Vietnam in their claims against Cambodia. He found it especially difficult to accept U.S. disinclination to support the Cambodian claim for international recognition of her borders. This was an issue of special concern to Sihanouk and, toward the end of 1962, he proposed a further Geneva Conference "to give Cambodia the benefit of the international provisions recently granted to Laos".[6]

This proposal by Sihanouk received only limited Western support. The general view was that Cambodia would do better to try to negotiate bilaterally with her neighbours. Sihanouk now appealed directly to the United States for help in gaining Thai and South Vietnamese acceptance of Cambodian independence, neutrality and territorial integrity. At the same time, Sihanouk was again accusing the Thais and South Vietnamese of aiding the Khmer insurgency, known as the Khmer Serai, led by Son Ngoc Thanh. Against this background of accusation and acrimony, Sihanouk's direct approach to the Americans fell by the wayside.[7]

During November 1963, Prince Sihanouk said publicly that the American establishment in Vietnam were indeed helping the Khmer Serai. He demanded American help to end Khmer Serai broadcasts against his régime. He said that if this were not done, he would replace Western aid with Communist aid. He was as good as his word. On 20th November, he requested the termination of American aid. If it was bluff, it was called. The Americans agreed to Sihanouk's demands.

A British effort to meet Sihanouk's aims through use of the Geneva machinery also proved unsuccessful. The path now lay downhill. During February 1964, South Vietnamese air attacks against Viet

Cong positions in Eastern Cambodia caused casualties among Khmer villagers. At the beginning of March, the United States indicated that the agenda for any conference on Cambodia should include the establishment of Commissions to determine the frontiers of Cambodia.[8] For Sihanouk this was too much, and with President Kennedy, for whom he had great respect, now dead, he turned decisively the other way. The recognition which he sought, from his standpoint as of right, was of Cambodia's existing frontiers. On 10th March, Cambodian arms purchasing missions set out for Peking and Moscow. The next day, 11th March, the British and American embassies in Phnom Penh were sacked by organised mobs.[9] Six years later, to the day, it would be the turn of the North Vietnamese and Viet Cong embassies to be sacked in the same way. But this episode belongs later. The aftermath of the 1964 embassy incidents, and of subsequent caustic exchanges between Washington and Phnom Penh, was a breach in United States-Cambodian diplomatic relations. This took place on 3rd May 1965. For the Communist diplomatic effort in Cambodia, in the years before war came to Cambodia, this was a high water mark.

During the mid 1960s, Sihanouk established diplomatic relations with the North Vietnamese and with the National Liberation Front of South Vietnam (the Viet Cong). At the same time, as stated by President Johnson, Sihanouk also accepted Chinese proposals that Cambodia should assist the supply of the Vietnamese Communists. But the Communists pressed too hard. Internal insurgencies continued within Cambodia, and Sihanouk suspected links between "internal and external Communists". In May 1967, he reaffirmed his country's determination to defend its neutrality against any enemy "whether it be the Viet Minh or the United States". In the same year he observed: "The Vietnamese war is increasingly becoming the Cambodian War."[10]

In January 1968, Sihanouk publicly acknowledged for the first time that his country's Eastern provinces were being used by Communist Vietnamese forces both as a sanctuary and as a source of supplies.[11] This public statement was another turning point of a sort. Up to this moment, it had been Sihanouk's policy to deny the presence of Communist forces in his country. From now on, the issue became more specific. In March 1969, Sihanouk displayed a map showing in detail the areas used by Communist forces. In October, he gave the number of North Vietnamese and Viet Cong forces operating within the country as 40,000. This compared with a total Cambodian army strength of 35,000. Sihanouk had cause for concern. The Communist Vietnamese presence in Eastern Cambodia was not popular with his people. And, by this time, it was common knowledge in Phnom Penh that a supply line to the Communist Vietnamese operated through

Cambodia. The transport organisation was the Hak Lee Trading Company, whose premises and trucks were attacked and burnt by Cambodian demonstrators in the immediate aftermath of the 1970 coup against Sihanouk.

Sihanouk's apprehensions for the future of Cambodia, squeezed between Vietnam and Thailand were well founded in history. They were also influenced by the events which had taken place at the very beginning of his reign. At that time, the then Japanese authority had supported the Thais in their annexation of the Cambodian border provinces of Siam Reap and Battambang, a major Cambodian rice area. Later, during the 1950s, there had been further difficulties with Thailand. These came to a head in a dispute over the ancient Buddhist temple of Preah Vihear, in Northern Cambodia. The issue was whether the ruined temple which had been occupied by the Thai police in 1953, was Cambodian or Thai. In 1962, the International Court at the Hague passed judgment in favour of Cambodia, but the issue remained an open sore.[12] Charge and counter charge abounded. Bangkok accused Phnom Penh of allowing Communist elements to infiltrate Thailand. Phnom Penh accused Bangkok of seeking to establish a rebel government within Cambodia.

Sihanouk was even more concerned with his Eastern border, and the absence of diplomatic relations between Phnom Penh and Bangkok was matched by the absence of diplomatic relations between Phnom Penh and Saigon. Cambodian diplomatic relations were with the Communist Vietnamese. Unfortunately for Sihanouk, the Communists proved less responsive to his gestures than he had hoped, and the national call of those who deposed Sihanouk was publicly based on his failure to limit the consolidation of Communist Vietnamese influence in Eastern Cambodia.

The area handbook on Cambodia prepared by the American University "to be useful to military and other personnel who need a convenient compilation of basic facts" describes in the following terms the Sihanouk era which came to an end in 1970:[13] "Until deposed in March 1970 Prince Sihanouk was, for nearly two decades, a towering figure in Cambodian politics and government. He was popular and accessible to the bulk of the population, although his popularity seemed to diminish somewhat, beginning in the late 1960s. His leadership was only rarely questioned at home, except by small numbers of dissidents and by an equally limited number of intellectuals and students in the cities ... Prince Sihanouk was able to keep the country out of the Vietnam war through diplomatic juggling based on an ostensible policy of non alignment. Dominant as he was, however, the Prince was not without problems, foremost among them being the mounting pressure of the Vietnam war." Most of the foreign diplomats in Cambodia at the time would endorse this view.

Certainly Sihanouk recognised the strength of the Communist Vietnamese position and its actual and latent threat to Cambodia. Above all, he recognised the significance of Communist China to the South East Asia scene. Yet he himself was no Communist. His writings before his deposition in March 1970 expressed this endlessly. Likewise, even his broadcasts after that date from Peking. His national objective, like those who deposed him, was the maintenance of the Khmer (Cambodian) identity. His method of achieving this objective was to rely above all upon China. By his nimble footwork on the international stage, he also managed to preserve the peace of his country.

Sihanouk's own words written shortly before his deposition, spell out his problem.[14] "If the Vietnam war were to end in an American defeat on the ground, a sort of Dien Bien Phu, Asian Communism, despite all its present assurances, would have no reason to spare us .... Yet if my own Buddhist Cambodia has to die, my sole wish is that when Communism becomes inevitable it should be a Cambodian Communism, knowing how to keep its distances from "brother" governments of Saigon, Hanoi, Bangkok, Vientiane. I would wish for a Communist Cambodia which, even if it cannot be a Yugoslavia, will at least have the sense to seek China as its protector rather than Vietnam or Thailand." A nationalist objective, however muted.

In January 1968, shortly before the North Vietnamese/Viet Cong Tet offensive, which had been largely mounted from within Cambodia, Sihanouk had said for the first time that the Communists were using the Eastern part of his country. He also stated publicly that, if he were forced to resign because of Communist provoked chaos, the alternative would be a takeover by the Cambodian army and the establishment of a pro-American government.[15] In February 1969 he repeated his concern.

In April 1969, following a message from President Nixon expressing United States recognition of the sovereignty, neutrality and territorial integrity of Cambodia, steps were taken for the restoration of diplomatic relations between the two countries. In June 1969, these relations were formally restored.[16]

During April, there had indeed been positive action against the Communist Vietnamese. In an effort to apply pressure, delivery was held up on a Chinese arms shipment which had arrived at Sihanoukville for the Communist forces.[17] Sihanouk's numerous published statements at this time confirm his deep personal concern over the Communist stronghold in the Eastern part of Cambodia. In August 1969, with an estimated 40,000 Communist Vietnamese entrenched in Cambodia, Prince Sihanouk named Lon Nol as his new Prime Minister.

General Lon Nol was a figure of the right, who had previously been Prime Minister during 1966. Although the full story of the internal pressures building up in Cambodia at the end of 1969 and the beginning of 1970 is by no means clear, events now had their own momentum. At the end of 1969, when Lon Nol was out of the country receiving medical treatment, and Prince Sirik Matak was acting for him, there had been a National Congress, a special meeting of Sihanouk's national movement, the Sangkum. A number of observers thought the occasion went badly for Sihanouk.

After this, early in January 1970, there were reports that Sihanouk was unwell. On 6th January, he too left for extended medical treatment in France in advance of planned visits to the Communist leaders in Moscow and Peking to seek their help in securing the withdrawal of North Vietnamese and Viet Cong troops from Cambodia. During his absence the pace quickened, and the published news included the following:

On 31st January, there was an announcement that the State Casino on the waterfront at Phnom Penh would be closed. This was a casino authorised by Sihanouk with gambling facilities for all pockets, and the "percentage" went to the Government. It was a noisy, busy establishment and opposition to it brought together two separate groups: on the one hand those who disapproved of gambling as irreligious and, on the other, those who saw profit for themselves if the State monopoly of gambling were ended and the "industry" returned to private enterprise. The casino was seen by some as an indicator of Sihanouk's authority, and its closure as an important political pointer. Reports of the event must even have reached Peking, as Sihanouk recounts that, on May Day 1970, Mao Tse-tung raised the subject with him. Mao apparently observed that the Cambodian people enjoyed gambling, "it was better the profit go to the State than into the private pocket of gambling house owners".[18] Sihanouk adds, incidentally, that this conversation briefly delayed Mao's appearance as the signal to commence the firework display celebrating May Day; and that this delay led to much press speculation about Mao's health!

On 7th February, a Lebanese cargo aircraft said to contain £3 million worth of medicines for the Viet Cong, was held at Phnom Penh airport. A few days later the flags of Nationalist China and of South Vietnam were officially seen in Phnom Penh for the first time. The occasion was a meeting of the Mekong Committee. On 18th February, General Lon Nol returned from France. On 20th February, the Cambodian government required the suspension "for national security" of diplomatic bag traffic and, two days later, the country's bank note issue was changed. The effect of this was to render worthless the large stocks of Cambodian money held by the Viet Cong. On 4th March, the official news bulletin in Phnom Penh published details of alleged smuggling by Oum Manourine, the Minister for Ground Defence. Oum Manourine was a half-brother of Princess Monique, Sihanouk's wife, and was widely regarded as one of the people whom Sihanouk had left to "watch the shop" while he was away. The smear, true or false, was now close to the top, and in a few days' time would focus on Monique's partially Vietnamese origin (unpopular in various Cambodian circles) before turning fully on to Sihanouk himself.

On 6th March, the bulletin reported visits by General Lon Nol to Eastern Cambodia "to inspect Cambodian troops defending Cambodian territory against the Viet Cong". On 8th March, some anti-Viet Cong demonstrations took place in the border area. On 10th March, Prince Sihanouk said in Paris that "Communist Vietnamese strength in Cambodia is being reduced through the intervention of our Socialist friends in Peking", and announced that Pham Van Dong, the North Vietnamese Prime Minister would be visiting Phnom Penh during May.

The climax came the next day. On 11th March, the Embassies of the Provisional Revolutionary Government (Viet Cong) and of North Vietnam were sacked and left burning after well organised anti-Viet Cong demonstrations, and there was widespread belief in Phnom Penh that the man in charge of the demonstrations was Major Lon Non, a younger brother of Lon Nol, the Prime Minister. The National Assembly met and expressed support for the demonstration. From Paris, Prince Sihanouk sent a cable criticising the demonstration.[19] The government of General Lon Nol took little notice and, on 13th March, issued the form of an ultimatum requiring the withdrawal of North Vietnamese and Viet Cong troops from Cambodia by dawn on 15th March. It was an ultimatum from the weak to the strong. Unsurprisingly, it was ineffective, except perhaps to sharpen hostility still further. On 16th March, a first attempt to get Prince Sihanouk denounced by the National Assembly was unsuccessful. But the pressure was on. Next day, Oum Manourine resigned and, on 18th March, the National Assembly announced their dismissal of Prince Sihanouk from his post as Head of State. Prince Sihanouk heard the news in Moscow. He continued his planned journey the same day to Peking where he was met by Chou En-lai. A few days later, Sihanouk announced from Peking his intention to establish a government in exile. Meanwhile in Phnom Penh, where the Lon Nol Government had closed down all external communications on 18th March, and news reaching the international press was restricted, the American Embassy faced an addition problem of unusual diplomatic complexity.

On 15th March a U.S. munitions ship, the Columbia Eagle had been brought into Cambodian water by two hippy hi-jacker crew members. Amidst the turmoil of the coup, Mr. Rives, the hardpressed United States Chargé d'Affaires, strenuously sought local United Nations and independent diplomatic verification of the genuine nature of the incident, and of the cargo (of napalm). Inevitably, however, there were rumours of guns on board. Equally inevitably, the episode was latched on to by those hostile to America who were determined to suggest CIA complicity in the coup against Sihanouk.

Some words from Michael Leifer's *Peace and War in Cambodia* are relevant to the background:[20] "The protracted struggle, which has transformed the condition of Cambodia will be seen to have arisen only in part from the presence on Cambodian territory of the forces of the Vietnamese Communists. The precipitating factor was an internal conflict between Prince Sihanouk and members of his government led by General Lon Nol and Prince Sirik Matak, who resented the suffocating omnipotence of the Cambodian Head of State."

In the later 1960s, Prince Sihanouk super-impressed his presence in Cambodia. His voice was always on the radio. His pictures were in the newspapers every day. The films on show in Phnom Penh were those he himself directed. Indeed, he frequently used these films to poke fun at the frailties and foibles of the Cambodian upper crust below his own Royal level. At Palace showings of his films, Sihanouk would contribute a personal running commentary about the goings on portrayed. Sometimes he even used members of the upper crust as actors to portray venal characters like themselves. It was a game with obvious pitfalls. But after almost thirty years of great authority, it may have been compulsive behaviour given the nature of Prince Sihanouk's character. The consequences were to prove tragic both for the Prince and for his country. Sihanouk was the only Cambodian of authority capable of the high wire act needed to keep the worst of the Vietnam war away from Cambodia. He sought to save the Cambodian people from suffering. Unfortunately for him and for his country his personal ways made him too many enemies near the top within his own State.

Baron Walter von Marschall who headed the Federal German mission in Phnom Penh for almost five years has shrewdly summed up the deposition of Sihanouk in a few lines:[21] "The decisive element in the coup and its overriding cause were the determination of a small but influential group to secure the profits of power ... they stirred anti-Vietnamese sentiment in the country only in order to gain popular support for their coup against Prince Sihanouk ... and foolishly let themselves be swept away by the tide of anti-Vietnamese feeling they created."

In the Spring of 1970, the Americans knew that Sihanouk was limiting arms supplies to the Communist Vietnamese. They also knew that he was seeking help in Moscow and Peking to ease the Communist weight on Cambodia; and that he was about to accept an American Ambassador. With this background, would those at the top in Washington have wanted Sihanouk's downfall? Action lower down, American like any other, can rarely be fully probed. But to most of those on the spot, a top American initiative appeared very far indeed from the open and shut case taken for granted in a number of circles elsewhere.

On this very basic issue of United States involvement in the March 1970 events, Baron von Marschall's words are as follows:[22] "Since it has often been claimed that the CIA staged the coup d'état of 18th March 1970 it should be mentioned that all the events that led to the overthrow of Sihanouk can be fully and satisfactorily explained on purely Cambodian grounds." Von Marschall adds that the Soviet and other Eastern European diplomats who remained in the Cambodian capital long after the deposition of Prince Sihanouk, "repeatedly expressed amusement at naive belief in the omnipotent rôle of the CIA." This was so.

[1] Johnson, p. 135.

[2] *The American University, Cambodia*, p. 204.

[3] Sihanouk: *My war with the C.I.A.*, p. 87.

[4] *Ibid.* p. 107.

[5] *Ibid.* p. 110.

[5] *Ibid.* p. 110.

[6] *C.O.I. The Khmer Republic*, p. 15.

[7] *The American University, Cambodia*, p. 217.

[8] *C.O.I. The Khmer Republic*, p. 17.

[9] *Ibid.* p. 17.

[10] *The American University*, p. 208.

[11] *Ibid.* p. 208.

[12] *American University*, p. 213.

[13] *American University*, p. 213.

[14] Sangkum, February 1970.

[15] *American University*, p. 218.

[16]*South East Asia Quarterly,* Winter 1971, p. 59.

[17]*American University,* p. 314.

[18]Sihanouk, p. 209.

[19]*American University,* p. 209.

[20]Leifer: *Peace and War in Cambodia, South East Asia Quarterly,* Winter 1971, p. 59.

[21]Dr. Walther Baron von Marschall, 1975 *RCDS,* p. 97.

[22]*Ibid.* p. 98.

The army going to war by bus — Cambodia, April 1970.

Repairing a road after Communist attack — Cambodia, May 1970.

Above and below: Sacking of the Communist Vietnamese Embassies. DRV (Hanoi) and NLF (Vietcong) — Phnom Penh, 11 March 1970.

Khmer soldiers (Artillery Division) seen relaxing here — Cambodia, late 1970.

Cambodia — Vietnam border area (Parrots Beak). Block-house left over from the French War.

Boy soldiers of the Lon Nol army guarding the Bat Hoay Bridge — Cambodia, late 1971.

18 The Nature of the Cambodian War: 1970 – 1975

FOR a few days after the coup the new Cambodia was left in peace. The Government repeated its determination to secure the country's territorial integrity, but stressed its peaceful intentions. British help was sought to secure the return of the International Control Commission to police the frontier. Lon Nol also told the international press that he hoped the United Nations might be able to achieve a peaceful solution to the country's problems. Then came the North Vietnamese reaction from the frontier strongholds. It was direct attack with the aim of overthrowing the new Cambodian Government. The first of the many journalists to become casualties of the Cambodian war lost their lives. Among them was Sean Flynn the son of the film star Errol Flynn. Elements of three regular North Vietnamese divisions pushed forward and, daily during April 1970, there were reports of their troops closing in on Phnom Penh.

By mid-April, all of North-East Cambodia was in their hands. On 20th April, the Phnom Penh Government announced that the North Vietnamese now held several positions within thirty miles of the capital, and that Vietnamese in Cambodia were helping the North Vietnamese and their Viet Cong allies. Patriotic sentiment and latent anti-Vietnamese feeling among the Khmers burgeoned. Large numbers of students joined up to reinforce the small Cambodian Army, whose effectives were barely half the size of the North Vietnamese military strength in the country. The hundred thousand or more Vietnamese in Phnom Penh were rounded up and restricted, and a number suffered harm. There were days of drama. The international press, including the London Times, published photographs of dozens of dead bodies, bound together, floating in the Mekong. It was accepted in Phnom Penh that these included the leaders of the Viet Cong cells in the city. The Government of General Lon Nol, which had given itself the title "The Salvation Government," nailed its colours to the mast as the Communist threat to the capital developed further.

Now, for a while, there appeared an impressive unity between government and people. Whatever happened before and after, these were days when it really did seem that the Cambodian conflict was a

167

classic case of a small nation battling for its existence. It certainly seemed this way, for example, to Norman Kirk, who visited Phnom Penh at this time, shortly before becoming Prime Minister of New Zealand. In the early days there seemed no reason to doubt Lon Nol's patriotism. Nor, at this time, was there reason to believe his leadership would decay to ignominy.[1] This came later.

In April 1970, there was certainly an invasion of Cambodia. It was a North Vietnamese invasion, spearheaded by regular army troops of great military skill and experience. Against them, was a hastily recruited student army which fought bravely but lacked training and supplies. Whatever feelings these young men may have had towards Prince Sihanouk, they believed they were fighting for the existence of their country against its traditional enemy. Indeed, when Prince Sihanouk associated himself on 25th April 1970 with Pham Van Dong, the North Vietnamese leader, and with some others, in pledging support for the "liberation" of Cambodia, this action greatly damaged him within the country. In a sense, Sihanouk appeared to have joined the enemy. It was his association with the April declaration of the "Summit Conference of Indo-Chinese Peoples" which provided the "legal" basis for continued North Vietnamese intervention in Cambodia.

Now came the event which captured the headlines and bought time for the new government in Phnom Penh. But it was bought at the high price of obscuring the reality of the North Vietnamese attack. On 30th April (already 1st May in South East Asia), President Nixon announced joint United States/South Vietnamese operations inside Cambodia "to clean out enemy sanctuaries".[2] This United States intervention was limited to a twenty mile border area which had long been occupied by the Communist Vietnamese. President Nixon stressed that this was no "invasion of Cambodia" and, on 8th May, announced that all United States troops would be withdrawn by 30th June. Cambodia was to be no Vietnam. Colonel Alexander Haig (later to become General Haig), who at this time was an Assistant to Dr. Kissinger, visited Phnom Penh to assess the requirement.

On 30th June President Nixon reported to the American people as follows:[3]

(a) There would be no United States ground force personnel in Cambodia apart from those at the Embassy (and on this there was agreement with Congress that Embassy strength would not exceed 200).
(b) There would be no United States advisers with Cambodian units; but
(c) there would be certain agreed air operations.

In this 30th June report the President stressed that the United States Government "had neither connection with, nor knowledge of the events leading to the overthrow of Prince Sihanouk". He also made known the options he had considered as the Communist pressure on Phnom Penh had mounted during April. The President summed up the alternatives:

(a) Do nothing; which would have increased the risk to the remaining U.S. forces in South Vietnam and have retarded Vietnamisation.

(b) Intervene massively; which would not have been realistic as the United States had no wish to get drawn into the permanent direct defence of Cambodia.

(c) Attack the sanctuaries; limited in time (two months) and depth (twenty miles inside Cambodia). This course would aid the United States troop withdrawal programme from Vietnam as well as having other advantages.

The report went on to inform the people of the United States that a number of major operations had been launched with a mixed force of 32,000 American troops and 48,000 South Vietnamese troops. The objective was "supplies rather than personnel". This last may have been a rationalisation after the event. The Headquarters of the Communist Vietnamese in the South, COSVN, was sought but not found. Even so, the haul from the two month operation was considerable. The material captured included about 25,000 personal weapons, and about 2,500 crew served weapons, rocket launchers, mortars and so on. In addition, considerable quantities of ammunition were taken.

Yet, with the benefit of hindsight, the governing consequence was probably the effect upon American opinion. And this was not a success story for the Administration. The operation did indeed cause damage to the Communist Vietnamese logistic arrangements. But it failed with the American press and public opinion. In addition, as far as Cambodia was concerned, there were some worrying side effects. As the Communist Vietnamese retreated in the face of the attack upon them from the East, they spread deeper within Cambodia. The presence of South Vietnamese troops within the country also caused problems:[4] "despite government to government cordiality, Cambodian popular resentment manifested itself against South Vietnamese forces".

In a number of cases, the South Vietnamese undoubtedly behaved like an invading army (the distaste between the Khmers and the Vietnamese was mutual), and, after the mid-1970 operations, the Phnom Penh Government sought to do without Saigon help. Later on, Saigon forces did indeed try to capture Kratie in the North East from the Communists. But the attack, code-named *Total Victory*, turned out badly. Its lively commander, General Do Cao Tri was killed, and the operation ended with considerable loss of tanks and artillery to the Communists. Indeed in the aftermath, a number of Cambodian commentators in Phnom Penh came close to accusing the Saigon forces of helping the enemy.

Until the end of 1970, the anti-Vietnamese sentiment of the Cambodians sustained them against the regular North Vietnamese forces, estimated to be of the order of 50,000, who were seeking to grip the country by cutting communications from the capital. The situation continued to be fairly presented as invasion rather than Civil War, and, despite set-backs such as a very effective North Vietnamese sapper raid on Phnom Penh airport, the Cambodian armed forces maintained their spirit into the early part of 1971. Thereafter came decline. The leadership was not matching the courage of the individual Khmer soldiers. In the autumn of 1971, Cambodian Army morale suffered a grave set-back in an operation called Chenla II. This operation was intended to clear the road between Phnom Penh and Kompong Thom, a besieged provincial capital about a hundred miles away to the North. The Phnom Penh Government troops suffered heavy casualties on a high exposed road. Their failure was generally ascribed to poor direction and leadership, and tactical shortcomings in the face of experienced and highly mobile troops of the North Vietnamese First Division. The battle was one where the Communists let twenty thousand Cambodian soldiers advance up Highway 6 (the road to Kompong Thom) without opposition. And, in the way of the old Cambodia, families followed their menfolk. Then, when the supply lines were stretched thin, the Vietnamese chopped them up. The Cambodians were forced into enclaves which shrank and fell despite heavy American air support. A critical blow against the Cambodian Army was the destruction of an important bridge at Batheay about half way between the towns of Skoun and Kompong Thom. In this watery area the alertness of the young bridge guards failed against the Communist sappers. The final upshot was disaster. Baron von Marschall describes it as the Cambodian 'Stalingrad', and the turning point of the war.[5]

During 1971, there were also political and military problems of command and authority. These stemmed from Lon Nol's partial incapacitation by a stroke. 1970 had been a year of hope despite shortages of arms and material. 1971 turned into a year of disappointment for the Phnom Penh régime. Although the Army (Forces Armées Nationales Khmères–FANK) was bigger and had more equipment, it was increasingly being cast in the mould of the American method in Vietnam, and this was not necessarily a gain. In the early days,

Jonathan Ladd, a former Green Beret Colonel, who headed a small political/military group at the American Embassy, was widely regarded as an architect of the FANK success achieved in 1970. His watchword had been simplicity. His later problems with some of the military establishment in Washington have been described in detail in the press. Likewise the difficulties and stresses on Emory Swank, the conscientious and courageous United States Ambassador who had a very narrow escape from a Viet Cong assassination squad.

After the end of the Chenla II operation in December 1971, both the political and the military initiative passed to the Communists. The Red Khmer movement, under Khieu Samphan and others, began to be a force in its own right. What had begun as resistance to invasion now turned into Civil War. Once again, a balanced picture of the situation at this time is presented in the American University handbook on Cambodia.[6] "In 1972, popular political attitudes appeared to be in a state of unprecedented fluidity. Contributing factors were the prevailing uncertainty about the direction of the war against the Communist Vietnamese intruders; insecurity engendered by the alternate cycles of advance and retreat between the opposing forces of the government (FANK) and the insurgent (National United Front of Cambodia — (FUNK) forces, and the increasingly credible show of strength demonstrated by the local insurgent forces. These factors were responsible, to a degree for popular disinclination to become openly identified with either of the country's two principal political forces — the Republican Government in Phnom Penh and Prince Sihanouk's Government in Peking.

At this stage, there was still an important twist which distinguished the Cambodian conflict from the straightforward Communist/anti-Communist conflict in Vietnam. This was the public position of Prince Sihanouk in relation to Communism. In April 1970, in the month after his deposition, he had indeed associated himself with the Communist North Vietnamese action against Cambodia. Even so, he said in a subsequent broadcast from Peking, that he did not wish Cambodia to be "anyone's satellite". He declared "I may admire Communism but I am not a Communist. I am a Nationalist Cambodian like my ancestors". Sihanouk's Government still remained a Royal government. Its initial letters G.R.U.N.K. stood for the Gouvernement Royal d'Union Nationale du Kampuchea. But, from 1972 onwards, events moved increasingly against there ever being return to the Royal values of the past.

In Phnom Penh itself, the Lon Nol régime had sought to revert to a number of the practices of their former Head of State. Sihanouk liked to style himself a 'God King'. Those around Lon Nol increasingly sought to present him as a 'God President'. And, with remoteness at the top, an increasing burden of the war fell on the mass of common people. In the main these bore their trials with fortitude. But those who within the country were categorised as 'intellectuals' protested against what they saw as continued feudalism. Two years before it had been "down with Sihanouk". Now, they saw Lon Nol in the same light. Some left for France. But a number joined the Khmer Rouge.

During the 1960s, Sihanouk had used the term Khmer Rouge to describe the relatively small guerilla groupings in Cambodia which were hostile to him. To begin with, they were unorganised and separate. The few thousand Cambodian Communists who had joined Hanoi after the 1954 Geneva Conference had mostly stayed there. There were also those who had broken with Sihanouk around 1960. This group now provided a hard core for a Khmer Rouge movement directed against Lon Nol. Their numbers grew from those who volunteered to join them. Also from those who were pressed. In 1972 and 1973, the Communist cause in Cambodia passed to their hands. They were a formidable force. Now there really was Civil War.

1972 was a year when the Communist effort once again concentrated on cutting communications, and the Mekong river route into Phnom Penh became increasingly important. Then, in January 1973, came the Vietnam Peace Agreement. One of its articles (Article 20) required that foreign countries end military activities in Cambodia and Laos. This article was not observed by either party and, for some months, there was very heavy American bombing in support of the Phnom Penh Government. Mr. Elliot Richardson, the United States Secretary of Defence said:[8] "The constitutional authority rests on the circumstances that we are coming out of a ten year period of conflict. What we were doing is to encourage the observance of the Peace Agreement by engaging in air action at the request of the Cambodian Government". However, the United States Congress took a different view. By their order this bombing was ended on 15th August 1973.

In the dry season, at the turn of the year, the Khmer Rouge carried out a direct attack on Phnom Penh. But they suffered heavily and failed to achieve their objective. Twelve months later, a more methodical attack ended the war. This time, the river route to the capital was made the first target. The lifeline was successfully cut. Thereafter, the Khmer Rouge tightened their grip around the capital. Whatever opportunity there might have been for a reasonable transfer of power through Sihanouk was now past. On 1st April 1975, Lon Nol flew out of Phnom Penh leaving it to others to try to negotiate. According to General Saukam Khoy, Lon Nol had required a payment of $U.S. one million from his country's Treasury.[9] But a number of the other leaders of the stricken Republic showed high courage and character.

Long Boret, the last Prime Minister, who was very well respected and left a charming wife and family, had accompanied Lon Nol out of the country. But, although on the 'Death List' of the Khmer Rouge, he believed it was his duty to try to provide for an orderly transfer of power. He returned to Phnom Penh, and was killed by the Khmer Rouge when they took the city on 17th April 1975.

Prince Sirik Matak, the patrician figure long opposed to Prince Sihanouk, also stayed to the end. John Gunther Dean, the American Ambassador, offered him a seat on the helicopter flight which evacuated the United States Embassy on 12th April. Sirik Matak replied to the offer in these terms:

> Dear Excellency and Friend,
>   I thank you sincerely for your letter and your offer to transport me to freedom. I cannot, alas, leave in such a cowardly fashion. As for you, and in particular your great country, I never believed for a moment that you would have the sentiment of abandoning a people which have chosen liberty. You have refused us protection and we can do nothing about it. You leave, and it is my wish that you and your country will find happiness under the sky. But mark it well, that if I shall die here on the spot and in the country I love, it is too bad because we are all born and must die one day. I have only committed the mistake of believing in Americans. Please accept, Excellency, my dear friend, my faithful and friendly sentiments.

According to a number of witnesses, Sirik Matak maintained his bearing to the last. After a brief respite in the French Embassy, the time came for him to meet the new masters of Cambodia. A Khmer Rouge truck carrying an escort drove up. Sirik Matak who was neatly turned out gave his stick to one of the escorts "as if the soldier were a valet". Then he was driven off. Later he was killed.

The tragedy of the taking of Phnom Penh; of the forced exodus and of the killings and the other human misery, has been detailed in the world's newspapers. At the end, as at the very beginning, it was a Cambodian event.

[1] Von Marschall, p. 126.

[2] *American University, Cambodia*, p. 219.

[3] Public papers of President Nixon, 1970, p. 529.

[4] *American University, Cambodia*, p. 212.

[5] Von Marschall, p. 108.

[6] *American University, Cambodia,* p. 199.

[7] Von Marschall, p. 113.

[8] *Far Eastern Economic Review,* 30 April 1973, p. 15.

[9] Von Marschall, p. 115.

19   1969 – 1973:
Diplomatic Purpose

D ESPITE the shadow of Watergate, President Nixon's achievements in the field of foreign policy remain widely recognised. Pride of place is usually accorded to the final extrication of the United States from their ten years of direct military involvement in Indo-China. The course to this objective was announced in some detail early in President Nixon's first term, and was codified in his February 1970 message to Congress, *A New Strategy for Peace.*[1]

In his introduction to this new strategy, the President stressed the turning point now reached in world affairs:[2] "The post-war period in international relations has ended; then new nations were being born, often in turmoil and uncertainty; today these nations have their own spirit" .... "Once it was feared they would become fertile ground for Communist penetration; this fear misjudged their national pride" .... "Then we were confronted by a monolithic Communist world: today the nature of that world has changed ... its solidarity has been broken by the powerful forces of nationalism: the Marxist dream of international Communist unity has disintegrated". "Then the United States had a monopoly or overwhelming superiority of nuclear weapons: today the Soviet Union and the United States can inflict unacceptable damage on each other, no matter who strikes first". In this changing world, said the President, peace indeed called for strength; but also it called for willingness to negotiate.

President Nixon then referred to the "Nixon doctrine," first enunciated at Guam in the Western Pacific on 26th July 1969. The message from Guam had been that the United States would continue to participate in the defence of her allies and her friends. But there now had to be genuine partnership. The United States would no longer carry the whole burden for others.[3]

President Nixon's various public statements[4] emphasised the assessments made by his Administration. When it assumed office at the beginning of 1969 it was clear there was no easy choice on Indo-China. "The escalation of the war which would certainly deepen the internal division within the United States would not ensure success." Yet the immediate withdrawal strongly urged in a number of quarters was not so simple. In Nixon's own words:[5] "Precipitate disengagement, without regard to consequences, would have made impossible our efforts to forge a new foreign policy: it might have been domestically popular for a short time, but, as its consequences became clear, the agony of recrimination would have replaced the agony of war: overseas this course would have shaken the trust of our friends and have earned the contempt of our adversaries. We could not begin to build new partnerships by turning our back on people who had come to count on our support. And we could not set out to negotiate with adversaries by abandoning allies. There were however two possible courses of action which would be internationally responsible and responsive to domestic opinion. The fastest and most decisive course was to negotiate a settlement to end the war for all participants: we progressively defined the terms of such a settlement ... however we needed an alternative: thus we launched the process of progressively turning over defence responsibilities to the South Vietnamese and thereby reducing U.S. involvement. We also hoped this course would stimulate negotiation."

The U.S. objectives for South Vietnam were now clear. Washington had two main lines of policy: one of them negotiation, the other, Vietnamisation. The complaint from Indo-China, from the French years as well as the years of American build up, about lack of political direction and clear objectives could not be levelled against the Nixon Administration.

In September 1969, during the course of his address to the 24th session of the General Assembly, the President had said: "The people of Vietnam, North and South alike, have demonstrated heroism enough to last a century ... the people of Vietnam, North and South, have endured an unspeakable weight of suffering for a generation: they deserve a better fate." And, in the same speech, spelling out the Nixon Doctrine:[6]

"It is not my belief that the way to peace is by giving up our friends or letting down our allies. On the contrary, our aim is to place America's international commitments on a sustainable long term basis, to encourage local and regional initiative, to foster national independence and self sufficiency, and by so doing to strengthen the total fabric of peace."

At the time of this speech, the Americans had already (in May 1969) offered peace proposals embracing mutual withdrawal from the South of all non-South Vietnamese forces, and, alongside this withdrawal, internationally supervised elections.[7] The object was to let the people of the South decide their own future by secret ballot. They could become Communist should this be their free choice.

American diplomatic effort contributed, as well, to the parallel peace offer made by President Thieu on 11th July 1969. This envisaged free, internationally supervised elections and a mixed Electoral Commission on which all parties, including the Viet Cong, could be represented.[8] In 1969, the United States also took the three major steps which various well wishers had counselled would lead quickly to serious negotiations, namely:[9]

(a) A halt to the bombing of the North.
(b) The commencement of the withdrawal of U.S. forces from the South.
(c) Acceptance of the National Liberation Front (the Viet Cong) as a party to the negotiations.

During the year, there was, however, no significant response from Hanoi on negotiation. Vietnamisation prospered better. On the one hand, U.S. forces were cut by about one hundred thousand men: on the other, about half a million guns were supplied to the South Vietnamese Peoples Self Defence Force, the local Home Guard.[10] At the time, this seemed a vote of confidence by both the Americans and by President Thieu in the anti-Communist spirit of some of the most populous areas of the countryside of South Vietnam.

For the newspaper readers of the West, 1970 was the year of the Cambodian War. The American involvement imposed additional stress. At the same time, the offer to negotiate with Hanoi remained on the table. The drive toward Vietnamisation was also sustained. Once again, however, negotiations were sterile. The Communist demand was for something more than the elections in the South. They also sought that the Americans themselves should ensure that President Thieu was not a participant.[11]

Meanwhile, Vietnamisation appeared to be going ahead well. By the end of the year, American troop strength was nearly a quarter of a million men below its peak. At the same time, South Vietnamese forces continued to expand: indeed the Air Force of South Vietnam was on its way to becoming one of the largest Air Forces in the world, apart from those of the super powers. Vietnamisation showed through in the casualty lists.[12] During 1968, American dead had averaged more than a thousand a month. Inside two years, the figure had come down to about two hundred a month. Contact with the other side lay increasingly with the Saigon forces. The South Vietnamese army, which now numbered more than one million men, "was conducting twenty major combat engagements for every one involving U.S. forces: by the end of the year,

U.S. forces had shifted essentially to a defensive and base security rôle."[13] The fact that average monthly American draft calls were now down to 7,500, one quarter the 1968 figure, was further evidence that the burden of Vietnam was being lifted from the back of the American people. Even so, it did not appear that South Vietnam was about to fall to the Communists.

The really major development, which was about to come, was bound up in Nixon's reiteration that the configuration of power which had emerged from the Second World War was gone. With it had also gone the parameters which had determined United States foreign policy since 1945. Perhaps the words were drafted by Dr. Kissinger. But they were spoken by the President. His message read:[14] "Around the globe, East and West, the rigid bipolar world has given way to the fluidity of a new era of multilateral diplomacy. It is an increasingly heterogeneous and complex world, and the dangers of local conflict are magnified. But so too are the opportunities for creative diplomacy". The next year would see the United States seeking and exploiting such opportunities to the full.

1971 was justly held by President Nixon to be a watershed year. The new look, foreshadowed in his first two foreign policy reports to Congress, now became reality. Among the principal achievements were:

(a) An opening to China:[15] "The initiative was the fruit of almost three years of the most painstaking work ... it represents a necessary and giant step toward the creation of a stable structure of world peace."

(b) The beginning of a new relationship with the Soviet Union based on super power interests:[16] "We have succeeded in giving momentum to the prospects for more constructive relations through a series of concrete agreements which get at the basic causes of tension between our two countries."

(c) The laying of foundations for more realistic relationships with the rest of the world:[17] "Our friendships are constant, but the means by which they are mutually expressed must be adjusted as world conditions change: the continuity and vigour of our alliance require that our friends assume greater responsibility for our common endeavours."

The overall American objective was a stable peace.[18] "There was an exigent need to reshape the American rôle in Vietnam so that it contributed to, rather than hindered progress toward the national goal of stable world peace." In plain words, there was a need that Indo-China should fall into its place as a modest rather than a major piece on the chessboard of world affairs. On 15th July, there was the announcement from Washington and Peking which caught the imagination of the world:

"Premier Chou En-lai and Doctor Henry Kissinger, President Nixon's Assistant for National Security Affairs held talks in Peking from 9th to 11th July 1971. Knowing of President Nixon's expressed desire to visit the Peoples Republic of China, Premier Chou En-lai, on behalf of the government of the Peoples Republic of China has extended an invitation to President Nixon to visit China at an appropriate date before May 1972. President Nixon has accepted the invitation with pleasure. The meeting between the leaders of China and the United States is to seek the normalisation of relations between the two countries, and also to exchange views on questions of concern to the two sides."

1971 was, additionally, the year in which President Nixon announced that he would also be visiting Moscow during the course of 1972.[19] He would be the first President of the United States to make the journey. The leadership in Hanoi may have begun to wonder if their international support was being undercut by the diplomatic effort now being mounted by the United States administration.

Meanwhile, U.S. policy toward Hanoi still remained based on the twin prongs of readiness to negotiate to end the war, alongside progressive strengthening of the armed forces of South Vietnam to enable them to stand on their own. And, at this stage, Washington revealed that with the knowledge and approval of President Thieu, Dr. Kissinger had travelled to Paris for secret meetings with the North Vietnamese on twelve occasions between August 1969 and September 1971.[20] Kissinger had met seven times with both Le Duc Tho, of Hanoi's political leadership, and Xuan Thuy, head of the North Vietnamese delegation in Paris: Kissinger had also met Xuan Thuy on five other occasions. The secret talks had indeed been impressively secret. Even senior American officials at the main peace talks were unaware of what was going on.

Unlike the formal Paris peace talks taking place at the same time, the secret talks offered no element of "scoring". The American interest was to achieve a settlement which would stick — one which Hanoi might genuinely wish to keep. And, as the secret talks went on, the Americans shaped their offers increasingly toward the expressed Hanoi wish for a comprehensive settlement. Always, however, discussion came back to the same stumbling block. Hanoi consistently sought active United States co-operation in overthrowing the leadership of President Thieu in Saigon. They had similarly sought French co-operation against Ngo Dinh Diem, almost twenty years before, in 1954 and 1955, in the immediate aftermath of the Geneva Conference. Shades perhaps too of the days in 1963 when a U.S. dimension had indeed settled the fate of Ngo Dinh Diem.

In May 1971, the United States offered total American withdrawal in return for a prisoner exchange and an Indo-China ceasefire, leaving other outstanding issues for resolution by the Indo-Chinese parties themselves. This was insufficient for Hanoi who continued to insist that political questions had to be fully incorporated in any settlement, and the Hanoi nine point plan tabled in June included, as an integral term, the demand for the removal of the existing Saigon government.[21]

By now, the existence of two sets of talks in Paris, one declared, the other secret, were beginning to complicate the American position. During July the Communist side *publicly* presented another set of peace proposals, the Seven Points of the National Liberation Front. This focussed on South Vietnam. Hanoi's secret proposals at this time were covering the whole of Indo-China. The United States were faced therefore at the same time with a secret Communist proposal on their private channel which differed from the Communist proposal of the open negotiations.

The United States were told that the North Vietnamese interest lay mainly in their secret proposals. But, as time passed, the North Vietnamese themselves berated the U.S. administration for not responding to the public proposals of the National Liberation Front of South Vietnam. This increased domestic difficulty for the President's administration. A number of Americans felt strongly that their government was not doing all it should to achieve a negotiated settlement. Both for domestic reasons, and also to show forcefully to Hanoi the U.S. commitment to its secret negotiating position, the American President now made public the hitherto secret negotiations with the Vietnamese Communists.[22]

Meanwhile, Vietnamisation continued steadily forward. By the end of 1971 U.S. troop levels were down by nearly 400,000 from their 1968 peak figure of 550,000 when General Westmoreland was still bidding for more. Moreover, publicly forecast reductions would soon bring the U.S. force level down to 70,000. The American Administration understandably drummed home the statistics. From the peak average of one thousand American dead a month, the figure at the end of 1970 had come down to about two hundred. By the end of 1971, this key figure was down to less than fifty.[23] American air attack sorties in South Vietnam also declined dramatically, as the strong South Vietnamese Air Force increasingly took the weight of local operations.

Perhaps most significant of all, the South Vietnamese had attempted during 1971 their first major independent offensive operation, Lamson 719. This operation into Southern Laos in February 1971 somewhat parallelled the Cambodian sanctuary operations of the previous year. On both occasions, the objective was to cut communications, destroy supplies and blunt Communist military strength. In February 1971, the Saigon offensive directly straddled the Ho Chi Minh trail. It was a complex operation mounted in difficult terrain against a well prepared enemy. Adverse weather, which affected supporting air operations, added to the task. In addition, there was unexpected contact with North Vietnamese tanks. The operation which had only very limited success also aroused controversy in the Western press.

Yet, in fairness, it should be noted that not a single South Vietnamese soldier went anywhere except where tens of thousands of North Vietnamese soldiers had been entrenched for years.[24]

It now seemed that South Vietnam might show the capacity and resolution to maintain its own national identity.

The Saigon government's state of mind was reflected in the eight point proposal offered in Paris on 25th January 1972, with the full agreement of President Thieu.[25] The proposal called for respect for the Geneva Agreements of 1954 and 1962; for settlement by the Indo-Chinese parties themselves of their differences, including the rôle of the North Vietnamese forces — and for international supervision. Its main elements provided that within six months of agreement there would be:

(a) complete withdrawal of all U.S. and allied forces from South Vietnam;
(b) exchange of prisoners throughout Indo-China;
(c) ceasefire throughout Indo-China;
(d) new Presidential elections in South Vietnam.

The provisions of the proposal regarding Presidential elections in South Vietnam were in themselves of special interest.

(a) The election would be organised by an independent body representing all political forces in South Vietnam, including the Viet Cong.
(b) The election would be internationally supervised.
(c) President Thieu would resign one month before the election.
(d) All U.S. troops would be out of South Vietnam before the election.

There does not appear to have been any direct North Vietnamese response to the 25th January offer. But a sign of Communist Vietnamese movement on the issue most central to the mood of the

American people had appeared at the end of 1971. The several hundred men of the U.S. Armed Forces held prisoner by the Communists were the "Achilles' heel" of the American negotiating position. Alongside the normal diplomatic pressure, Colonel Frank Borman, the distinguished astronaut, travelled abroad to seek support for the cause of the prisoners. But apparently without success. There had also been a dramatic but unsuccessful commando rescue attempt at Son Tay in November 1971. This may however have been a failure for the best. It is difficult to believe that the majority of the prisoners could have been extricated without casualties. In addition, those left behind would almost certainly have suffered more, and, through the political mists, a possible end of captivity could now dimly be perceived. Shortly before Christmas 1971, the Communists released a large number of letters from the prisoners of war. In some cases these letters provided the first evidence that the men concerned were still alive. This move was aimed directly at United States public opinion.

At the same time, Hanoi pursued its military aim within Vietnam. The four Military Regions of South Vietnam were numbered One to Four, from North to South. And, whatever the military activity elsewhere, it was always appreciated by Saigon and by the U.S. Military Command that direct Communist attack across the demilitarised zone into Military Region One was a high card which Hanoi would play if circumstances were ripe. In plain words, the card was open invasion by large scale regular elements of the North Vietnamese army: repetition of the North Korean attack on the South.

The government of North Vietnam sensed an opportunity in the Spring of 1972. At this time, the United States were fully committed to Vietnamisation, and a Presidential election was due in the Autumn. The date also bore on U.S. relations with China and with Russia. During February, President Nixon had visited China. In May, he was to visit the Soviet Union. Toward both these friends of Hanoi, U.S. policy was now one of détente. The leaders of North Vietnam may have calculated that the American reaction to an attack across the 17th parallel would be minimal.

On 30th March 1972, General Giap's troops poured through the demilitarised zone established nearly twenty years before at Geneva. It was a very heavy attack indeed. There was the back up of modern ground war, including tanks and artillery. Shortly afterwards, Giap's army captured Quang Tri, the first provincial capital in South Vietnam to fall to them. The old imperial capital at Hué, which had suffered so heavily during the Tet offensive of 1968 was once again threatened. In the South there was also strong Communist activity, notably near An Loc.

This was the long foreseen conventional war and, in the past, strong American formations had been posted in Military Region One to "guard the bolt". Because of Vietnamisation these American formations were no longer in the line, and, although strong U.S. air support was put into the battle, there was anxiety for a while that the South Vietnamese Army might not be able to hold the attack from the North. But despite heavy casualties the South Vietnamese held, and after prolonged and very heavy fighting, Quang Tri was eventually recaptured from the Communists.

As the military action deepened, the United States sought de-escalation through diplomatic channels.[26] A variety of alternatives were suggested: mutual de-escalation; a de facto ceasefire; some partial withdrawal of North Vietnamese forces: and also more comprehensive solutions for peace. These proposals were all rejected. On the North Vietnamese side, the argument was that it was the United States which was the aggressor: the United States had no right to be involved at all.

In President Nixon's view, the moment was now crucial. It was the eve of his visit to Moscow. In his own words, "The United States could not passively acquiesce in all out aggression fuelled by the arms of outside powers and conducted in disregard of international agreements and understandings .... The enemy attacks challenged America's credibility and thus the chances of stability around the world ... How could the President of the United States go to a summit meeting while an ally was being overrun with the help of arms supplied by the country he was visiting?" To use the descriptive Asian term, was Mr. Nixon's America a paper tiger?

On 8th May, Nixon announced the resumption of air and naval attacks on North Vietnam, "to interdict the flow of troops and material to the South".[27] In addition, the President announced the mining of North Vietnamese ports. This measure had long been advocated by the United States Navy. At the same time, Hanoi was offered a settlement based upon a ceasefire, the return of the American prisoners of war, the withdrawal of all American forces from Vietnam and the cessation of all American military action in Vietnam. Hanoi was also informed of American readiness to continue secret negotiations.

The reaction from Hanoi was in some ways predictable. At home, they sought to harness patriotic opinion against the renewed bombing. On the world stage, they sought to convince the people of the United States, that this new phase of American activity was a major threat to innocent civilian life. The chosen issue was that the American bombing threatened the dykes and dams in the Red River delta.

In some ways this was a flashback to the opening months of the war against the French, twenty-six years before. On that occasion, the

French had to some extent been able to turn the issue to their own advantage by stressing the French effort to maintain the system. The upshot had indeed been an exchange of surprisingly felicitous messages between Ho Chi Minh and General Salan, the French military commander in the North.

This time, the circumstances were of course different. The whole of North Vietnam was in Communist hands, and, with the rainy season due shortly to reach its peak, the leadership in Hanoi no doubt had genuine anxiety about the country's dyke system. Anxiety could also have extended to what the United States might do. It was common sense, therefore, to make an issue in advance, and, despite American official announcements to the effect that the dykes were not being attacked, a few stray American bombs gave Hanoi the propaganda leverage it sought.

Foreign diplomats, visiting journalists, and sympathetic celebrities such as Jane Fonda, were taken to visit the damage, most of it away from Hanoi, where a serious effort to cause harm would have had most effect. The episode is mentioned as an example of the significance of presentation: also as a reminder of the importance of close control of military action in a tight politico-military situation.

The American air attacks were not directed against the dykes. But they were undoubtedly heavy compared to previous attacks. Perhaps because of this, the North Vietnamese decided, during July, to resume the secret negotiations with the Americans in Paris. Their negotiating position continued to retain a core unacceptable to the Americans, the imposition in Saigon of a coalition government inclined toward Communist control. Again to quote President Nixon:[28] "Until October 1972, therefore, the basic stumbling block remained North Vietnam's demand that political victory be handed to them as a precondition for settling all military questions: in that case, of course, the latter would become totally irrelevant since the very issue that the struggle was all about would have been settled."

What suddenly changed in October 1972 was that the North Vietnamese themselves presented a plan in Paris which was very close to the American position. Perhaps Hanoi now realised that Nixon would continue as President for a second term. Perhaps there were military aspects which the North Vietnamese saw to their advantage. Whatever the reason, Hanoi now separated military questions from the main political issues. They spelt out specific solutions to the former, leaving the rest for later. In particular, they dropped the requirement for the resignation of President Thieu, as a first step toward settlement.

The Hanoi plan was published on 8th October. Intensive diplomatic activity followed. After years in which delay was the norm,

Hanoi now sought final signature of a settlement on 31st October. This time, it was the United States, on the verge of its Presidential election which found the time-table too rushed. The North Vietnamese negotiators were privately told that while the United States was prepared in principle to accept the draft agreement hammered out between the two sides, the 31st October date for signature could not be met.

President Nixon gave three reasons for this:[29]

(a) "During the last half of October we received mounting evidence that the Communists were planning to take advantage of the ceasefire with military offensives. Our South Vietnamese friends would have minimum time to prepare for the new situation. It also made imperative the need to tighten up certain aspects of the agreement, including the supervisory mechanism. Failure to settle on international machinery would mean that any violation would occur in an unsupervised context."

(b) "We ran into opposition in Saigon. Our South Vietnamese ally wanted many changes in the agreement, and more time for consultation. We were not prepared to accept all their proposals but ... we believed a country that had suffered so much was entitled to have its views fully considered. We made clear, however, that we could maintain the integrity of the draft settlement."

(c) "At the very time we were conducting delicate negotiations with Saigon, Hanoi's leadership made public comments suggesting the possibility of a coalition government, which both sides had firmly agreed was not envisaged in the settlement. These and other ambiguities had to be put to rest."

President Nixon subsequently reported to Congress: "Peace certainly was near in late October — the ending of a twelve year conflict was reached twelve weeks later."[30] Yet the twelve weeks were critical. And, whether the view is for or against the Nixon-Kissinger line, the events of this period are central to any consideration of the lessons of Vietnam. President Nixon "decided to bring home to both parties that there was a price for continuing the conflict."

Toward the North, the President decided that it had to be made clear that its own territory could not be immune while it waged war against the South: moreover, that the United States wished to see an end. During the week before Christmas, bombing was recommenced North of the 20th Parallel. But this was not like some of the bombing of the past. It was very heavy indeed, and intended to be felt to hasten the recommencement of purposeful negotiations. And it caused numerous civilian as well as military casualties. President Nixon said the decision to order this bombing was one of the most difficult foreign affairs decisions which he had to make as President. As for the South, they were also told that the United States was determined to settle — on the lines of the draft agreement previously in train. Saigon was told that the terms they sought were not possible of achievement.

The upshot was a return to negotiation. Dr. Kissinger was assured that North Vietnam sought serious talks, and on New Year's Eve American bombing North of the 20th parallel was once again suspended. During January, the negotiating process was rapid. From 8th to 15th January Dr. Kissinger and Le Duc Tho met continuously, and a ceasefire agreement and associated protocols were elaborated into final agreed form. Likewise, the South Vietnamese were carried into agreement.

On 23rd January, representatives of the United States and of North Vietnam, respectively Dr. Kissinger and Le Duc Tho, with the concurrence of the Saigon government and of the Viet Cong, initialled "The Agreement on ending the War and Restoring Peace in Vietnam". This was the end of the road, even though the formal signing of the agreement by Mr. Rogers, the American Secretary of State, and Nguyen Duy Trinh, the North Vietnamese Foreign Minister, did not take place until 27th January.

The text of this agreement is at Appendix D. Its main points were:

(a) An internationally supervised ceasefire would begin from 2400 GMT 27th January.
(b) Within sixty days, all Americans held prisoners of war throughout Indo-China would be released.
(c) During the same sixty-day period all American forces would be withdrawn from South Vietnam.
(d) The people of South Vietnam would have the right to self-determination — specifically "the South Vietnamese people shall decide the political future of South Vietnam through genuinely free and democratic general elections under international supervision." (Article 9 b)

In his address to the people of the United States, announcing this agreement, President Nixon had this to say: "We must recognise that ending the war is only the first step toward building the peace: all parties must now see to it that this is a peace that not only ends the war in South East Asia but contributes to peace in the whole world."[31]

He also paid tribute to his predecessor, President Johnson, who had died the previous day, almost five years after the historic announcement that he "would not seek and would not accept nomination for the Presidency", and that he "was now taking the first steps to de-escalate the war." Events during 1973 would give some preliminary pointers to what had actually been achieved for peace on Vietnam. They would also give pointers on Laos and Cambodia, where the agreement signed in Paris imposed on all its parties the obligation to uphold the 1954 agreement on Cambodia, and the 1962 agreement on Laos: "foreign countries shall end all military activities in Cambodia and Laos, totally withdraw from and refrain from reintroducing into these two countries troops, military advisers, munitions and war material .... The internal affairs of Cambodia and Laos shall be settled by the peoples of each of these countries without foreign interference." (Article 20 b and c)

The January settlement was followed, a few weeks later, by a major international conference in Paris designed to set the seal of international approval on the agreement which had been reached. This conference was attended by representatives of twelve governments; namely: Canada, The Peoples Republic of China, The United States, France, The Provisional Revolutionary Government of South Vietnam (The Viet Cong), the Democratic Republic of Vietnam (Hanoi), The Republic of Vietnam (Saigon), Hungary, Indonesia, Poland, The Soviet Union and Britain. The Secretary General of the United Nations was also present.

On 2nd March 1973 the Conference issued an agreed declaration, the text of which is also at Appendix D. Given the disparate nature of the representation at the Conference, the achievement of this agreement was a considerable diplomatic feat in its own right. Besides supporting the Paris Agreement, the "act of the international conference" provided for the International Commission for Control and Supervision to report through the parties to the Agreement to the governments taking part, and also for the Secretary General to receive such reports for his information. Thus the special British position, as Co-Chairman of the 1954 conference with ongoing responsibility, now came to an end.

A British involvement had commenced in 1945, when forces of Lord Mountbatten's South East Asia Command carried out the post-war occupation task in Southern Indo-China. Almost a decade later, Anthony Eden had performed a crucial rôle at Geneva in achieving a settlement of the French war in Indo-China. The March 1973 Conference marked the formal termination of the residual British rôle in Indo-China. On 5th March, Mr. Anthony Royle (later Sir Anthony), the Parliamentary Under Secretary of State at the Foreign and

Commonwealth Office, reported on the Conference to the House of Commons.[32] He stressed the importance attached by the British Government to the withdrawal of foreign troops from Laos and Cambodia, and the need for an end to foreign interference. He then went on to add these words, which reached to the heart of the situation: "No documents, no words, indeed no conference, can ensure the maintenance of peace in Vietnam. This, as I have indicated, must rest with the parties concerned on the ground. If they are determined that the agreement will work it will. If they are not so determined it will not. If the act of the Conference is observed, both in the letter and in the spirit it will, Mr. Speaker, serve well the cause of peace."

The arrangements to achieve settlement in Vietnam were parallelled by arrangements affecting Laos. On 21st February 1973, a ceasefire agreement was also signed for Laos. Its terms included the withdrawal of all foreign troops within 60 days of the formation of a new coalition government; and, although the new government did not arrive for a year, Laotians ceased to shoot each other. On 3rd April 1974, more than a decade after the collapse of the coalition blessed by the international conference in Geneva in July 1962, Prince Souphannouvong returned to Vientiane. He was warmly greeted by Prince Souvanna Phouma, his half-brother.

On 5th April, the Laotian monarch King Savang Vatthana signed Royal decrees setting up a new Provisional Government of National Union. It was a Coalition Government. The Cabinet had twelve ministers; five from the Vientiane side, five from the Pathet Lao, plus two others acceptable to both parties. On the all-important matter of the withdrawal of foreign troops, the United States and Thailand observed the Laos ceasefire terms. The Thai military in Laos, who at one time had numbered some thousands, were fully withdrawn in May 1974. The very last of the Americans involved in the Laos war went at about the same time. But the North Vietnamese stayed on.

Although there was token North Vietnamese withdrawal in certain areas, reliable press reports said that more than 20,000 North Vietnamese troops still remained along the Ho Chi Minh Trail. This part of the wider conflict continued. For Laos, as for Vietnam, events had not yet run their course.

Meanwhile, some aspects of the Vietnam settlement proceeded with reasonable smoothness, notably the withdrawal of U.S. troops and the return of the American prisoners of war, although the accounting for the missing (Article 8 b) brought yet more casualties. Other aspects, between the Indo-Chinese parties, proceeded much less smoothly, and the fighting which continued in South Vietnam, Laos and Cambodia revived tension between the United States and North Vietnam.

Difficulty also arose on the International Control Commission, originally manned by Canada, Poland, Indonesia and Hungary. Canada withdrew, to be replaced by Iran.

Once again it fell to Dr. Kissinger and Le Duc Tho to negotiate, and the upshot was a joint communique, issued in Paris on 13th June, this time publicly agreed to by all four parties, the United States, North and South Vietnam and the Provisional Revolutionary Government of South Vietnam (Viet Cong).

The communique called for scrupulous implementation by all the parties of the ceasefire provisions of the January Peace Agreement; specifically, it required "the high commands of the two South Vietnamese parties to issue identical orders to all regular and irregular armed forces and police under their command to strictly observe the ceasefire agreement throughout Vietnam."

At his press conference after the signing of the 13th June communiqué Dr. Kissinger was asked what would make it work better than the 27th January agreement. The reply was predictable. Kissinger realistically observed that there was nothing in a communiqué to make it work: "Words alone cannot produce peace; it is the combination of words, intention and performance."[33] American extrication had been achieved, and their prisoners of war brought home. But, as the year of the agreement and the communiqué came to an end, peace had still to return to Indo-China.

[1] President Nixon: United States Foreign Policy for the 1970s — Report to Congress, 18th February 1970.

[2] *Ibid.* pp. 2–4.

[3] President Nixon: Weekly compilation of Presidential documents, 4th August 1969.

[4] President Nixon's Foreign Policy Reports to Congress: 1970, 1971, 1972.

[5] 1972 Report, p. 39.

[6] President Nixon's address to the U.N. General Assembly, 18 September 1969.

[7] Nixon: Foreign Policy for the 1970s, p. 49.

[8] *Ibid.* p. 49.

[9] *Ibid.* p. 50.

[10] *Ibid.* p. 51.

[11] Nixon: Report to Congress, 25 February 1971, p. 26.

[12] *Ibid.* p. 24.

[13] Nixon: Report to Congress, 9 February 1972, p. 39.

[14]Nixon: Report to Congress, 25 February 1972, p. 6.

[15]Nixon: Report to Congress, 9 February 1972, pp. 7 & 8.

[16]*Ibid.* pp. 7 & 8.

[17]*Ibid.* p. 7.

[18]*Ibid.* p. 9.

[19]*Ibid.* p. 13.

[20]*Ibid.* p. 40.

[21]*Ibid.* p. 40.

[22]*Ibid.* p. 41.

[23]*Ibid.* p. 39.

[24]*Ibid.* p. 45.

[25]*Ibid.* p. 41.

[26]Nixon: Report to Congress, 3 May 1973, p. 20.

[27]*Ibid.* p. 20.

[28]*Ibid.* p. 22.

[29]*Ibid.* p. 22.

[30]*Ibid.* p. 23.

[31]U.S. State Department; Documentation on the Vietnam Agreement, p. 2.

[32]Statement in House of Commons, 5 March 1973.

[33]U.S. Documentation on the Vietnam Agreement. White House Release of 14 June 1973. Transcript of Dr. Kissinger's press conference in Paris on 13 June 1973.

20   *The Last Lap*

1974 turned out to be a bad year for the Governments in Saigon, Phnom Penh and Vientiane. It was a year when almost everything got worse for them. American help diminished substantially, and the resignation of President Nixon in August was seen by many as also marking the end of the road for President Thieu in South Vietnam. Another blow at this time, was the very severe cut imposed by the United States Congress in the military aid programme for the fiscal year ending in July 1975. The immediate effect was to put certain limits upon fuel and ammunition expenditure for the South Vietnamese armed forces. But stocks were still substantial. The wider effect related to confidence, and the South Vietnamese economy accelerated downhill. Inflation increased further. Likewise, the gap between imports and exports. Reports of oil strikes off-shore failed to stem the mood of economic and political deterioration.

In September 1974, there were major demonstrations against President Thieu in the Northern city of Hué. These were led by a Roman Catholic priest called Father Thanh. Thanh charged that corruption at the top hampered the battle against "Godless Communism". Although there was no intention to help the Communist cause, the practical effect was to undermine the authority of the Government in Saigon.

The Saigon press disregarded the censorship to publish the news. Soon there were disturbances in Saigon itself. President Thieu responded by reshuffling his Cabinet, and by dismissing some senior Generals. But, whether deserved or not, the finger of blame now pointed directly toward President Thieu himself. Air Marshal Nguyen Cao Ky took the opportunity to press for a government with a new look, for a government of *National Salvation*. This pressure can hardly have helped the cause of resistance to Hanoi. But in any case the situation of the South was by this time beyond all help.

The North Vietnamese probes, which were soon to win the South, began in January 1975. At the beginning of the month, the Communists over-ran Phuoc Long Province in the Mekong Delta adjoining Cambodia. This was the first province to fall completely to the Communists. Press reports suggested that the Communists used this operation to "test the water" on American reaction against them. There was none. Indeed, almost the reverse. Doctor Kissinger's advocacy made little impression on Congress, where those directly responsible to the electorate sensed American weariness with Indo-China. There was increased Congressional reluctance to continue to provide military aid to the Saigon régime. By this time too, the fabric of anti-Communist unity in Saigon was very thin indeed.

Early in March, the Communist forces began a limited offensive in the Central Highlands of Vietnam. It involved a number of the road cutting operations in which they were so especially adept. This Communist offensive was given little publicity at the time. Various reasons have been adduced for this. One of them was that there may have been some division of opinion in Hanoi as to whether the time was right for the coup de grâce. But in any case it was not part of General Giap's military philosophy to announce an offensive until its success was certain. The same was true of Giap's Deputy and Field Commander in the South, General Van Tien Dung, who, two decades earlier, had helped Giap muster the Viet Minh strength which overwhelmed Dien Bien Phu. This success now came quickly. The first major centre to fall was Ban Me Thuot, close to the Cambodian border. This exposed the cities of Pleiku and Kontum and, on 15th March, both these places were lost. With them fell the whole of the Central Highlands area. South Vietnam was close to being cut in two. At about this time President Thieu brought back to Saigon from the North some of the most effective units of the Army of South Vietnam (ARVN). Press reports at the time suggested that he did this to ensure the presence of loyal troops in Saigon, where he must now have expected a coup against him. But the action sparked the final rout. It was not General Giap's way to be hesitant when an enemy was on the run. Giap's forces pressed home their opportunity and advantage.

Quang Tri and Hué and Danang, close to the 17th parallel, now fell with little resistance. The Communists gained the immense military base stocks of the First Corps area, and took large numbers of prisoners. Within days of the probe in the Central Highlands, two-thirds of the country had fallen to Hanoi. Remaining South Vietnamese forces were now withdrawn to screen Saigon. But, after the loss of a string of coastal towns to the North, and the fall of Xuan Loc, a strategic centre East of the capital, it was clear beyond all doubt that time had at last run out for President Thieu and his régime. The tanks and trucks which the Communists had captured further North, were now being used to help hasten the Communist's encirclement of Saigon. As at Dien Bien Phu, there had been an underestimation of the Communist logistic capability. Subsequent reports stated that several regular Communist divisions had been swiftly assembled around Saigon, compared to the five ARVN divisions left to defend the capital.[2]

On 21st April, the day Xuan Loc fell, President Thieu announced his resignation. There were echoes of Prince Sirik Matak's last statement in Phnom Penh. Thieu's speech blamed the Americans in general, and Dr. Kissinger in particular, for the way things had gone. At the same time, in what may have been an attempt to rationalise his withdrawal, he suggested his resignation might revive American support.[3] "I have resigned today as the United States is scrutinising aid: after my resignation there may be more."

Thieu's burden had been heavy. It is also fair to say that he may just possibly have hoped that the Communists would negotiate evenly with a successor. After a few days of uncertainty, the task of facing the new masters fell into the hands of General Duong Van Minh (Big Minh), who had briefly led the South after the 1963 coup against Ngo Dinh Diem. It quickly became apparent that there could not be a negotiated solution, and that the only formula was surrender. On 30th April, General Minh announced unconditional surrender to the Communists.

The days between the fall of President Thieu and the final unconditional surrender of Saigon, were used by the Americans to achieve the evacuation of the fifteen hundred or so Americans still in Vietnam, and about six or seven thousand specially chosen South Vietnamese.[4] These included those most closely associated with the Americans. Some of the Saigon leaders, like President Thieu, made their own arrangements to escape. Others like Air Marshal Ky, were taken to America. In the end, in the face of great hazard and difficulty, almost two hundred thousand more South Vietnamese somehow managed to get away. Some of them escaped in open boats across the South China Sea to Borneo and the Malayan Peninsula. Many others reached Thailand and the Philippines. For almost all of them, the United States was the land where they wished to rebuild their lives.

The pattern of the events of a fortnight before, when Phnom Penh fell to the Khmer Rouge, has already been outlined. The Communist occupation of Saigon under General Tran Van Tra' was a more civilised operation. There were strict instructions on behaviour, and directives for "re-education". But there were no mass killings, and a number of international journalists were permitted to stay and report. One of them was a French reporter, Roland-Pierre Paringaux, who observed the contrast between North and South.[5] "The two parts of Vietnam are like Sparta and Byzantium: they are like the two ingredients of sweet and sour sauce, difficult to mix so that it will remain tasty for all." The observation echoed the views of Salan and other Frenchmen thirty years before.

In 1976, the refugee exodus from South Vietnam continued. But with this significant difference from 1975. In the beginning, the people who wanted to get away from the South were largely those who in one way or another were tied to the Thieu régime and the American connection: government officials and the middle classes. By 1976, however, the escapers were often ordinary Vietnamese fishermen and farmers — frequently people with little money who did not speak French, let alone English.

Vientiane was the last of the Indo-China capitals to 'fall.' The event came gradually, and was muted and without bloodshed. In practice the city was in Pathet Lao hands from the beginning of May, even though the formal announcement of "complete liberation" did not come until later. The final act for Laos was the establishment in December of a Peoples Democratic Republic. There, as previously mentioned, the abolition of the Monarchy, and the political demise of Prince Souvanna Phouma, had some apparent content of style and sympathy.[6] The former King and the former Prime Minister were named as Counsellors: the former as Counsellor to the President, the latter as Counsellor to the Government. Their true status, however, is by no means clear.

Some of the immediate local aftermath of the Communist victories in Indo-China was briefly touched upon in the chapter on "The Other Side". The reunification of Vietnam was formalised during 1976. In military terms, the now unified Socialist Republic is among the most formidable powers of South East Asia, and it would only be natural for other nations in the area to wonder how the power may be used. Perhaps above all this would apply to Cambodia. Unless a legacy of centuries of distrust changed overnight — and this was hardly likely — Cambodia would still seek to remain a Khmer state. Basic Khmer reserve toward the Vietnamese would not change. The old frictions, together with some new ones such as offshore oil rights, would make for Cambodian wariness of any Vietnam.

On September 9th, 1975 Prince Sihanouk returned to Phnom Penh from Peking on board a Chinese aircraft. It was said that he was disillusioned with what he saw, but his public statements continued to put a brave face on the new circumstances.[7] A little later, Sihanouk left the country again, but this time only briefly. He spoke at the United Nations on 4th October.[8] He asserted Khmer independence, and said his country reserved its right to defend itself against aggression and, despite what he had seen in the previous few weeks, he then courageously returned to Phnom Penh. In an interview at about this time with Wilfred Burchett, Sihanouk sought to offer some explanation for the Khmer Rouge excesses after their takeover. Burchett reported that *the main thing* for Sihanouk remained the fact that *red or not* his country had retained its identity.[9]

Not long after, there were news reports which suggested that the men in command in Cambodia included a shadowy figure called Pol Pot and another, Ieng Sary, who appeared to have a foreign affairs rôle. By May 1976, Chou En-lai, who had been a personal and powerful friend of Sihanouk, was dead. Soon after this, Sihanouk ceased to be the Cambodian Head of State and his personal safety became uncertain. In Sihanouk's place Khieu Samphan became President, and a foreign affairs post was formally entrusted to Ieng Sary. Despite the diminishment in Sihanouk's status, there were, however, reports that President Tito had not forgotten his old friend in the hour of need, and had asked his Ambassador in Phnom Penh to show interest in Sihanouk.

What was already clear to the outside world, was that the Cambodians now bowed to their own distinct and extremely ferocious form of Communism. Even so, it was reported in October 1976; "They may have read a lot of Marx but the ideology of the present Khmer leadership is virulent Khmer nationalism".[10] By comparison, the new régime in Laos seems less severe. Although the country has ceased to be a Monarchy, it does not appear to have dropped all its traditional values. For Laos and Cambodia, as indeed for other countries in South East Asia, the full regional dimension of Hanoi, in the aftermath of its victory has yet to be determined.

Meanwhile, the narrative should perhaps touch briefly upon three contemporary matters as the Communists achieved their victory in Indo-China: the Mayaguez incident in May 1975; the reaction of Asian leaders outside Indo-China to the Communist success; and, last but not least, the reactions to the events of the Americans themselves. The Western view of life tends to be linear. Events are expected to move forward and have direction. Within Asia, the wheel of life is a more familiar concept. Events come round again. In some of its obscurities, the Mayaguez episode off the Cambodian coast at the end of the Cambodia war, recalled the obscurities of the Colombia Eagle episode in the same waters in March 1970, in the final days of peace for the old Cambodia.

The bare facts of May 1975 were the boarding by the Cambodians, on 12th May, off their coast, of the American freighter Mayaguez. On one count, this incident could have taken place on the high seas: on another, in territorial waters.[11] Next day, there was United States air action against some of the Cambodian gunboats in the area. There was also United States diplomatic activity in Peking, said to have involved Prince Sihanouk. In the absence of apparent Cambodian response to an American broadcast calling for the ship's release, there was a sharp United States attack on 15th May against Koh Tang island where the ship — but not the crew — had been detained. There were also air attacks against targets in mainland Cambodia. By this time, the new Phnom Penh Government is said to have announced it had no intention of detaining the Mayaguez, and had no wish to stage provocation.[12] But the time scale must have been too tight for the message to have much chance of affecting events. All of these incidents took place at a time when Cambodian domestic and international behaviour aroused apprehension. It does seem, however, that the Mayaguez crew were already being released when the attacks took place. In a report at the time, the journalist, William Shawcross suggested that Dr. Kissinger played up the episode for wider political purpose — to stress that the United States still had teeth.[13] Shawcross reported that, when the Singapore Prime Minister had been in Washington about a week before the incident, he (Mr. Lee Kuan Yew) had said the Administration were looking for a crisis. Whatever the full story of the incident, the upshot was a loss of more American lives.

It would have been surprising if Dr. Kissinger had not noted the reaction of some of the Asian leaders most aligned to American policy to the fall of Indo-China.[14] The South Korean President, Park Chung Hee drew the moral "in the end you count on nobody but yourself". President Marcos of the Philippines observed that "closer links with the Communist States appeared the only way to ensure security and survival". He also enquired "whether commitments by the United States Presidents were binding or were merely forms of psychological re-assurance". From Singapore, Mr. Lee Kuan Yew offered the balanced view that it made sense for the countries of South East Asia to establish "correct and if possible cordial relations" with the Communist régimes. But at the same time, it made no sense to give up on the United States until the dust had settled — until the full significance of the Communist takeover in Vietnam had become clear.

The longer term United States reaction is still taking shape. The immediate United States reactions were predictable. President Ford offered the fair observation;[15] "we must first of all face the fact that what has happened in Indo-China has disquieted many of our friends, especially in Asia." Jane Fonda commented that "to say that Vietnam had fallen was like saying that the thirteen colonies had fallen two centuries ago". Almost equally predictably, General Westmoreland said that people who attempted to dismiss the domino theory were "all wet". The former Vice President Hubert Humphrey, who had been so much associated with the years of President Johnson's stress, wisely said that what had been learnt was that there were not American answers for every problem in the world. He added, the particularly perceptive remark that the United States had made judgements about

Asia based on experience in Europe: the Asian scene was different. With complete candour, he added, "it is clear there is blame enough for all of us. I include myself". George Ball, who had been a realist in the days of President Johnson, once again commented realistically. His words in 1975 echoed his advice a decade before. From now on, America must be critical and cautious in the commitment of its power. America needs to be very sure that when its forces are committed in support of American interests, that these interests are more than marginal. In Vietnam they had been marginal.

In the immediate aftermath of Hanoi's success, snap opinions were sought from many of the Americans most concerned in the longest war in American history. One of the deepest judgements came from Dean Rusk, Secretary of State, first under President Kennedy, later under President Johnson. "We do need to be sure what we mean when we talk about collective security: if it's going to cost us 50,000 dead every decade, we are not very secure, and our security isn't collective .... Yet there is a caution for young people .... When they reject the mistakes of their fathers, not to make the mistakes of their grandfathers." Dean Rusk was warning against the risk of a United States return to extreme isolationism.

[1] Asia Handbook 1976, p. 309.

[2] Far Eastern Economic Review, 12 September 1975, p. 37.

[3] Asia Handbook 1976, p. 310.

[4] U.S. Defence Department Statement quoted in Time magazine, 12 May 1975, p. 16.

[5] Time Magazine, 12 May 1975, p. 14.

[6] Far Eastern Economic Review, 19 December 1975, p. 16.

[7] Far Eastern Economic Review, 14 November 1975, p. 11.

[8] Far Eastern Economic Review, 24 October 1975, p. 15.

[10] Far Eastern Economic Review, 23 October 1976, p. 23.

[11] Far Eastern Economic Review, 30 May 1975, p. 12.

[12] Ibid. p. 11.

[13] Far Eastern Economic Review, 30 May 1975, p. 11.

[14] Time Magazine, 12 May 1975, p. 8.

[15] Ibid. p. 8.

21   The Balance Sheet

APART from the plain fact that Hanoi won in Vietnam, it is not really possible to offer a simple balance sheet for the decades of conflict in Indo-China. Time has not stood still. The colonialism, which up to the Second World War, appeared entrenched and settled in so much of Asia and Africa has virtually disappeared. At any rate this is true of Western European colonialism. Even since the 1950s and 1960s, much has changed. President Kennedy's objectives in Indo-China proudly proclaimed the American concept of the right to liberty: — and young America applauded. But events and mood have their own pace. The configurations of power, both regional and global, have shifted considerably within the last twenty years. The decades of conflict in Indo-China certainly brought their own pattern of change. Yet a number of events which were foreseen as part of this change did not emerge. These also have a place in the balance. Nor should the random factor be ignored. Chance played its part, and no one can tell how Hanoi would have fared without the bonus of Watergate. But the fact remains that Hanoi won. Perhaps the only valid measure which can be applied to a historical development of the sort experienced in Indo-China is the price of change.

The casualties within Indo-China are to be measured in millions. These include the Cambodians, Laos and Vietnamese of both sides. In addition, the French left behind 75,000 dead in Indo-China, and hundreds of thousands were maimed. For the Americans, the price was almost as heavy. Their killed exceeded 56,000. Their wounded numbered more than 300,000.

Yet in a sense there were always two conflicts. One of them, and this held throughout — was the fighting within Indo-China itself. This was the war on the ground where the casualties were suffered. Here the human balance was sadly adverse, and none of the governments and parties engaged, whether internal or external to Indo-China, can evade their share of responsibility for this suffering. The other, was a conflict which claimed no direct casualties, although it seemed at times to be on an almost global scale. There were moments, when it really did appear to some of the leaders in the West, that Communist strength and will might be tilting the world power balance from a position of leverage in

South East Asia. From this second conflict, the balance now appears more neutral. The fuse of Indo-China did not set the world ablaze. Indeed, the present stability and development of South East Asia beyond Indo-China, suggests some element of local compensation.

It will probably be the judgement of history that, despite anxious moments in 1954, and, again, in the 1960s, Indo-China was not in fact the scene of anything approaching full scale East/West challenge. It is a statement of the obvious that North Vietnam was greatly helped by the Soviet Union and by Communist China. But the two great Communist States no more saw eye to eye over matters of Indo-China than they did over matters elsewhere. Their policies over Cambodia offer a good example. Moscow and Peking saw the situation in different terms. When Sihanouk was deposed, the Chinese quickly withdrew their Mission from Phnom Penh. The Soviet and Polish and other Eastern European Missions remained in the Cambodian capital for some years.

The challenge, first to Paris, later to Washington, finally to Saigon, came from within North Vietnam itself. This challenge was exemplified in the personality of Ho Chi Minh, and the close group of Hanoi colleagues who maintained their cohesion and will for so long. Their dynamic was Vietnamese Nationalism and Vietnamese Communism. The two motivations marched together. Both stemmed above all from Hanoi.

It is true that events in Laos briefly contained elements of great power confrontation. But remoteness weighed against Laos as a major battlefield. In President Kennedy's words, the country hardly merited the engagement of the great powers. In direct global terms, Indo-China as a whole never escalated to the pitch of Berlin at the time of the blockade. Nor did it compare in hazard with the Cuban missile crisis, when the Russians sought to challenge America on her doorstep.

On the other hand, a number of experienced observers believe that there were moments during the Dulles years when the Chinese might have believed that the Americans were challenging *them* on their doorstep. This was notably the case in 1954. This was before China possessed nuclear weapons. But in any case Dulles was not President. Above him stood the steady authority and great military experience of President Eisenhower. Events did not follow the Korean pattern. The Chinese reaction to developments in Indo-China never matched their reaction to the advance of General MacArthur's armies to the Yalu River.

This view of the limited dimension of the war as fought in Indo-China relates to the basic geography and history; and to the fact that it takes two to escalate to a world conflict. But it does not diminish the impact of the conflict on the global stage. Hanoi always saw the need to gain impact on a world front in order to achieve its aims within Vietnam, and elsewhere within Indo-China. A pointer to Hanoi progress towards its local objectives can be gained from a consideration of the three agreements, spanning nearly thirty years of conflict, to which her leadership was party. These three agreements were, the Franco/Vietnamese Convention of 6th March 1946; the Geneva Agreement of 1954; and the Paris Agreement of 1973. They are worth setting out, once again, as signposts marking the determination of Ho Chi Minh and his colleagues. The 1946 Agreement signed by Ho Chi Minh and Sainteny promised "French readiness to ratify decisions taken by the populations consulted by referendum" (Article 1). The declaration of the 1954 Geneva Conference said: "The Vietnamese people should be entitled to decide their future by secret ballot under international supervision." The 1973 Agreement, initialled by Dr. Kissinger and Le Duc Tho, and subsequently ratified by the American Secretary of State and by the Foreign Minister of the Democratic Republic of Vietnam, stated that the reunification of Vietnam should be carried out step by step. It went on to add that this reunification should be achieved through peaceful means, on the basis of discussion and agreement between North and South Vietnam (Article 15); and "that the South Vietnamese people shall themselves decide the political future of South Vietnam through genuinely free and democratic general elections under international supervision". In 1975 Hanoi achieved military victory, and the unity of Vietnam under Hanoi was formally accomplished the following year.

With the increasing breakdown of the monolithic structure of the Communist world, it became more and more clear that Indo-China was less than vital in the world setting. Yet this is a view with all the comfortable benefits of hindsight. For a long time, the challenge of Indo-China was seen by many in larger terms than mere Hanoi expansionism. Almost up to the time of Richard Nixon's Presidency, there seemed a direct linkage with Western interests of real substance, quite apart from reputation. Yet for France, what had once seemed a vital interest later appeared more of a mirage. What had seemed so important could be viewed more coolly. Likewise, for the United States, there were the years when Indo-China seemed of the highest importance in strategic terms. There were the special years of trauma during the Johnson Presidency, when the domino theory was in full flood.

This theory gained sway in Washington, in spite of the CIA's cool assessment at the time, that "a continuation of the spread of Communism in the area would not be inexorable, and that any spread which did occur would take time; time in which the total situation might change in any number of ways unfavourable to the Communists". The upshot of the acceptance of the domino theory was that the United States increasingly became drawn into Vietnam; and thereby into the near vital interest of its own military and political reputation. Whatever the geopolitics, prestige was now engaged.

It was perhaps as well for the world that the Russians recognised the limitations of their own interest in Indo-China. They did not put their reputation on the line to the same extent. The Soviet Union put some limit on the sophistication of the arms supplied to Hanoi. And, within Vietnam they refrained from sending their own forces into action, whether as volunteers or otherwise. It is true that Russian ships carried military cargo to Haiphong in considerable quantity. But the Russian Navy made no attempt to challenge the United States Navy off-shore. The Russians saw beyond Indo-China in their relations with the United States. Their leaders also had in mind the growing and direct clash of interest between Communist Russia and Communist China in areas more significant to them to the North. The sum of these factors limited major threat to world peace, and risk of East/West nuclear exchange.

In strategic terms, there also appeared at times some possible contradictions in the positions taken by the United States and China. The Chinese saying is frequently quoted "the neighbour of my neighbour is my friend". This illuminates Chinese wariness of the States directly on her borders. Yet if, as was often suggested during the 1950s, the United States objective was containment of China, then a strong Vietnam, albeit Communist but unlikely to be a Chinese vassal, might have helped America toward this objective. Under the leadership of Ho Chi Minh, such a Vietnam might have become an Asian Yugoslavia. There was also the converse. If it were a consideration to limit a neighbour's power, Chinese help to Hanoi might be of question-able value to her interests. In short, the American national interest in the 1950s, and for a while later, might perhaps have been served by a strong and united Vietnam like Communist Yugoslavia; that of China, by a divided and weakened Vietnam.

By way of contrast, there was a consistency about the detached Russian view of the Indo-China situation. By the yardstick of the Soviet national interest, their objectives in the area were usually much more closely conceived than those of the United States or China. In the immediate postwar years, when France and Western Europe looked a possible prize, Soviet support for Ho Chi Minh was muted. Moscow sensed that the larger Soviet interest in France itself might not be served by such action. Only later, did Moscow come out fully for Ho

Chi Minh. Yet, even in 1956, Soviet policy on Vietnam envisaged the establishment of two States, each of them a member of the United Nations. This concept, which irritated Hanoi, related to wider Soviet views, notably toward two Germanys. Although it is in some ways incidental to the Indo-China story, it is one of the ironies of life that some of those in the West who have pressed most strongly for the right of the Vietnamese people to be unified should hold such a very different view when it comes to the unification of Germany.

At a later stage, Soviet policy toward Hanoi was of course influenced by Sino-Soviet considerations. And well before the end of the Indo-China saga, it was abundantly clear that Moscow saw the interests of Hanoi as less important than its own objective of détente with the United States, and acted accordingly.

At the same time, Moscow always appreciated that the Soviet interest would only gain from differences between the United States and China in South East Asia. In addition, the situation offered useful spin off on a wider stage. In national terms, Indo-China was less than vital both for France and for the United States. But in both cases the war in Vietnam rallied elements in these countries against their established order in a way which can hardly have displeased Moscow. This internal dimension for the West was among the more significant fall-out from the years of conflict.

In France, the pressures contributed to the upheavals which led finally to the re-assumption of power by General de Gaulle, and to the years of French reserve toward the United States which then followed.

Within the United States, there was internal division for almost two decades. It is true that some of the sharpness diminished with the decision by President Johnson not to consider a further term. The end of the 'draft', and the application by President Nixon of a policy of *Vietnamisation,* carried this further. As far as America was concerned, it was natural that the diminishment of direct involvement should ease dissension. Even so, the rumblings of the Vietnam controversy contributed to the clashes between the Nixon Administration and the press which came to a head with the publication by the New York Times in June 1971 of the Pentagon Papers. The investigation into the leak of these previously secret documents about Indo-China had links with the so-called White House "plumbers". Soon there would be Watergate. In the United States, as in France, the Vietnam involvement caused damage to many established reputations.

It is hardly a comparison of like with like to set the Indo-China situation in its early days alongside the situation in India at about the same time. Britain was fortunate in 1946 in having a sense of achievement; in particular, as far as India was concerned, because of the victory over the Japanese in Burma. France may have felt a need to win a laurel of victory in Indo-China through the effort of her own armies. In terms of national sentiment, Britain was better placed than France to concede to the post-war tide of Asian nationalism. Yet, it was a situation which, with different personalities, could have had a different upshot.

Britain was fortunate at that time in the men responsible for policy over India. The Prime Minister was Mr Attlee, whose sense of principle and purpose was well known. The Viceroy was Lord Mountbatten, the distinguished and forward-looking Admiral, who had already proved himself as the war-time Supreme Allied Commander in South East Asia. Indeed, it was in this latter capacity that he had given counsel to General Leclerc about the new situation he would find in Indo-China. Mountbatten was a descendant of Queen Victoria, and was indeed a nephew of the last Tsar of Russia. The partnership of Attlee and Mountbatten was geared firmly to the progressive idea of independence for India. And it was altogether too strong a partnership to be vulnerable to query of its patriotism. Moreover, the social standing of the Mountbattens was able to influence British opinion in India and at home toward whole-hearted acceptance of the transfer of power. Within Indo-China, there was no such force.

The nearest French equivalent to Attlee and Mountbatten might perhaps have been a partnership of Léon Blum and General Leclerc: Blum, had he been able to head a strong enough government; Leclerc, as the French representative in Indo-China. Even so, what has to be accepted as fact is that the Prime Minister of France, when the war with the Viet Minh broke out on 19 December 1946, was none other than the justly respected leader of the Popular Front, Leon Blum himself. There can only be speculation about what might have happened had Léon Blum controlled events differently. A pattern of events might have emerged in Indo-China resembling the pattern achieved in India. Certainly, Sainteny believed that the risk of concessions to Ho Chi Minh was one which the French should have taken; and, that the people of Vietnam should have been allowed to decide their future by referendum. No doubt this would have given power to Ho Chi Minh. Sainteny's views on this were as follows.[1] "Ho Chi Minh was as much a Nationalist as a Communist. The Communist régime would perhaps be less harsh today had we yielded at the beginning ... have we not arrived at a much worse result with the war".

The British also had to face the long emergency in Malaya. In some ways this was a situation more comparable to Indo-China. This was also a situation where very strongly motivated Communist groups sought to capture the independence movements. But the leaders were

Chinese and, in this case, there were communal factors along with others to limit the Communist infiltration of the community. In Malaya, the man at the centre when the storm broke in 1948 was Mr. Malcolm MacDonald, the then Governor-General of the British territories in South East Asia. MacDonald, who was the son of the first Labour Prime Minister in Britain, was himself a former Cabinet Minister. He immediately assessed a requirement for effective counter measures against the Communist guerrillas. At the same time, he saw this had to be coupled with a real promise of independence as soon as possible. Direct responsibility within Malaya lay with successive High Commissioners and Directors of Operations. Sir Henry Gurney, who was killed in a Communist ambush, and Field Marshal Sir Gerald Templer were perhaps the best known. In the end, success was achieved. The hallmarks of this success were protection of the people, denial of food and facilities to the Communists, flexibility, fighting close to the ground, a powerful intelligence system and, above all, awareness of "the battle of the hearts and minds".

The casualties and suffering of the Indo-China conflict impose diffidence on those seeking to comment from the outside on the lessons of the struggle. The bitterness and the prolonged nature of the fighting suggest the complexity, and the fact that the people most directly involved saw their interests as engaged. But there cannot be much argument that a great power involves itself at its peril in committing its forces in a distant region where, for one reason or another, it may not easily be able to deploy its full strength. The hazard increases if there is some interest, but not a really vital one. This is, because once involved, prestige and credibility become hostages. From then on, disengagement becomes all the more difficult. It was probably as well for Britain, for example, that operations were maintained in a low key during the "confrontation" launched by President Soekarno of Indonesia.

Yet, if a great power does feel obliged to make threats, they do need to be real. It would still seem to be the hallmark of a great power not to be seen as a "paper tiger". This philosophy was at the heart of the Nixon handling of Vietnam events at the end of 1972. And it can hardly be denied, that the strong American action at this time helped achieve the Paris Peace Agreement. Yet, alongside the credibility of power to an enemy, and the credibility of power to an ally, a responsive democratic society also requires credibility toward itself : — a sense of ethical acceptability. There is a certain sense of how far it is right to go — how hard to press. Common sense and ethic can come together in a situation of major confrontation, in allowing the other side an escape gap. There was an example of this in 1962. Although a number of the top military advisers in Washington counselled otherwise, the idea of providing an escape gap for the Soviet Union was close to the heart of President Kennedy's masterly handling of the Cuban missile crisis.[2]

It was natural that Western debate and discussion about Indo-China should so often revert to the assessment, first of the French, later the American interests. It was also natural to consider the ethic of involvement. But sometimes the argumentation was like a gramophone record which was stuck. It often remained based upon matters already past. Maintenance of the aim is basic military doctrine. At the same time, reasonably continuous re-assessment of a nation's interest safeguards against fossilised policy. This is not a matter exclusively for Government. In a free society, this is also a fair rôle for the press as it seeks to serve the community.

Yet fairness to a country's soldiers counts too. The importance of military confidence needs to be recognised. Without confidence, few battles are won. Yet misplaced confidence is an equally disastrous formula. Except in the bombing around Hanoi at the end of 1972, Western trust in the use of its air power in Indo-China was misplaced. Excessive claims were made and accepted about the effect of bombing on the Communist Vietnamese supply trails. In somewhat similar fashion, the enemy casualty figures issued by the United States Command in Saigon were heavily weighted by casualties assumed to have been caused by air attack. As mentioned earlier, these sometimes amounted to no more than an assumption that a certain tonnage of bombs should have done some definite amount of damage. The casualties claimed were indeed so numerous that the war should have been won if they represented reality. But the war went on.

The ill-founded faith in air power, as an offensive weapon against a guerilla enemy, was common both to the years of French and American involvement. There was also, at times, underestimation of the enemy himself. Apparent lack of military style may have contributed. As example, French and American Generals more than once failed to appreciate the logistic capability of the Communist Vietnamese. It took time to realise the true quality of the soldier in the black pyjamas.

It would be utterly wrong and foolish to diminish in any way the courage and effort of the hundreds of thousands of young Americans who fought in Indo-China. What can fairly be said however is that American military techniques often appeared to operate against the wider American military purpose. Extravagances such as the saturation bombing of country areas by B52s, although intended to save American lives, almost certainly did the American cause more harm than good. Yet American military frustration was understandable. What most commanders sought was contact with the enemy. But the enemy was elusive. Too often, the upshot was fire to no purpose. And, when that failed, yet more fire.

To some extent, the concept of "gearing-up" may have been born of procedures successfully applied in the later years of World War II when the Allies had overwhelming material superiority against weakened conventional German forces in the West. The Americans looked back too on the pulverising of Japanese positions in relatively small islands isolated from external sources of supply. As a World War II example, the Burma campaigns would have been a better guide.

American military techniques in Indo-China were also sometimes associated with the personal industrial leadership philosophies of Mr. MacNamara, the United States Defence Secretary under Presidents Kennedy and Johnson. The emphasis was on military weight, and strong logistic and administrative support. Yet the very scale of the American presence in Vietnam in the late 1960s probably operated against them. Perhaps, above all, the draft built up hostility within the United States itself. This point was never lost on Ho Chi Minh and the North Vietnamese leadership. Their strategy was aimed as much at the American people, as the forces in the field. And, as in ju jitsu, the weight of an adversary was used to make the fall harder.

Moreover, to the extent that America chose to take the load of the war, it was almost inevitable that local effort would diminish. Late in the day, the French appreciated the crucial value of Vietnamisation in achieving a counter force to their enemy. Likewise, the Americans. In both cases the experience was dearly bought. In the late 1960s and early 1970s, there was American understanding, but it came too late. In Vietnam, and in Cambodia, over-Americanisation of methods worked for the enemy. Laos was a separate case. In Laos, the so-called "clandestine war" remained relatively contained in terms of American involvement, and more nearly accorded with the modest counter insurgency concepts of President Kennedy.

The direct results of the French and United States campaigns in Indo-China are already part of military history. But the indirect effects on the French and United States armies also belong in the balance. Among the consequences of the Indo-China conflict which still have to be weighed, is the effect of "revolutionary warfare" on conventional armies charged with defeating such warfare. In Indo-China, although the two Western armies concerned were conventional forces, they were in a sense examples of different species. The French Army was a professional force. The American Army was a conscript force. It is no disrespect to say that their separate and distinctive wars cut deep into the ethos of both.

In the case of the French expeditionary force, the officer corps was French. But conscripts from France were excluded from her Indo-China War. Because of this, a large proportion of the French troops engaged, belonged to the Colonial Army and to the Foreign Legion. For the people of France, the impact of their war fell largely therefore on a relatively narrow band of professional leadership, and the mass of the French people were not directly affected. With the Americans the position was different. Their army was indeed conscript. The nation as a whole was more engaged than France had been. But the direct impact hit an altogether different group to those who had suffered in France. Despite conscription, the war again bore most severely on one particular group. In this case the men hardest hit were those who could not claim some exemption. On the whole, the least well off.

At the two different levels in both countries, the practical experience of those involved drove home what seemed to be the hard truth of "revolutionary war": that this sort of war was total, embracing every aspect of the lives of those involved. The lesson was learnt that the object of such war is to capture in one way or another the will of the people. The vital battleground to be won are the people themselves.

In the aftermath of Dien Bien Phu, General Navarre sought to distinguish the *pays réel* of France from the *pays légal*. Many other French soldiers believed that the army had a special rôle in relation to the *pays réel* and, that in certain circumstances, this amounted to a duty. The concept is by no means uncommon elsewhere. An apparent failure of Parliamentary Government can tend an army toward intervention. Likewise, any development within a State of private armies separate from the National army. Or the maintenance of professional forces for too long in a *no win* situation. The issues are complex. It does seem that internal security is a growing commitment for a number of armies. The "winning of hearts and minds" is increasingly a part of the baggage of the professional soldier.

For the French, the tragedy of Indo-China was soon followed by war in Algeria. And, after the Indo-China experience, it was natural that many French officers should themselves be attracted by the concept of total war. They lent toward the use, in support of the State, of the same total measures which the insurgents employed against it. In 1957, French paratroop forces under General Massu, a veteran of the Indo-China War, reasserted the French grip on Algiers in a series of measures determinedly followed through to ensure obedience. When the Liberation Front ordered a general strike in Algiers, and the closure of shops, Massu remorselessly insisted they stay open, and made his will effective. Giap's teaching in Indo-China had now been absorbed by his adversaries. Colonel Argoud, Chief-of-Staff to Massu, put the point bluntly to Paris. "In revolutionary war the main objective is to gain everyone's commitment through the conquest of hearts and minds. This can only be done if justice plays its rôle adequately. In disposing of the adversary — the one who acts in secret as well as the one who throws the grenade — justice should be exemplary. Examples are set through severity and speed." The French military action, which felled the Fourth Republic and brought de Gaulle to power in 1958, was founded in the creed of the army as trustee of the State. Within three years, however, when the trick was tried a second time, the rough justice of life turned the tables on the military leaders disputing de Gaulle's Algerian policy.

In France, the direct impact of Indo-China was mainly at the middle to senior level of a professional officer group. In the end, they intervened. The upshot, was the demise of the Fourth Republic, and the Gaullist decade of tight authoritarian control of the State. In the United States, the final effect was almost the complete reverse.

In the early days of the American involvement in Vietnam, the policy of the Administration was not out of line with the mood of America. The election results offer their proof. But increased involvement failed to achieve results. The consequent sense of disappointment must be among the larger factors responsible for the American change of mood. It can never be said for certain if the draft, and the increased cost of the Vietnam war, and the lack of success of it all, was the main direct cause of social unrest in America. Probably not. But there can be no doubt at all that there was a considerable connection.

The Vietnam involvement coincided with a period of change within America. The Youth Culture was running strongly. It fed television and radio, and was itself fed by them; and the Indo-China war almost became a television series. The impact of the Youth Culture weighed against a number of previously accepted values, notably, in relation to the deprived, and to the authority of the State. This tide was very well sensed by the leadership in Hanoi.

Meanwhile, there was a parallel tendency for successive Washington Administrations to take more upon themselves. But, as complexity built upon complexity, the risk of failure increased. And the consequences of failure related increasingly to authority itself. In no aspect of American policy was this more true than in relation to Vietnam. The reality was perceived by President Johnson, when he finally refused General Westmoreland's request that United States strength in Vietnam be increased from over half a million to approaching three quarters of a million. For the United States, this reality was later carried forward by President Nixon and Dr. Kissinger. Finally by Congress itself.

Even so, there is still a view that all that went wrong was failure: that if success had been achieved the mood and the rationalisation would have been different. If the lack of vital Soviet or Chinese interest had been appreciated earlier, the Christmas 1972 bombing which secured American extrication could have come years before. Perhaps this is so. But it is still doubtful if the final upshot would have been different for Vietnam itself.

Most of the time, the main task of civilised Governments and their diplomacy is to work toward the achievement of interests within a framework of peace. And, for those whose work touches the affairs of others, there does seem a basic truth. A local solution is usually more likely to last than a verdict, however well-meaning, handed down from the outside. Where there are local people, who are at least prepared for rational discussion of the issues in conflict, this is a major step toward peaceful settlement. It is true that in the Indo-China conflict it will never be firmly established if more extreme influences gained from Ho Chi Minh's lack of success at the conference table in 1946. But some of the French people engaged believe this was so. What is certainly known is that the unfortunate Doctor Thinh, the first President of the "Republic of Cochin China", killed himself when he realised that the colonial power would not let him deliver real independence to his own people. The apparent lack of interest on the part of the Emperor Bao Dai may have stemmed from much the same sort of frustration. Later years gave more and more examples of those on the outside "knowing best", and subsequently being proved wrong.

It is a statement of the obvious that it is unwise to underestimate the strength of local feeling. Yet it is done. Apart from the special case of Europe, there could now be a contemporary tide, almost worldwide, by no means away from co-operation, but certainly toward some separation, and toward the local interest. The failure of a number of post-war Federations in Africa and the West Indies, and also in Asia, suggests that nationalism in its local sense of identification with nearby territory remains a potent force. Certainly there is regional co-operation. But it is a co-operation of consent.

Late in the day, the French came around to Vietnamisation — to letting Vietnamese fight their own battles. And, during the Eisenhower years, there was caution about direct American involvement, in spite of the urgings of Mr. Dulles and some others. President Eisenhower saw further than a number of his top advisers, and sensed the hazard of American involvement in a major conflict on the Asian mainland. Yet, it is only fair to those who held responsibility in Washington in the 1960s, to add that it looked as if South Vietnam would fall to the Communists if America did not help. Misjudgment lay in the methods, and in the assessment of the consequences for America if Saigon fell. The leaning toward a larger American rôle gained sway to culminate in the events of 1968, and the courageous re-assessment finally made by President Johnson. Subsequently, the Americans adopted Vietnamisation, and came to a more relaxed view on Communism in Vietnam if this were the local solution.

The realities of national motives, as distinct from international ideology were appreciated by President Kennedy.[3] It has been said that "the stark Dulles contrast between the god anointed apostles of free enterprise and the regimented hordes of atheistic Communism" was a bore to him. Indeed, in 1958, Kennedy called on Americans to renounce the proposition that "conflict with Communism should be seen as a moral crusade requiring the unconditional surrender of the enemy". Kennedy tended to discount the rôle of dogma in Soviet policy. But, at the same time, he recognised that Communist ideology gave the Soviet Union a lever in the Third World which they would, where appropriate, seek to use for their national purposes. This leverage was not a force to be used as a matter of course. Where it was not appropriate to Soviet national purposes it would not be applied.

Whether the confrontation was national or ideological, President Kennedy recognised the virtue of resolution; a quality which he distinguished from rigidity. Above all, however, he saw the test for mankind, not in terms of a final battle between democratic good and Communist evil, but as an "obscure and intricate drama where men, institutions and ideals, all bedevilled by the sin of self righteousness threatened to rush humanity to the edge of destruction, and where salvation lay in man's liberation from myth and fanaticism".

Delicate questions arise about human rights in other nations. And of honesty concerning such human rights. The reality of the twentieth century is that the world is not all of a kind. And even when there are international conventions about human rights, this does not prevent differences of interpretation from arising. The external interest and above all, the maintenance of international peace, usually requires some element of modus vivendi between governments. This applies irrespective of the manner in which governments have achieved power. In foreign relations the other side has often to be taken as it comes. Only the very sure, and indeed, only those prepared that a price be paid, if this has to be, can afford the attitudes of moral certainty such as were shown by Dulles during the 1950s.

In a free society, the press spans both the internal and the external scene. It has been described by Walter Lippmann as resembling the beam of the searchlight, moving restlessly, bringing one episode, then another out of darkness into vision. At the same time,

Lippmann carefully distinguished between *light* and *right*: he added "men cannot do the work of the world by this light (the press) alone".

In the West, the 'censors' are in a sense the journalists themselves as they develop their stories, and in Indo-China it needs to be recorded that they frequently risked their lives as they sought their material: within Cambodia, press casualties were particularly heavy. The other 'censors' are the editors who decide what to print. Where there are alternative accounts, the reader can indeed pick and choose. But realistic judgement must recognise the way the Indo-China War was generally reported: the same judgement must recognise the power exercised by the Western press as the Indo-China situation evolved — the media themselves were not hesitant in using their right to decide what was news and what was not. Yet what is of interest, looking back to the early days of both the French and the American involvement, is the extent to which the press in both countries appeared on the whole to be sympathetic to their own government's policies. Disenchantment came later. It is a question for separate answer whether it was the political/military failure against the Communists which in the end turned the press.

Within Indo-China, the power of the press was recognised. Until his deposition, Sihanouk sought to keep most of the overseas press out of Cambodia. In general, the only foreign journalists allowed to work in the country were those he believed favourable to his viewpoint. As for Vietnam, during the American war, relatively few Western journalists gained entry permits to enable them to report from the North. Reporting from the South was easier. Yet sometimes, those who allowed reporting as a privilege, seemed to gain a better press than those who admitted journalists freely.

The full history of the Indo-China conflict has yet to be written. Among the matters for research are bound to be the manner in which, first France, and then the United States, established the nature of their interests as hostilities developed. But, at the risk of saying what is manifest, the years of French and United States involvement gave an extra edge to the already sharp regional conflict.

What can also be said, is that there was truth in General Navarre's cri de coeur after Dien Bien Phu, that successive French governments failed to indicate their objectives in Indo-China to the commanders on the spot. Was the war for French interests? If so, that was one thing. Or was it an anti-Communist campaign on behalf of the United States? That was something very different indeed. Likewise, for the United States, the objective in Indo-China was at times uncertain. What was constant, however, was the fact that a great power which had made a commitment was substantially committed. Its prestige was engaged. The barrack room chant "We're here because we're here" summed up a very great deal.

The memorandum on American aims, submitted in the early days of the Johnson administration by John McNaughton, the then Assistant Secretary for Defence, indeed assessed American aims as 70% to avoid a humiliating defeat to the country's reputation as a guarantor; 20% to contain China, and a bare 10% for South Vietnamese freedom. In a sense the commitment made America captive. For successive American leaders, a personal sense of honour and duty became engaged.

For the United States in Vietnam, the legacy went back to the early 1950s and, to a large extent, to the convictions and moral judgements of its then Secretary of State. The warning of Indo-China is the extent to which a great power can be captured by a distant commitment. However worthy the cause, the need for caution in commitment could be the lesson for a great power — Communist or non-Communist. Beyond this, there also stands the need for caution in striking a strong 'moral' position from which escape may be difficult. Caution applies, above all, in the commitment of large ground forces. Crusading can have its hazards, and this can apply to all. There is a sensible distinction to be made between a military situation which can be quickly resolved, and presented as a 'fait accompli', and one which of its nature is likely to be prolonged. The prudent crusader seeks enough, but not too much, and is flexible. President Kennedy bid reasonably, both over Laos in 1961 and over Cuba a year later. In both instances sufficient was achieved. In a world where weapons of mass destruction are numbered in their tens of thousands it is only too clear that a high stake makes for hazard. Even so, Dean Rusk's warning to America of the risk in excessive withdrawal from world events stands as wise counsel. As already mentioned, it was American withdrawal from the Korean Peninsula which triggered the Korean War. The origins of the Korean War hold their lesson, as well as the events in Indo-China. The maintenance of international peace seems still to hinge upon super power balance.

But perhaps these words push at an already open door as far as the United States and the Soviet Union are concerned. The recently published book, "Gunboat Diplomacy", contains some passages which approach to the heart of the matter. "The conflicts in Indo-China and the Middle East have shown how far the Super Powers will go — and they may in future be prepared to go further — at the expense of their clients in order to avoid direct confrontation" ... "if men were sensible, governments would resolve their disputes without threat or use of force — if men accepted the logic of their own lunacy there would be no limit to the force they employed".[5] Most of the time, of course, the realities lie somewhere in between.

The mutual safety considerations of the existing Super Powers may already be pointing them away from further, far off, large scale land involvement. The United States has had its experience in Indo-China, and the Soviet Union may have drawn its own lesson from this American experience. Perhaps the maritime presence, which is a smaller hostage to fortune in a developing situation, will once again have the major rôle. Or armed action by "Agency States". Only the future can show. It may also show the global danger of unbalance.

There is a related issue. Domestic pressures within a great power can eventually diminish a cause which its government previously considered vital to its international standing. This too seems a statement of the obvious. Yet the history of the Second World War reveals relatively few efforts by either side to go behind the back of the governments against them, direct to the people of the other side. But as a central aspect of *"Peoples War"* this was something well understood by Ho Chi Minh. It may not always be wise for lesser powers to count on the promised help of the government of a greater power. The nation's public opinion may or may not be behind its government. This could be the really important factor. There is nothing new in this. The concept of alliance becomes no less valid even though allies are realistic about what really may happen when the chips are down.

Indo-China was probably seen for too long through a magnifying glass by those on the outside. There is a legend of Laos that, many centuries ago, a Chinese general entrusted with the defence of South China, installed bronze drums in the waterfalls which abound in Laos as they do in Northern Burma and Tonkin. The general did this to make up for his shortage of troops. The water falling on the drums suggested the noise of armies and a strong Chinese presence. The noise magnified the reality. President Kennedy's assessment of Laos was that prestige and commitment apart, "this was not a land worthy of engaging great powers". In the aftermath, even Indo-China as a whole might be viewed in the same cool light. Even so, geography will always impose an interest for China. And this Chinese interest will be a limiting factor for any wider Vietnamese ambitions over Indo-China.

There are the lessons of Indo-China which apply to the larger powers. For the West, these could involve pricing disengagement as well as involvement. There are also reminders about that blend of local feeling, in which geography and origin, and pride and self-interest, all loom large; in a word, Nationalism. The world is a safer place when its realities are recognised. Differences between neighbours are as old as

history. As already suggested, the intervention of a distant third party
can give extra edge to their local conflict. And, for all the swiftness of
communication in the modern world, and the speed with which central
military effort can be deployed, weight often seems to lie with the local
interest. Perhaps this is because the local interest is permanently
engaged. The fact that a force can come in from the outside also means
it can go back whence it came. Passion is usually stronger in those who
are geographically rooted. The decades of conflict in Indo-China have
demonstrated the strength of purpose of those engaged on the spot. The
world has been shown what can and cannot be achieved, and made
lasting and effective from the outside. Perhaps this is the principal
reminder of the thirty or more years of war. If it may be said, it is a
reminder with a significance far beyond Indo-China.

[1] Sainteny, p. 101.

[2] Lord Harlech, BBC broadcast, 27 January 1974.

[3] Schlesinger, p. 271.

[4] Schlesinger, p. 272.

[5] James Cable: *Gunboat Diplomacy,* p. 172.

Appendix A

PRELIMINARY FRENCH-VIETNAMESE CONVENTION, 6TH MARCH 1946

It has been agreed between the following distinguished parties:

The Government of the French Republic, represented by M. Sainteny, Delegate of the French High Commission — acting on the authority of Vice Admiral Georges-Thierry d'Argenlieu, French High Commissioner, Plenipotentiary of the French Republic on the one hand, and the Government of the Republic of Vietnam, represented by its President, M. Ho Chi Minh and the Special Delegate of the Cabinet, M. Vu Hong Khanh on the other hand.

1.   The French government recognises the Republic of Vietnam as a free State, having its government, its parliament, its army and its finances, and being part of the Federation of Indo-China and of the French Union. As far as the reunion of the three "Ky"* is concerned, the French government undertakes to ratify the decisions taken by the population consulted by referendum.

2.   The government of Vietnam declares itself ready to welcome with friendliness the French army when, according to the international agreements, it takes over from the Chinese forces. An auxiliary agreement, appended to the present preliminary Convention will establish the conditions upon which the take-over operations will be carried out.

3.   The aforementioned stipulations will come into effect immediately. As soon as the signatures have been exchanged, each of the distinguished contracting parties will take all necessary measures to cease the hostilities at once, to maintain its forces in their respective positions and to create the favourable climate necessary to an immediate start of friendly and open negotiations. These negotiations will, in particular, cover:

a)   the diplomatic relations of Vietnam with foreign countries

b)   the future status of Indo-China

c)   the French economic and cultural interests in Vietnam.

Either Hanoi, Saigon or Paris could be chosen for the conference.

Signed at Hanoi, 6th of March 1946
Signed: Ho Chi Minh, Vu Hong Khanh
Signed: Sainteny

*Tonkin, Annam and Cochinchine

AUXILIARY AGREEMENT

It has been agreed, as follows, between the distinguished parties involved in the preliminary Convention representing the Government of the French Republic and the Government of Vietnam:

1) The relief forces will consist of:

   a) 10,000 Vietnamese, with their Vietnamese officers within the jurisdiction of the military authorities of Vietnam.

   b) 15,000 French, including the French forces, now present on the territory of Vietnam, north of the 16th parallel. These forces must consist solely of French of metropolitan origin, with the exception of the forces guarding the Japanese prisoners.

   The totality of these forces will be under the French High Command assisted by Vietnamese delegates. The progression, installation and utilization of these forces shall be defined during a conference of Chiefs of Staff, representatives of the French and Vietnamese military authorities, which will be held as soon as the French units are disembarked. At all levels, mixed commissions will be established to ensure that the liaison between French and Vietnamese forces will be carried out in a friendly spirit of cooperation.

2) The French relief troops shall be divided into three categories:

   a) The units responsible for the Japanese prisoners of war.

   These units shall be repatriated as soon as they have achieved their purpose, consequent upon the withdrawal of the Japanese prisoners and, in any case, within a maximum time of 10 months.

   b) The units which, in collaboration with the Vietnamese army, are responsible for keeping public order and maintaining the security of the Vietnamese territory. These units shall be relieved by 1/5th per annum by the Vietnamese army: this relief shall thus effectively be accomplished within a period of 5 years.

   c) The units responsible for the defence of the naval and air bases.

   The duration of the mission entrusted to these units shall be defined in further conferences.

3) Wherever French and Vietnamese troops will be stationed, demarcation (and billetting) zones will be properly defined.

4) The French government undertakes not to utilise the Japanese prisoners for military purposes.

Signed: Sainteny, Salan
Signed: Vo Nguyen Giap

Appendix B

MODUS VIVENDI OF THE
14TH SEPTEMBER 1946

JOINT DECLARATION
OF THE GOVERNMENT OF THE FRENCH
REPUBLIC AND OF THE DEMOCRATIC
REPUBLIC OF VIETNAM

The Government of the French Republic and the Government of
the Democratic Republic of Vietnam have firmly decided to pursue — in
a spirit of reciprocal trust — the policy of agreements and collaboration
set out by the preliminary Convention of the 6th March 1946, further
defined during the French-Vietnamese conferences at Dalat and
Fontainebleau.

Persuaded that only this policy corresponds to the permanent interests of the two countries and the democratic tradition they lay claim to,
the two governments, while referring to the Convention of the 6th March
1946 which remains in force, consider that the moment has come to mark
a new progress in the development of the relations between France and
Vietnam, awaiting conditions allowing a total and final agreement.

In a spirit of friendship and mutual understanding, the Government of the French Republic and the Government of the Democratic
Republic of Vietnam have signed a modus vivendi which, within the
restricted agreements, will bring provisional solutions to the most
important questions of immediate interest arising between France and
Vietnam.

Concerning the referendum foreseen by the preliminary Convention of the 6th of March, the two governments reserve the right to
decide its time and terms at a later date.

They are convinced that the whole of the measures contained in the
modus vivendi will contribute to re-establishing in the near future, a
climate of peace and confidence ensuring, early final negotiations.

They believe therefore that they could consider resuming, in the
month of January 1947, the French Vietnamese discussions which were
held recently.

Paris, the 14th of September 1946

217

FRENCH-VIETNAMESE MODUS VIVENDI

ARTICLE ONE   Vietnamese nationals in France and French nationals in Vietnam will enjoy the same freedom of establishment as the subjects of the respective countries, as well as the freedom of opinion, education, commerce, movement and, more in general, all democratic rights.

ARTICLE TWO   French properties and companies in Vietnam will not be subjected to a more rigorous treatment than, that accorded to the properties and companies of Vietnamese subjects, particularly regarding taxes and labour legislation. This equality of status shall be recognised by right of reciprocity to properties and companies of Vietnamese nationals in the territories of the French Union.

The status of French properties and companies in Vietnam can only be modified by common agreement between the French Republic and the Democratic Republic of Vietnam.

All French property which has been requisitioned by the Government of Vietnam, or the property of which persons or companies have been deprived of by the Vietnamese authorities, shall be handed back to their owners or to their rightful claimants. A mixed commission shall be set up to establish the terms and conditions under which this resolution will take place.

ARTICLE THREE   In order to re-establish from this moment, the cultural relations which France and Vietnam both desire to develop, French educational systems of various degrees can function freely in Vietnam.

They will adhere to the official French programs. By special agreement, these establishments will receive those buildings required to function properly. They will be open to Vietnamese students.

Scientific research and the establishment and functioning of scientific institutes shall be open to French nationals throughout Vietnamese territory. Vietnamese nationals will enjoy the same privilege in France. The Pasteur Institute will be granted its previous rights and property.

A mixed commission will fix the conditions under which the "Ecole Francaise d'Extreme-Orient" will start its activities again.

ARTICLE FOUR   The government of the Democratic Republic of Vietnam will first call upon French nationals every time it requires advisers, technicians or experts. The priority awarded to French nationals will only cease if and when France will not be able to supply the requested personnel.

ARTICLE FIVE   As soon as the present problem of monetary harmonisation will have been resolved, one single and same currency shall circulate in the Territories under the authority of the government of the Republic of Vietnam and in the other territories of Indo-China.

This currency is the Indo-Chinese piastre issued at present by the "Banque de l'Indo-Chine" until the creation of a currency board. The statute of the currency board shall be studied by a mixed commission where all the members of the Federation will be represented. The objective of this commission will also be the coordination of currency and exchanges. The Indo-Chinese piastre will be part of the franc zone.

ARTICLE SIX   Vietnam forms, with the other countries of the Indo-Chinese Federation, a Custom Union. Consequently, there will be no internal custom barrier and the same tariffs shall be applied everywhere for entrance into and exit from the Indo-Chinese territory.

A commission for the coordination of customs and external trade which can be the same as the one instituted for the currency and exchanges, will study the measures required for the application of customs duties and will prepare the organisation of the customs of Indo-China.

ARTICLE SEVEN   A mixed commission for the coordination of communications shall study the appropriate measures to re-establish and improve the communications between Vietnam and the other countries of the Indo-Chinese Federation and the French Union: transport by land, sea and air, postal, telephone, telegraph and radio-electric communications.

ARTICLE EIGHT   Pending the conclusion, by the French Government and the Government of the Democratic Republic of Vietnam, of a final agreement settling the question of diplomatic relations of Vietnam with foreign countries, a mixed French-Vietnamese commission shall work out provisions required to ensure consular representation of Vietnam in neighbouring countries and its relations with foreign consuls.

ARTICLE NINE   The French Government and the Government of the Democratic Republic of Vietnam, anxious to ensure as soon as possible the restoration of public order in Cochin China and in South Annam, indispensable for the free development of democratic liberties, as well as for the resumption of commercial transactions, and conscious of the favourable repercussions they can have on the cessation of all acts of hostility and violence, agree on the following measures:

a) all acts of hostility and violence shall be ended by both parties

b) Agreements between the French and Vietnamese Chiefs of Staff shall establish conditions of implementation and control of the measures which have been jointly agreed upon

c) it has been agreed that prisoners who at present are detained for political motives, shall be released, with the exception of those prosecuted for crimes and delicts of common law. This shall also apply to persons imprisoned during operations.

Vietnam guarantees that no proceedings, will be instituted and that no act of violence shall be tolerated against persons on account of their attachment or allegiance to France. Reciprocally, the French government guarantees that no proceedings shall be instituted and that no act of violence shall be tolerated against persons for reasons of allegiance to Vietnam.

d) The enjoyment of democratic liberties, defined in Article One, shall be guaranteed reciprocally.

e)   Unfriendly propaganda shall be stopped by both parties.

f)   The French Government and the Government of the Democratic Republic of Vietnam shall collaborate to make it impossible for nationals of ex-enemy powers to create trouble.

g)   A representative of the Democratic Republic of Vietnam, and approved by the French Government, shall be accredited to the High Commissioner to establish the cooperation necessary for the execution of the present agreements.

ARTICLE TEN   The Government of the French Republic and the Government of the Democratic Republic of Vietnam agree to endeavour jointly to bring to conclusion special agreements for all questions which might arise, having regard to the improvement of their friendly relations, and to prepare the road to a final general treaty. The negotiations shall therefore be restarted as soon as possible and not later than the month of January 1947.

ARTICLE ELEVEN   All measures of the present modus vivendi — executed in duplicate — shall come into effect on the 30th of October 1946.

Paris, 14th September 1946

For the Provisional
Government of the French Republic,
The Minister of French Overseas Territories,

Signed: Marius Moutet

For the Government
of the Democratic Republic of Vietnam,
The President of the Government,

Signed: Ho Chi Minh

For certified copy, corresponding to the original,
The Secretary of the Indo-Chinese Commission,

Signed: P. Messmer

Appendix C(i)

FINAL DECLARATION OF THE GENEVA CONFERENCE, 21 JULY, 1954([1])

Final Declaration, dated the 21st July, 1954, of the Geneva Conference on the problem of restoring peace in Indo-China, in which the representatives of Cambodia, the Democratic Republic of Viet-Nam, France, Laos, the People's Republic of China, the State of Viet-Nam, the Union of Soviet Socialist Republics, the United Kingdom, and the United States of America took part.

1. The Conference takes note of the agreements([1]) ending hostilities in Cambodia, Laos and Viet-Nam and organising international control and the supervision of the execution of the provisions of these agreements.

2. The Conference expresses satisfaction at the ending of hostilities in Cambodia, Laos and Viet-Nam; the Conference expresses its conviction that the execution of the provisions set out in the present declaration and in the agreements on the cessation of hostilities will permit Cambodia, Laos and Viet-Nam henceforth to play their part, in full independence and sovereignty, in the peaceful community of nations.

3. The Conference takes note of the declarations made by the Governments of Cambodia and of Laos of their intention to adopt measures permitting all citizens to take their place in the national community, in particular by participating in the next general elections, which, in conformity with the constitution of each of these countries, shall take place in the course of the year 1955, by secret ballot and in conditions of respect for fundamental freedoms.

4. The Conference takes note of the clauses in the agreement on the cessation of hostilities in Viet-Nam prohibiting the introduction into Viet-Nam of foreign troops and military personnel as well as of all kinds of arms and munitions. The Conference also takes note of the declarations made by the Governments of Cambodia and Laos of their resolution not to request foreign aid, whether in war material, in personnel or in instructors except for the purpose of the effective defence of their territory and, in the case of Laos, to the extent defined by the agreements on the cessation of hostilities in Laos.

5. The Conference takes note of the clauses in the agreement on the cessation of hostilities in Viet-Nam to the effect that no military base under the control of a foreign State may be established in the regrouping zones of the two parties, the latter having the obligation to see that the

([1]) Further Documents relating to the Discussion of Indo-China at the Geneva Conference. "Miscellaneous No. 20 (1954)", Cmd. 9239.

zones allotted to them shall not constitute part of any military alliance and shall not be utilised for the resumption of hostilities or in the service of an aggressive policy. The Conference also takes note of the declarations of the Governments of Cambodia and Laos to the effect that they will not join in any agreement with other States if this agreement includes the obligation to pàrticipate in a military alliance not in conformity with the principles of the Charter of the United Nations or, in the case of Laos, with the principles of the agreement on the cessation of hostilities in Laos or, so long as their security is not threatened, the obligation to establish bases on Cambodian or Laotian territory for the military forces of foreign Powers.

6.   The Conference recognises that the essential purpose of the agreement relating to Viet-Nam is to settle military questions with a view to ending hostilities and that the military demarcation line is provisional and should not in any way be interpreted as constituting a political or territorial boundary. The Conference expresses its conviction that the execution of the provisions set out in the present declaration and in the agreement on the cessation of hostilities creates the necessary basis for the achievement in the near future of a political settlement in Viet-Nam.

7.   The Conference declares that, so far as Viet-Nam is concerned, the settlement of political problems, effected on the basis of respect for the principles of independence, unity and territorial integrity, shall permit the Viet-Namese people to enjoy the fundamental freedoms, guaranteed by democratic institutions established as a result of free general elections by secret ballot. In order to ensure that sufficient progress in the restoration of peace has been made, and that all the necessary conditions obtain for free expression of the national will, general elections shall be held in July, 1956, under the supervision of an international commission composed of representatives of the member States of the International Supervisory Commission, referred to in the agreement on the cessation of hostilities. Consultations will be held on this subject between the competent representative authorities of the two zones from 20 July, 1955, onwards.

8.   The provisions of the agreements on the cessation of hostilities intended to ensure the protection of individuals and of property must be most strictly applied and must, in particular, allow everyone in Viet-Nam to decide freely in which zone he wishes to live.

9.   The competent representative authorities of the Northern and Southern zones of Viet-Nam, as well as the authorities of Laos and Cambodia, must not permit any individual or collective reprisals against persons who have collaborated in any way with one of the parties during the war, or against members of such persons' families.

10.   The Conference takes note of the declaration of the Government of the French Republic to the effect that it is ready to withdraw its troops from the territory of Cambodia, Laos and Viet-Nam, at the request of the Governments concerned and within periods which shall be fixed by agreement between the parties except in the cases where, by

agreement between the two parties, a certain number of French troops shall remain at specified points and for a specified time.

11. The Conference takes note of the declaration of the French Government to the effect that for the settlement of all the problems connected with the re-establishment and consolidation of peace in Cambodia, Laos and Viet-Nam, the French Government will proceed from the principle of respect for the independence and sovereignty, unity and territorial integrity of Cambodia, Laos and Viet-Nam.

12. In their relations with Cambodia, Laos and Viet-Nam, each member of the Geneva Conference undertakes to respect the sovereignty, the independence, the unity and the territorial integrity of the above-mentioned States, and to refrain from any interference in their internal affairs.

13. The members of the Conference agree to consult one another on any question which may be referred to them by the International Supervisory Commission, in order to study such measures as may prove necessary to ensure that the agreements on the cessation of hostilities in Cambodia, Laos and Viet-Nam are respected.

Appendix C(ii)

GENEVA CONFERENCE ON THE PROBLEM OF RESTORING PEACE IN INDO-CHINA: U.S. UNILATERAL DECLARATION

Mr Bedell Smith (United States): Mr Chairman, Fellow Delegates, as I stated to my colleagues during our meeting on July 18, my Government is not prepared to join in a Declaration by the Conference such as is submitted. However, the United States makes this unilateral declaration of its position in these matters:

The Government of the United States being resolved to devote its efforts to the strengthening of peace in accordance with the principles and purposes of the United Nations.

Takes Note of the Agreements concluded at Geneva on July 20 and 21, 1954, between (*a*) the Franco-Laotian Command and the Command of the People's Army of Vietnam; (*b*) the Royal Khmer Army Command and the Command of the People's Army of Vietnam; (*c*) the Franco-Vietnamese Command and the Command of the People's Army of Vietnam, and of paragraphs 1 to 12 of the Declaration presented to the Geneva Conference on July 21, 1954.

The Government of the United States of America:

Declares with regard to the aforesaid Agreements and paragraphs that (i) it will refrain from the threat or the use of force to disturb them, in accordance with Article 2 (Section 4) of the Charter of the United Nations dealing with the obligation of Members to refrain in their international relations from the threat or use of force; and (ii) it would view any renewal of the aggression in violation of the aforesaid Agreements with grave concern and as seriously threatening international peace and security.

In connexion with the statement in the Declaration concerning free elections in Vietnam, my Government wishes to make clear its position which it has expressed in a Declaration made in Washington on June 29, 1954, as follows:

In the case of nations now divided against their will, we shall continue to seek to achieve unity through free elections, supervised by the United Nations to ensure that they are conducted fairly.

With respect to the statement made by the Representative of the State of Vietnam, the United States reiterates its traditional position that peoples are entitled to determine their own future and that it will not join in an arrangement which would hinder this. Nothing in its declaration just made is intended to or does indicate any departure from this traditional position.

We share the hope that the agreement will permit Cambodia, Laos and Vietnam to play their part in full independence and sovereignty, in the peaceful community of nations, and will enable the peoples of that area to determine their own future.

Appendix D(i)

TEXT OF AGREEMENT ON ENDING THE WAR AND RESTORING PEACE IN VIETNAM, PARIS 27 JAN 1973

White House press release dated January 24

AGREEMENT ON ENDING THE WAR
AND
RESTORING PEACE IN VIETNAM

The Parties participating in the Paris Conference on Vietnam,

With a view to ending the war and restoring peace in Vietnam on the basis of respect for the Vietnamese people's fundamental national rights and the South Vietnamese people's right to self-determination, and to contributing to the consolidation of peace in Asia and the world,

Have agreed on the following provisions and undertake to respect and to implement them:

Chapter I

THE VIETNAMESE PEOPLE'S
FUNDAMENTAL NATIONAL RIGHTS

Article 1

The United States and all other countries respect the independence, sovereignty, unity, and territorial integrity of Vietnam as recognized by the 1954 Geneva Agreements on Vietnam.

Chapter II

CESSATION OF HOSTILITIES—WITHDRAWAL OF TROOPS

Article 2

A cease-fire shall be observed throughout South Vietnam as of 2400 hours G.M.T., on January 27, 1973.

At the same hour, the United States will stop all its military activities against the territory of the Democratic Republic of Vietnam by ground, air and naval forces, wherever they may be based, and end the mining of the territorial waters, ports, harbors, and waterways of the Democratic Republic of Vietnam. The United States will remove, permanently deactivate or destroy all the mines in the territorial waters, ports, harbors, and waterways of North Vietnam as soon as this Agreement goes into effect.

The complete cessation of hostilities mentioned in this Article shall be durable and without limit of time.

226

Article 3

The parties undertake to maintain the cease-fire and to ensure a lasting and stable peace.

As soon as the cease-fire goes into effect:

(a) The United States forces and those of the other foreign countries allied with the United States and the Republic of Vietnam shall remain in-place pending the implementation of the plan of troop withdrawal. The Four-Party Joint Military Commission described in Article 16 shall determine the modalities.

(b) The armed forces of the two South Vietnamese parties shall remain in-place. The Two-Party Joint Military Commission described in Article 17 shall determine the areas controlled by each party and the modalities of stationing.

(c) The regular forces of all services and arms and the irregular forces of the parties in South Vietnam shall stop all offensive activities against each other and shall strictly abide by the following stipulations:

—All acts of force on the ground, in the air, and on the sea shall be prohibited;

—All hostile acts, terrorism and reprisals by both sides will be banned.

Article 4

The United States will not continue its military involvement or intervene in the internal affairs of South Vietnam.

Article 5

Within sixty days of the signing of this Agreement, there will be a total withdrawal from South Vietnam of troops, military advisers, and military personnel, including technical military personnel and military personnel associated with the pacification program, armaments, munitions and war material of the United States and those of the other foreign countries mentioned in Article 3 (a). Advisers from the above-mentioned countries to all paramilitary organizations and the police force will also be withdrawn within the same period of time.

Article 6

The dismantlement of all military bases in South Vietnam of the United States and of the other foreign countries mentioned in Article 3 (a) shall be completed within sixty days of the signing of this Agreement.

Article 7

From the enforcement of the cease-fire to the formation of the government provided for in Articles 9(b) and 14 of this Agreement, the two South Vietnamese parties shall not accept the introduction of troops, military advisers, and military personnel including technical military personnel, armaments, munitions, and war material into South Vietnam.

The two South Vietnamese parties shall be permitted to make periodic replacement of armaments, munitions and war material which have been destroyed, damaged, worn out or used up after the cease-fire, on the basis of piece-for-piece, of the same characteristics and properties, under the supervision of the Joint Military Commission of the two South

Vietnamese parties and of the International Commission of Control and Supervision.

Chapter III

THE RETURN OF CAPTURED MILITARY PERSONNEL
AND FOREIGN CIVILIANS, AND CAPTURED AND
DETAINED VIETNAMESE CIVILIAN PERSONNEL

Article 8

(a)   The return of captured military personnel and foreign civilians of the parties shall be carried out simultaneously with and completed not later than the same day as the troop withdrawal mentioned in Article 5. The parties shall exchange complete lists of the above-mentioned captured military personnel and foreign civilians on the day of the signing of this Agreement.

(b)   The parties shall help each other to get information about those military personnel and foreign civilians of the parties missing in action, to determine the location and take care of the graves of the dead so as to facilitate the exhumation and repatriation of the remains, and to take any such other measures as may be required to get information about those still considered missing in action.

(c)   The question of the return of Vietnamese civilian personnel captured and detained in South Vietnam will be resolved by the two South Vietnamese parties on the basis of the principles of Article 21 (b) of the Agreement on the Cessation of Hostilities in Vietnam of July 20, 1954. The two South Vietnamese parties will do so in a spirit of national reconciliation and concord, with a view to ending hatred and enmity, in order to ease suffering and to reunite families. The two South Vietnamese parties will do their utmost to resolve this question within ninety days after the cease-fire comes into effect.

Chapter IV

THE EXERCISE OF THE SOUTH VIETNAMESE PEOPLE'S
RIGHT TO SELF-DETERMINATION

Article 9

The Government of the United States of America and the Government of the Democratic Republic of Vietnam undertake to respect the following principles for the exercise of the South Vietnamese people's right to self-determination:

(a)   The South Vietnamese people's right to self-determination is sacred, inalienable, and shall be respected by all countries.

(b)   The South Vietnamese people shall decide themselves the political future of South Vietnam through genuinely free and democratic general elections under international supervision.

(e)   Foreign countries shall not impose any political tendency or personality on the South Vietnamese people.

Article 10

The two South Vietnamese parties undertake to respect the cease-fire and maintain peace in South Vietnam, settle all matters of contention through negotiations, and avoid all armed conflict.

Article 11

Immediately after the cease-fire, the two South Vietnamese parties will:

—achieve national reconciliation and concord, end hatred and enmity, prohibit all acts of reprisal and discrimination against individuals or organizations that have collaborated with one side or the other;

—ensure the democratic liberties of the people: personal freedom, freedom of speech, freedom of the press, freedom of meeting, freedom of organization, freedom of political activities, freedom of belief, freedom of movement, freedom of residence, freedom of work, right to property ownership, and right to free enterprise.

Article 12

(a)   Immediately after the cease-fire, the two South Vietnamese parties shall hold consultations in a spirit of national reconciliation and concord, mutual respect, and mutual non-elimination to set up a National Council of National Reconciliation and Concord of three equal segments. The Council shall operate on the principle of unanimity. After the National Council of National Reconciliation and Concord has assumed its functions, the two South Vietnamese parties will consult about the formation of councils at lower levels. The two South Vietnamese parties shall sign an agreement on the internal matters of South Vietnam as soon as possible and do their utmost to accomplish this within ninety days after the cease-fire comes into effect, in keeping with the South Vietnamese people's aspirations for peace, independence and democracy.

(b)   The National Council of National Reconciliation and Concord shall have the task of promoting the two South Vietnamese parties' implementation of this Agreement, achievement of national reconciliation and concord and ensurance of democratic liberties. The National Council of National Reconciliation and Concord will organize the free and democratic general elections provided for in Article 9(b) and decide the procedures and modalities of these general elections. The institutions for which the general elections are to be held will be agreed upon through consultations between the two South Vietnamese parties. The National Council of National Reconciliation and Concord will also decide the procedures and modalities of such local elections as the two South Vietnamese parties agree upon.

Article 13

The question of Vietnamese armed forces in South Vietnam shall be settled by the two South Vietnamese parties in a spirit of national reconciliation and concord, equality and mutual respect, without foreign interference, in accordance with the postwar situation. Among the questions to be discussed by the two South Vietnamese parties are steps to reduce their military effectives and to demobilize the troops being reduced. The two South Vietnamese parties will accomplish this as soon as possible.

Article 14

South Vietnam will pursue a foreign policy of peace and independence. It will be prepared to establish relations with all countries irrespective of their political and social systems on the basis of mutual respect for independence and sovereignty and accept economic and technical aid from any country with no political conditions attached. The acceptance of military aid by South Vietnam in the future shall come under the authority of the government set up after the general elections in South Vietnam provided for in Article 9(b).

Chapter V

THE REUNIFICATION OF VIETNAM AND THE RELATIONSHIP BETWEEN NORTH AND SOUTH VIETNAM

Article 15

The reunification of Vietnam shall be carried out step by step through peaceful means on the basis of discussions and agreements between North and South Vietnam, without coercion or annexation by either party, and without foreign interference. The time for reunification will be agreed upon by North and South Vietnam.

Pending reunification:

(a) The military demarcation line between the two zones at the 17th parallel is only provisional and not a political or territorial boundary, as provided for in paragraph 6 of the Final Declaration of the 1954 Geneva Conference.

(b) North and South Vietnam shall respect the Demilitarized Zone on either side of the Provisional Military Demarcation Line.

(c) North and South Vietnam shall promptly start negotiation with a view to reestablishing normal relations in various fields. Among the questions to be negotiated are the modalities of civilian movement across the Provisional Military Demarcation Line.

(d) North and South Vietnam shall not join any military alliance or military bloc and shall not allow foreign powers to maintain military bases, troops, military advisers, and military personnel on their respective territories, as stipulated in the 1954 Geneva Agreements on Vietnam.

Chapter VI

THE JOINT MILITARY COMMISSIONS, THE INTERNATIONAL COMMISSION OF CONTROL AND SUPERVISION, THE INTERNATIONAL CONFERENCE

Article 16

(a) The Parties participating in the Paris Conference on Vietnam shall immediately designate representatives to form a Four-Party Joint Military Commission with the task of ensuring joint action by the parties in implementing the following provisions of this Agreement:

—The first paragraph of Article 2, regarding the enforcement of the cease-fire throughout South Vietnam:

—Article 3 (a), regarding the cease-fire by U.S. forces and those of the other foreign countries referred to in that Article;

—Article 3 (c), regarding the cease-fire between all parties in South Vietnam;

—Article 5, regarding the withdrawal from South Vietnam of U.S. troops and those of the other foreign countries mentioned in Article 3 (a);

—Article 6, regarding the dismantlement of military bases in South Vietnam of the United States and those of the other foreign countries mentioned in Article 3 (a);

—Article 8 (a), regarding the return of captured military personnel and foreign civilians of the parties;

—Article 8 (b), regarding the mutual assistance of the parties in getting information about those military personnel and foreign civilians of the parties missing in action.

(b) The Four-Party Joint Military Commission shall operate in accordance with the principle of consultations and unanimity. Disagreements shall be referred to the International Commission of Control and Supervision.

(c) The Four-Party Joint Military Commission shall begin operating immediately after the signing of this Agreement and end its activities in sixty days, after the completion of the withdrawal of U.S. troops and those of the other foreign countries mentioned in Article 3 (a) and the completion of the return of captured military personnel and foreign civilians of the parties.

(d) The four parties shall agree immediately on the organization, the working procedure, means of activity and expenditures of the Four-Party Joint Military commission.

Article 17

(a) The two Vietnamese parties shall immediately designate representatives to form a Two-Party Joint Military Commission with the task of ensuring joint action by the two South Vietnamese parties in implementing the following provisions of this Agreement:

—The first paragraph of Article 2, regarding the enforcement of the cease-fire throughout South Vietnam, when the Four-Party Joint Military commission has ended its activities;

—Article 3 (b), regarding the cease-fire between the two South Vietnamese parties;

—Article 3 (c), regarding the cease-fire between all parties in South Vietnam, when the Four-Party Joint Military Commission has ended its activities;

—Article 7, regarding the prohibition of the introduction of troops into South Vietnam and all other provisions of this article:

—Article 8 (c), regarding the question of the return of Vietnamese civilian personnel captured and detained in South Vietnam:

—Article 13, regarding the reduction of the military effectives of the two South Vietnamese parties and the demobilization of the troops being reduced.

(b) Disagreements shall be referred to the International Commission of Control and Supervision.

(c) After the signing of this Agreement, the Two-Party Joint Military Commission shall agree immediately on the measures and organization aimed at enforcing the cease-fire and preserving peace in South Vietnam.

Article 18

(a) After the signing of this Agreement, an International Commission of Control and Supervision shall be established immediately.

(b) Until the International Conference provided for in Article 19 makes definitive arrangements, the International Commission of Control and Supervision will report to the four parties on matters concerning the control and supervision of the implementation of the following provisions of this Agreement:

—The first paragraph of Article 2, regarding the enforcement of the cease-fire throughout South Vietnam:

—Article 3 (a), regarding the cease-fire by U.S. forces and those of the other foreign countries referred to in that Article;

—Article 3 (c), regarding the cease-fire between all the parties in South Vietnam;

—Article 5, regarding the withdrawal from Vietnam of U.S. troops and those of the other foreign countries mentiones in Article 3 (a);

—Article 6, regarding the dismantlement of military bases in South Vietnam of the United States and those of the other foreign contries mentioned in Article 3 (a);

—Article 8 (a), regarding the return of captured military personnel and foreign civilians of the parties.

The International Commission of Control and Supervision shall form control teams for carrying out its tasks. The four parties shall agree immediately on the location and operation of these teams. The parties will facilitate their operation.

(c) Until the International Conference makes definitive arrangements, the International Commission of Control and Supervision will report to the two South Vietnamese parties on matters concerning the control and supervision of the implementation of the following provisions of this Agreement:

—The first paragraph of Article 2, regarding the enforcement of the cease-fire throughout South Vietnam, when the Four Party Joint Military Commission has ended its activities:

—Article 3 (b), regarding the cease-fire between the two South Vietnamese parties:

—Article 3 (c), regarding the cease-fire between all parties in South Vietnam, when the Four-Party Joint Military Commission has ended its activities:

—Article 7, regarding the prohibition of the introduction of troops into South Vietnam and all other provisions of this Article:

—Article 8 (c), regarding the question of the return of Vietnamese civilian personnel captured and detained in South Vietnam;

—Article 9 (b), regarding the free and democratic general elections in South Vietnam;

—Article 13, regarding the reduction of the military effectives of the two South Vietnamese parties and the demobilization of the troops being reduced.

The International Commission of Control and Supervision shall form control teams for carrying out its tasks. The two South Vietnamese parties shall agree immediately on the location and operation of these teams. The two South Vietnamese parties will facilitate their operation.

(d)   The International Commission of Control and Supervision shall be composed of representatives of four countries: Canada, Hungary, Indonesia and Poland. The chairmanship of this Commission will rotate among the members for specific periods to be determined by the Commission.

(e)   The International Commission of Control and Supervision shall carry out its tasks in accordance with the principle of respect for the sovereignty of South Vietnam.

(f)   The International Commission of Control and Supervision shall operate in accordance with the principle of consultations and unanimity.

(g)   The International Commission of Control and Supervision shall begin operating when a cease-fire comes into force in Vietnam. As regards the provisions in Article 18 (b) concerning the four parties, the International Commission of Control and Supervision shall end its activities when the Commission's tasks of control and supervision regarding these provisions have been fulfilled. As regards the provisions in Article 18 (c) concerning the two South Vietnamese parties, the International Commission of Control and Supervision shall end its activities on therequest of the government formed after the general elections in South Vietnam provided for in Article 9 (b).

(h)   The four parties shall agree immediately on the organization, means of activity, and expenditures of the International Commission of Control and Supervision. The relationship between the International Commission and the International Conference will be agreed upon by the International Commission and the International Conference.

Article 19

The parties agree on the convening of an International Conference within thirty days of the signing of this Agreement to acknowledge the signed agreements: to guarantee the ending of the war, the maintenance of peace in Vietnam, the respect of the Vietnamese people's fundamental national rights, and the South Vietnamese people's right to self-determination; and to contribute to and guarantee peace in Indochina.

The United States and the Democratic Republic of Vietnam, on behalf of the parties participating in the Paris Conference on Vietnam, will propose to the following parties that they participate in this International Conference: the People's Republic of China, the Republic of France, the Union of Soviet Socialist Republics, the United Kingdom, the four countries of the International Commission of Control and Supervision, and the Secretary General of the United Nations, together with the parties participating in the Paris Conference on Vietnam.

Chapter VII
Regarding Cambodia And Laos

Article 20

(a)   The parties participating in the Paris Conference on Vietnam shall strictly respect the 1954 Geneva Agreements on Cambodia and the 1962 Geneva Agreements on Laos, which recognized the Cambodian and the Lao people's fundamental national rights, i.e., the independence, sovereignty, unity, and territorial integrity of these countries. The parties shall respect the neutrality of Cambodia and Laos.

The parties participating in the Paris Conference on Vietnam undertake to refrain from using the territory of Cambodia and the territory of Laos to encroach on the sovereignty and security of one another and of other countries.

(b)   Foreign countries shall put an end to all military activities in Cambodia and Laos, totally withdraw from and refrain from reintroducing into these two countries troops, military advisers and military personnel, armaments, munitions and war material.

(c)   The internal affairs of Cambodia and Laos shall be settled by the people of each of these countries without foreign interference.

(d)   The problems existing between the Indochinese countries shall be settled by the Indochinese parties on the basis of respect for each other's independence sovereignty, and territorial integrity, and non-inteference in each other's internal affairs.

Chapter VIII
The Relationship Between The United States And The Democratic Republic Of Vietnam

Article 21

The United States anticipates that this Agreement will usher in an era of reconciliation with the Democratic Republic of Vietnam as with all the peoples of Indochina. In pursuance of its traditional policy, the United States will contribute to healing the wounds of war and to postwar recontruction of the Democratic Republic of Vietnam and throughout Indochina.

Article 22

The ending of the war, the restoration of peace in Vietnam, and the strict implementation of this Agreement will create conditions for establishing a new, equal and mutually beneficial relationship between the United States and the Democratic Republic of Vietnam on the basis of respect for each other's independence and sovereignty, and non-interference in each other's internal affairs. At the same time this will ensure stable peace in Vietnam and contribute to the preservation of lasting peace in Indochina and Southeast Asia.

Chapter IX
OTHER PROVISIONS

Article 23

This Agreement shall enter into force upon signature by plenipotentiary representatives of the parties participating in the Paris Conference on Vietnam. All the parties concerned shall strictly implement this Agreement and its Protocols.

DONE in Paris this twenty-seventh day of January, one Thousand Nine Hundred and Seventy-Three, in Vietnamese and English. The Vietnamese and English texts are official and equally authentic.

For the Government of the United States of America	For the Government of the Republic of Vietnam
WILLIAM P. ROGERS Secretary of State	TRAN VAN LAM Minister for Foreign Affairs
For the Government of the Democratic Republic of Vietnam	For the Provisional Revolutionary Government of the Republic of South Vietnam
NGUYEN DUY TRINH Minister for Foreign Affairs	NGUYEN THI BINH Minister for Foreign Affairs

AGREEMENT ON ENDING THE WAR
AND RESTORING PEACE IN VIETNAM

The Government of the United States of America, with the concurrence of the Government of the Republic of Vietnam,

The Government of the Democratic Republic of Vietnam, with the concurrence of the Provisional Revolutionary Government of the Republic of South Vietnam.

With a view to ending the war and restoring peace in Vietnam on the basis of respect for the Vietnamese people's fundamental national rights and the South Vietnamese people's to self-determination, and to contributing to the consolidation of peace in Asia and the world.

Have agreed on the following provisions and undertake to respect and to implement them:

(Text of Agreement Chapters I–VIII — As stated on pgs 226–234)

Chapter IX
OTHER PROVISIONS

Article 23

The Paris Agreement on Ending the War and Restoring Peace in Vietnam shall enter into force upon signature of this document by the Secretary of State of the Government of the United States of America and the Minister for Foreign Affairs of the Government of the Democratic Republic of Vietnam, and upon signature of a document in the same terms by the Secretary of State of the Government of United States of America, the Minister for Foreign Affairs of the Government of the Republic of Vietnam, the Minister for Foreign Affairs of the Government of the Democratic Republic of Vietnam, and the Minister for Foreign Affairs of the Provisional Revolutionary Government of the Republic of South Vietnam. The Agreement and the protocols to it shall be strictly implemented by all the parties concerned.

DONE in Paris this twenty-seventh day of January, One Thousand Nine Hundred and Seventy-Three, in Vietnamese and English. The Vietnamese and English texts are official and equally authentic.

For the Government of the United States of America	For the Government of the Democratic Republic of Vietnam
WILLIAM P. ROGERS Secretary of State	**NGUYEN DUY TRINH** Minister for Foreign Affairs

Appendix D(ii)

DECLARATION OF THE
INTERNATIONAL CONFERENCE

Paris, March 2.—The full text of the declaration of the international conference on Vietnam is as follows:

The Act of the International Conference on Vietnam.

The Government of Canada, the Government of the People's Republic of China, the Government of the United States of America, the Government of the French Republic, the Provisional Revolutionary Government of the Republic of South Vietnam, the Government of the Hungarian People's Republic, the Government of the Republic of Indonesia, the Government of the Polish People's Republic, the Government of the Democratic Republic of Vietnam, the Government of the United Kingdom of Great Britain and Northern Ireland, the Government of the Republic of Vietnam, and the Government of the Union of Soviet Socialist Republics in the presence of the Secretary General of the United Nations.

With a view to acknowledging the signed agreements, guaranteeing the ending of the war, the maintenance of peace in Vietnam, the respect of the Vietnamese people's fundamental national rights, and the South Vietnamese people's right to self-determination, and contributing to and guaranteeing peace in Indo-China:

have agreed on the following provisions, and undertake to respect and implement them:

Article 1: The parties to this Act solemnly acknowledge express their approval of and support the Paris Agreement on ending the war and restoring peace in Vietnam signed in Paris on January 27, 1973, and the four Protocols to the Agreement signed on the same date (hereinafter referred to respectively as the Agreement and the Protocols).

Article 2: The Agreement responds to the aspirations and fundamental national rights of the Vietnamese people, ie, the independence, sovereignty, unity and territorial integrity of Vietnam, to the right of the South Vietnamese people to self-determination, and to the earnest desire for peace shared by all countries in the world. The Agreement constitutes a major contribution to peace, self-determination, national independence, and the improvement of relations among countries. The Agreement and the Protocols should be strictly respected and scrupulously implemented.

Article 3: The parties to this Act solemnly acknowledge the commitments by the parties to the Agreement and the Protocols to strictly respect and scrupulously implement the Agreement and the Protocols.

237

Article 4:   The parties to this Act solemnly recognise and strictly respect the fundamental national rights of the Vietnamese people, ie. the independence, sovereignty, unity, and territorial integrity of Vietnam, as well as the right of the South Vietnamese people to self determination. The parties to this Act shall strictly respect the Agreement and the Protocols by refraining from any action at variance with their provisions.

Article 5:   For the sake of a durable peace in Vietnam, the parties to this Act call on all countries to strictly respect the fundamental national rights of the Vietnamese people, ie. the independence, sovereignty, unity, and territorial integrity of Vietnam and the right of the South Vietnamese people to self-determination and to strictly respect the Agreement and the Protocols by refraining from any action at variance with their provisions.

Article 6:   (A) The four parties to the Agreement or the two South Vietnamese parties may, either individually or through joint action, inform the other parties to this Act about the implementation of the Agreement and the Protocols. Since the reports and views submitted by the International Commission of Control and Supervision concerning the control and supervision of the implementation of those provisions of the Agreement and the Protocols which are within the tasks of the commission will be sent to either the four parties signatory to the Agreement or to the two South Vietnamese parties, those parties shall be responsible, either individually or through joint action, for forwarding them promptly to the other parties to this Act.

(B)   The four parties to the Agreement or the two South Vietnamese parties shall also, either individually or through joint action, forward this information and these reports and views to the other participant in the International Conference on Vietnam for his information.

Article 7:   (A)   In the event of violation of the Agreement or the Protocols which threatens the peace, the independence, sovereignty, unity or territorial integrity of Vietnam, or the right of the South Vietnamese people to self-determination, the parties signatory to the Agreement and the Protocols shall, either individually or jointly, consult with the other parties to this Act with a view to determining necessary remedial measures.

(B)   The International Conference on Vietnam shall be reconvened upon a joint request by the Government of the United States of America and the Government of the Democratic Republic of Vietnam on behalf of the parties signatory to the Agreement or upon a request by six or more of the parties to this Act.

Article 8:   With a view to contributing to and guaranteeing peace in Indo-China, the parties to this Act acknowledge the commitment of the parties to the Agreement to respect the independence, sovereignty, unity, territorial integrity, and neutrality of Cambodia and Laos as stipulated in the Agreement, agree also to respect them and to refrain from any action at variance with them, and call on other countries to do the same.

Article 9: This Act shall enter into force upon signature by plenipotentiary representatives of all 12 parties and shall be strictly implemented by all the parties. Signature of this act does not constitute recognition of any party in any case in which it has not previously been accorded.

Done in 12 copies in Paris this second day of March, 1973, in English, French, Russian, Vietnamese and Chinese. All texts are equally authentic. —Reuter.

Appendix E

AGREEMENT ON RESTORING PEACE AND ACHIEVING NATIONAL CONCORD IN LAOS
21 FEBRUARY 1973

In response to the august desire of His Majesty the King and the earnest aspirations of the people of all nationalities across the country for a prompt end to the war, the restoration and firm maintenance of lasting peace, the achievement of national concord, the unification of the country, the building of a peaceful, independent, neutral, democratic, unified and prosperous Laos in order to make a positive contribution to the consolidation of peace in Indochina and South-East Asia,

On the basis of the 1962 Geneva Agreement and the present realities in Laos,

The Vientiane Government side and the side of the Patriotic Forces have unanimously agreed upon the following:

GENERAL PRINCIPLES

Article 1

(a)   The Lao people's will is to firmly preserve and resolutely exercise their sacred, inviolable fundamental national rights namely independence, sovereignty, unity and territorial integrity of Laos.

(b)   The declaration on the neutrality of Laos on 9 July 1962 and the 1962 Geneva Agreement on Laos are correct bases for the Kingdom of Laos' foreign policies of independence, peace and neutrality. They must be respected and scrupulously observed by the Lao parties concerned, the United States of America, Thailand and the other foreign countries.

The internal affairs of Laos must be settled by the Lao people themselves, without foreign interference.

(c)   In pursuit of the supreme goal of restoring peace, consolidating independence, achieving national concord and unifying the country, and taking into consideration the present realities of Laos where there are two zones separately controlled by the two sides, the internal affairs of Laos should be settled in the spirit of national concord and on the principles of equality and mutual respect, free from pressure of annexation by either side.

(d)   To preserve national independence and sovereignty, achieve national concord and unify the country, the people's democratic freedom must be scrupulously observed, which comprise individual freedom, freedom of religion, freedom of speech, freedom of press, freedom of assembly, freedom of setting up political parties and organisations, freedom of election and standing for election, freedom of movement, freedom of residence, free enterprise and the right to private property ownership. All laws, regulations and institutions contrary to these freedoms shall be abolished.

MILITARY PROVISIONS

Article 2

Beginning from 12.00 hours (Vientiane time) on 22 February 1973 a total simultaneous ceasefire in-place shall be observed throughout the Lao territory, which will comprise the following measures;

(a)   Foreign countries end completely and definitively all their bombardments on the whole Lao territory, stop all their acts of intervention and aggression against Laos, and terminate their military involvement of all kinds in Laos.

(b)   The armed forces of foreign countries end completely and definitively all military activities in Laos.

(c)   The armed forces of the Lao parties completely discontinue all military acts that constitute hostilities on the ground and in the air.

Article 3

After the cease-fire comes into effect

(a)   All military acts of assault, annexation, threat or violation on the ground and in the air by one party against the areas under the temporary control of the other party are strictly prohibited.

(b)   All hostile military acts including the activities of bandits and commandos and armed activities and espionage on the ground and in the air are strictly prohibited.

In case one of the parties should want to supply its men in food by going through the zone under the control of the other party, the Joint Commission for Implementation of the Agreement will discuss this and define, upon common agreement, the concrete modalities for the supply.

(c)   All the raids and operations of terror, repression and infringement on the people's lives and property, and all acts of reprisal and discrimination against those who collaborated with the other side during the war shall be strictly prohibited; assistance shall be given to people who were forced to leave their native villages during the war to help them return there freely to earn their living according to their desire.

(d)   The introduction into Laos of all military personnel of all kinds of regular or irregular troops, and all kinds of armament and war material of foreign countries, except for the ones provided for by the 1954 and 1962 Agreements, shall be prohibited. In case a replacement of damaged or wornout armament and war material should prove necessary, the two parties will discuss it and will make decisions by common agreement.

Article 4

Within 60 days after the setting up of the Provisional National Union Government and the National Political Consultative Council, the total withdrawal from Laos of all military personnel, regular and irregular troops of foreign countries, and the dissolution of the military and para-military organisations of foreign countries shall be completed.

The 'special forces' organized, equipped, trained and commanded by foreigners shall be dissolved, and all the bases, installations and positions of these forces shall be dismantled.

Article 5

Each of the two parties shall return to the other party the persons, regardless of their nationalities, who have been captured and detained because of their collaboration with the other party during the war.

This return will be carried out according to modalities jointly defined by the two parties, and completed, at the latest, within 60 days after the setting up of the Provisional National Union Government and the National Political Consultative Council.

After the completion of the return of all the captured personnel, each of the two parties will have the obligation of seeking for those reported missing during the war, and of supplying the other party with information about them.

POLITICAL PROVISIONS

Article 6

Genuinely free and democratic general elections shall be organized to set up the National Assembly and set up a definitive National Union Government authentically representing the people of all nationalities of Laos. The modalities and time for these general elections will be discussed and agreed upon by the two sides.

Pending the general elections, the two sides, within 30 days after the signing of the agreement, shall complete the formation of a new Provisional National Union Government and a National Political Consultative Council to implement the provisions of the agreement and handle state affairs.

Article 7

The new Provisional National Union Government will comprise representatives of the Vientiane Government and of the Patriotic Forces with equal numbers, and two personalities who stand for peace, independence, neutrality, and democracy and who will be chosen by the two sides by common agreement. The future prime minister will not be included in the two equal numbers of representatives of the two parties. The Provisional National Union Government will be set up following a special procedure through direct investiture by His Majesty the King and will function in accordance with the principle of unanimity of the two sides. Its task is to implement the agreement and the political programme agreed upon by the two sides, especially to implement and maintain the cease-fire, safeguard lasting peace, observe all democratic freedoms of the people, practice a foreign policy of peace, independence and neutrality, co-ordinate the plans for economic construction and cultural development, and receive and distribute the common aid given by various countries to Laos.

Article 8

The National Political Consultative Council, organ of national concord, will comprise representatives of the Vientiane Government and the Patriotic Forces with equal numbers and a number of personalities approving peace, independence, neutrality and democracy to be chosen by the two sides. It will function in accordance with the principle of unanimity of the two parties. Its task is:

—To discuss with the Provisional National Union Government (PNUG) major questions relating to domestic and foreign policies, and present its views regarding these questions to the PNUG.

—To promise and help the PNUG and the two sides in the implementation of the agreement in order to achieve national concord.

—To examine and adopt together the laws and regulations for the elections and join the PNUG in organizing general elections to set up the National Assembly and a definitive National Union Government.

The procedure for the establishment of the National Political Consultative Council is as follows: The two parties will discuss it in detail and take a joint decision on this subject. This decision will then be submitted to the PNUG, which in turn will submit it to His Majesty the King for investiture. The same procedure will be applied to the dissolution of the National Political Consultative Council.

Article 9

The two sides agreed to neutralize the Royal capital of Luang Prabang and the Vientiane capital, and to find all measures to ensure the security and the effective functioning of the Provisional National Union Government and the National Political Consultative Council and prevent all sabotage or pressure by any force from within and without.

Article 10

(a)   Pending the election to the National Assembly and the setting up of the Provisional National Union Government, the two parties, in the spirit of Article 6 of Chapter 2 of the Zurich joint communique of 22 June 1961, will keep the areas under their temporary control, and endeavour to carry out the political programme of the Provisional National Union Government, as agreed upon by the two parties.

(b)   The two parties will step up the establishment of normal relations between the two zones, create favourable conditions for the population to move about, earn their living, exchange visits, and make economic, cultural and other exchanges with a view to consolidating national concord and unifying the country at an early date.

(c)   The two parties take note of the US Government's statement that it will contribute to the healing of the wounds of war and to the postwar reconstruction in the whole of Indo-China. The Provisional National Union Government will discuss this contribution with the US Government, as far as Laos is concerned.

THE COMMISSION FOR IMPLEMENTATION
OF THE AGREEMENT AND THE INTERNATIONAL
COMMISSION FOR SUPERVISION AND CONTROL

Article 11

The responsibility for the implementation of the agreement rests mainly with the two parties concerned in Laos. These two sides shall set up at once a Joint Commission for Implementation of the Agreement with equal numbers of representatives. The Joint Commission for Implementation of the Agreement shall begin functioning immediately after the ceasefire comes into effect. It will work in accordance with the principle of discussion and unanimous decision.

Article 12

The International Commission for Supervision and Control set up following the 1962 Geneva Agreement on Laos, composed of India, Poland and Canada, with India as Chairman, will continue its activities in accordance with the tasks, power and principles as provided for in the protocol of the said Geneva Agreement.

OTHER PROVISIONS

Article 13

The Vientiane Government party and that of the Patriotic Forces undertake to implement this agreement and continue negotiations to carry out all the provisions already agreed upon and settle the pending questions concerning them, in the spirit of equality and mutual respect so as to end the war, restore and preserve peace in a steady and durable manner, achieve national concord and national reunification, and ulitimately build a peaceful independent, neutral, democratic, unified and prosperous Laos.

Article 14

The agreement shall enter into force from the date of its signature.

Done in Vientiane on 21 February 1973 in the Lao language in five copies. One copy will be submitted to His Majesty the King, each party will keep one copy, and the Provisional National Union Government and the Political Consultative Council will keep each one copy for their files.

For the Party of the Vientiane Government	For the Party of the Patrotic Forces

PHAGNA PHENG PHONGSAVAN   PHAGNA PHOUMI VONGVICHIT
Plenipotentiary Special   Plenipotentiary Special
Representative of the   Representative of the
Vientiane Government   Patrotic Forces

From *Survival,* vol. 15, no. 3; May/June 1973.

Bibliography

Acheson, Dean *Present at the Creation* Hamish Hamilton, London 1970.
American University *Cambodia* (Country Handbook), Washington 1972.
Batos, Victor *Vietnam: Origin of U.S. Involvement* London 1967.
Bidault, Autobiography *Resistance*.
Bloodworth, Dennis *An Eye for the Dragon: South East Asia Observed,* London 1970.
Briggs, Laurence *The Ancient Khmer Empire* Philadelphia 1951.
Bouscaron *The Last of the Mandarins* Pittsburgh 1965.
Browne, Malcolm *The New Face of War* New York 1968.
Buttinger, Joseph *The Smaller Dragon: A Political History of Vietnam* New York 1958.
Cable, James *Gunboat Diplomacy* London 1971.
Cameron, James *Here is Your Enemy* New York 1965.
Catroux, General Georges *Deux Actes du Drame Indochinois* Paris 1959.
Central Office of Information *Vietnam*. Background to an International Problem, 1970. *Laos,* June 1970. *The Khmer Republic,* July 1971.
Churchill, Sir Winston *The Second World War, Volume IV* 1951, *Volume V 1952, Volume VI 1954*.
Decoux, Admiral *A la Barre de l'Indochine*.
Devillers, Philippe *Histoire du Vietnam de 1940 a 1952*.
Devillers, Philippe and Lacoutere, Jean *End of a War* London 1969.
Duncanson, Denis *Government and Revolution in Vietnam* London 1968.
Eden (Lord Avon) *Full Circle* London 1961.
Eisenhower, President D. *Mandate for Change* London 1963.
Elliot Bateman *Defeat in the East* London 1967.
Ely, General Paul *L'Indo Chine Dans la Tourmente* Paris 1964.
Fall, Bernard *Indo-Chine 1946-1962* Paris 1962. *Le Viet Minh* Paris 1960. *Hell Is a Very Small Place* New York 1966, *The Two Vietnams* New York 1967.
Far Eastern Economic Review and *Asia Handbooks*.
Fitzgerald, Frances *Fire in the Lake* London 1972.
Gettleman, Marvin *Vietnam: History, Documents and Opinions* United States (Fawcett Publications) 1965.
Giap, General Vo Nguyen *People's War* New York 1962.
Greene, Graham *The Quiet American*.
Halberstam, David *The Making of a Quagmire* London 1965. *The Best and the Brightest* London 1972.

245

Hammer, Ellen *The Struggle for Indo China* Stanford 1954.

Herr, Michael *Dispatches;* published in U.S., Alfred A. Knopf Inc., 1976, later in U.K., Pan Books.

Higgins, Margaret *Our Vietnam Nightmare* New York 1965.

Ho Chih Minh, President *On Revolution.* Selected writings 1920-1966 edited by Bernard Fall, New York 1967.

Johnson, President Lyndon *The Vantage Point* New York 1971.

Kelly, George *Lost Soldiers* Cambridge (Massachusetts) 1965.

Khoi, Le Thanh *Le Vietnam: Histoire et Civilisation* Paris 1955.

Lacouture *Vietnam Between Two Truces* London 1965.

Lancaster, Donald *The Emancipation of French Indo China* London 1954.

Larteguy, Jean *Les Centurions* Paris 1960. *Les Tambours de Bronze.*

Leifer, Michael *Cambodia: The Search for Security* London 1967.

Lyon Peter *Peace and War in South East Asia* London 1969.

McAleavy, Henry *Black Flags in Vietnam* London 1968. *The Modern History of China* London 1967.

MacDonald, Rt. Hon. Malcolm *Angkor* London 1958. *Titans and Others* London 1972.

Mecklin, John *Mission in Torment* New York 1965.

Mountbatten (Earl Mountbatten of Burma) *South East Asia.* Report to the Combined Chiefs of Staff, London (H.M.S.O.) 1951. *Post Surrender Task.* Report to the Combined Chiefs of Staff, London (H.M.S.O.) 1969.

Navarre, General Henri *Agonie de l'Indo Chine* Paris 1956.

New York Times *Pentagon Papers* London 1971.

Nixon, President Richard *Papers of the President.*

O'Ballance, Edgar *The Wars in Vietnam* Ian Allan, London 1975.

Osborne, Milton *The French Presence in Cochin China and Cambodia: 1859-1905* Cornell 1969. *The River Road to China* Readers Union 1975.

Pedrazzani, Jean *La France en Indo Chine: de Catroux a Sainteny* Paris 1973.

Pluvier, J.M. *South East Asia from Colonialism to Independence* Oxford 1974.

Pritt, D.N. 'Autobiography' *Right to Left* London 1965.

Randle, Professor *Geneva 1954* Princeton 1969.

Roosevelt, President *Public Papers and Addresses.*

Roy, Philippe *La Bataille de Dien Bien Phu* Paris 1963.

Sainteny, Jean *Histoire d'une Paix Manquée: Indo-Chine 1945-1947* Paris 1954. *Ho Chi Minh and his Vietnam: A Personal Memoir* Chicago 1972.

Salan, General Raoul *Memoirs: Fin d'un Empire* Paris 1971.

Schlesinger, Arthur *A Thousand Days: John F. Kennedy in the White House* London 1965.

Serong, Brigadier *The Future of South Vietnam* New York (National Strategy Information Centre) 1971.

Shaplen, Robert *The Lost Revolution* New York 1966.

Sihanouk, Prince Norodom (as related to William Burcell) *My War with the C.I.A.* London 1973.

Terzani, Tiziano *Giai Phong! The Fall and Liberation of Saigon* New York 1976. (Translated from the Italian by John Shepley.)

Thompson, Sir Robert *No Exit from Vietnam* London 1969.

Tournoux, J.R. *Secrets d'Etat* Paris 1960.

Tuchman, Barbara *Sand Against the Wind. Stilwell: The American Experience in China.*

Turner, Robert *Myths of the Vietnam War* New York (American Friends of Vietnam) 1972.

Von Marshall (Dr Walther Baron Von Marshall) *The War in Cambodia: Causes and Military Developments.* Published R.C.D.S. Studies 1975.

Warner, Denis *The Last Confucian* London 1963.

Wilson, Rt. Hon. Harold *A Personal Record: The Labour Government 1964-1960* London 1971.

Index

Names of Vietnamese indexed under style most used in the press, e.g. Vo Nguyen Giap under Giap at (G) whereas Pham Van Dong at (P).